THE SCIENCE OF SELF-CONTROL

The
Science
of
Self-Control

Howard Rachlin

HARVARD UNIVERSITY PRESS

Cambridge, Massachusetts

London, England · 2000

Library of Congress Cataloging-in-Publication Data

Rachlin, Howard, 1935–
The science of self-control / Howard Rachlin.
p. cm.
Includes bibliographical references and index.
ISBN 0-674-00093-5 (alk. paper)
1. Self-control.   2. Habit.   I. Title.

BF632.R3   2000
153.8—dc21   99-045204

For Nahid, Leila, and Greg

Acknowledgments

Grants from the National Institute of Mental Health and The National Institute on Drug Abuse supported the writing of this book and the research from which it derives.

My viewpoint here, called *teleological behaviorism,* was developed out of Skinnerian behaviorism from the research and theory of many deep thinkers, not all of whom are referenced in the text, but to whom I am grateful. The application of teleological behaviorism to self-control is based on George Ainslie's (1992) *Picoeconomics,* the papers reprinted in Gary Becker's (1996) *Accounting for Tastes,* and Richard Herrnstein's (1997) *The Matching Law.*

Contents

THE SCIENCE OF SELF-CONTROL

Introduction

When I was in my twenties, I used to think that there were two legitimate ways of knowing things—by intuition and by science. You could appreciate music, I thought, as a lover of music, without understanding how a musical composition is put together, without being able to read music. You could appreciate the stars, I thought, not as the "learn'd astronomer" in Walt Whitman's poem[1] does, but as the poet does—by just going out and looking at them. But today I think differently. I now believe that the appreciation of music by the musician or the musicologist is far superior to that by an unskilled, uneducated, but enthusiastic music lover like myself, and that the astronomer's love of stars is far superior to that of the uneducated stargazer.

I have a decent collection of LP records, amassed mostly when I was quite young. Recently I decided to replay them systematically—Tchaikovsky's Fifth Symphony, Dvorak's New World Symphony, and the like. Beyond a faint stir of nostalgia, I detect only irritation with my earlier self. The fact is that my appreciation of these works was on such a low level that, all unconsciously, in the forty or so years since I played the records, I have become profoundly tired of them. The musicologist, on the other hand, is still finding value in these very works. The musicologist can understand these pieces on a higher level, a more abstract level, that is inaccessible to me. So while I, propelled by my yawns, go from Tchaikovsky, to Vivaldi, to Beethoven, to Bartok, to Ellington, searching for something new (to me), the musicologist casts the net widely, beyond my intuitive capacities.

The same goes for the astronomer. You and I can go out and look at the stars for only so long. After a while a good dinner and a glass of wine begin to exert their appeal. But when we have finished, the astronomer has barely begun. What is our sharp intake of breath at seeing the Milky Way on a clear summer's night compared to the discovery of a new world in one of those stars? Here (with my own punctuation) is my dictionary's definition of *supernova:*

SUPERNOVA

Astron. A star that suddenly increases very greatly in brightness
Because of an explosion disrupting its structure,
And ejecting debris at speeds of up to a tenth that of light,
And temperatures of hundreds of thousands of degrees.
Within the resulting shell of material may be left

A pulsar or a black hole.

Though frequently observed in other galaxies,
Only three have been recorded in our own Galaxy:
By Chinese astronomers in 1054,
By Tycho Brahe in 1572, and
By Kepler in 1604.

Surely the poet would have learned more—even about poetry itself—by staying and listening to the astronomer than by going out and looking at the stars. But, you may argue, I have not understood the point of Whitman's poem. The point may be not that looking at the stars is better than listening to the astronomer but that after listening to the astronomer, the poet comes to appreciate looking at the stars even more. Maybe. But the question then becomes, At what point should we stop listening to the astronomer and start looking at the stars themselves? The answer, I would say, is not until we can look at them as the astronomer looks at them—as the musician or musicologist hears a symphony, as the painter or art critic sees a painting, as the poet reads a poem, as the radiologist perceives a CAT scan. True, we cannot simultaneously become an astronomer, a musician, a poet, a radiologist. But we should not fool ourselves into thinking that our appreciation of their fields, no matter how enthusiastic, is as meaningful as theirs. The appreciation of the amateur is inferior to the appreciation of the professional.

The hard thing to grasp is that this fact applies to psychology—to the understanding of the human mind, to the understanding of our own minds—as well as it applies to any other area of knowledge. This book undertakes to understand the mind—your mind, the minds of other people, the minds of other organisms—not as the amateur does, by intuition, by insight, by introspection, but as the professional does, by careful observation, by experiment, by deduction, by making predictions about one's own behavior and the behavior of others and testing the power of those predictions. Not by *insight*, but by what Aristotle called *nous*, or *outsight*, the ability humans have to perceive a series of particular facts as a single abstract entity. To be scientists, that is, of our selves. Or, to paraphrase another poet, to be masters of our fates and captains of our souls.

Consider the squirrel who "saves" nuts. By depositing nuts into a tree hollow during the fall, the squirrel is providing for its own survival when winter comes. But the squirrel is not really saving nuts. Rather, it wakes up one autumn morning and suddenly finds depositing nuts in a tree-hollow to be valuable in itself. We know that is so because the squirrel will continue depositing nuts even when they are systematically removed from the cache. The squirrel simply does what it likes to do. The temporal extent of its interest can remain narrow while Mother Nature (genetic predisposition) takes care of the long view. A squirrel in its natural environment does not have and does not need self-control.[2]

Human civilized life, however, is different. By our own past experience, by listening to and observing others, by attending school and church, by reading, we learn a series of rules that we believe we ought to obey. As long as the actual acts of obedience are some distance in the future, we do intend to obey them. These rules, however, are often in conflict with our immediate inclinations. We want to do X in the present and Y in the future where X and Y are incompatible acts; if we do X now, we won't be able to do Y later. The problem is that we can only act in the present. The future *as future* never arrives. The gambler may intend to stop gambling; the alcoholic may intend to stop drinking; the workaholic may intend to spend more time with his family; the depressed individual may intend to get out and engage herself with the world. Those acts (saving money, drinking moderately, working moderately, socializing moderately), form a pattern of obedience to learned rules. They seem easy to do as long as they are to be done in the future. Meanwhile, now, we prefer to do X (place the bet, have the drink, work a few more hours, stay in bed). We cannot seem to avoid the fact that the future keeps converting itself into the present, and *in* the present, at the very point where we *can* act, we always prefer X.

If, like the squirrel, we always did what we momentarily preferred, Mother Nature would not take care of us. Instead our behavior would begin to obey another rule, to follow another pattern, a rule or pattern we never chose. The alcoholic does not choose to be an alcoholic. Instead he chooses to drink now, and now, and now, and now. The pattern of alcoholism emerges in his behavior (like saving emerges in the behavior of the squirrel) without ever having been chosen.

Consider the following allegory:

THE DRUNKARD'S PROGRESS

a. *Social drinking.* To overcome his natural shyness, John drinks at parties, on dates, and on nights out with friends. He finds it easier to approach women and to keep a conversation going if he has first had a couple of scotches. He has also gotten into the habit of having a glass or two of red wine with dinner and, once in a while, a scotch to relax before going to bed.

b. *The primrose path.* John marries Jane. The marriage is initially quite normal—that is to say, there are often arguments. To calm down after an argument, John needs a scotch in addition to the one just before bed. If there is no scotch, vodka or gin or bourbon will do. The arguments get worse. Sex deteriorates. Finally there is a divorce, a messy and expensive one. Now John is alone. He needs two, maybe three, drinks to really relax in the evening. Then he wakes up in the middle of the night with heart pounding and finds that a scotch will put him back to sleep. His hangover the next morning is cured by still another scotch. Meanwhile, his social life is unsatisfying. He tries to meet women at parties, but finds he needs a few drinks before going and, once there, tends to be boisterous or argumentative. He goes out on dates but cannot sustain a relationship. It becomes more and more difficult to get himself to attend social functions, movies, or concerts—where he cannot be drinking. It is much more comfortable to spend the evening at the local bar, where he knows all the other regulars, than by himself at home or even on a date. He begins to go to the bar every night. His work starts to suffer. He begins to have one or two vodkas with lunch, or instead of lunch. Everyone at work notices that he is not himself. He behaves inappropriately at meetings and with customers. He is passed over for promotion and gets no raise. Finally his boss calls him in and tells him that he is in danger of being fired.

c. *Just say no.* Still, he does not consider himself to be an alcoholic. He believes that his drinking is just a temporary reaction to his divorce. In fact, he is shocked to discover that anyone views him as an alcoholic. Nevertheless, to satisfy his boss, he resolves to cut back his drinking to one scotch a night. For a few days he manages to stick to his resolution but is miserable almost all the time, especially in the knowledge that an extra drink or two would alleviate the misery. He decides to have his one drink at the bar. Why not? If it's only one, what's the difference where he has it? But once at the bar he discovers that, before he knows it, he has already had several drinks. Now he realizes that cutting back isn't going to be so easy. He may need a little help to stop drinking.

d. *Alcoholics Anonymous.* He begins to attend AA meetings at a local church. There he is forced to confront his alcoholism. He hears the stories of others who identify themselves as alcoholics. He cannot deny that *they* are indeed what they say they are; he is able to see his own behavior as similar to theirs. In that light, he concludes that he must be an alcoholic too. The following syllogism is inescapable: (1) a person who behaves like an alcoholic is an alcoholic; (2) I am behaving like an alcoholic; (3) therefore I am an alcoholic. John decides to rely on logic rather than instinct, and to stop drinking completely. He is an intelligent person, used to following rules, and the AA method begins to work. He is grateful for the unconditional social support of the group. He is especially close to Walter, a fatherly man who volunteers to be his mentor within the program. Walter is available at any time of the day or night. Whenever John feels the need for a drink, he can call Walter and discuss his urges. The help is not so much what Walter says as his comforting and approving presence. John slips a few times, but Walter is completely understanding. Once, at a critical time, Walter got dressed in the middle of the night, came over, and the two men talked for hours, not necessarily about alcoholism, but about life in general. John feels closer to Walter than he ever felt toward any of his friends or even his wife. Weeks, months, a whole year passes without a drink and John is apparently safely on the wagon. His social life picks up and his job performance has never been better.

e. *What sort of a life is this?* Although John is much happier than he was as an alcoholic, his life is still far from perfect. In fact, looking back, he sees his days as a social drinker in a sort of rosy glow. Currently, he feels unbalanced. He is working too hard and not enjoying himself as much as he might. He feels sort of stuffy. He tries to avoid places where alcohol is readily available, but it is difficult to do so. It is tiresome having to explain to people he meets that he cannot have even one drink because he is an alcoholic. When he does explain, they see him as defective and weak, not someone with whom to develop a long-term relationship. On the other hand, if he doesn't explain, they think he is too much on guard or incapable of relaxing. He tends to socialize only with friends from the days before he became an alcoholic, but they know better than to invite him to join them when they go out for a few drinks. Finally, he does go to a party and with some effort does not drink. He compensates by acting a little drunk anyway, but he cannot forget that he is acting—indeed, he *must* not forget it or he would surely take a drink. He does not have a good time. Images of a better life surround him—in the form of the memories of his social drinking days and in the form of his social drinking friends. It seems as though he has gone from one extreme to the other. Why can't he achieve a happy medium?

f. *Relapse.* The vast majority of former alcoholics and other drug abusers relapse (Brownell et al., 1986). John is no exception. To be a social drinker and achieve a better life, two things are required: (1) not drinking most of the time, and (2) drinking moderately on social occasions. John tells himself that he already has licked number 1, the hard part. Only number 2, the easy part, remains. If he had to assign numbers to degrees of happiness, John would give a 0 to being an alcoholic, an 8 to being a teetotaler as he is now, and a 10 to being a social drinker. He has laboriously climbed all the way from 0 to 8. Why not try for 10?

Heart in hand, he embarks on this dangerous course. To his surprise he succeeds. He starts going to parties, drinks moderately while there, and feels a freedom and a pleasure that wash over his whole life. His happiness has gone from 8 to 10, maybe even 11. But he has entered on the primrose path. Tolerance begins to build up. To maintain the exalted state he has achieved, John needs to drink ever so slightly more each week. Simultaneously, and unconsciously, John begins to increase the number of drinks he has on social occasions and the number of social occasions he attends. Finally, he begins to expand his definition of what constitutes a social occasion—from parties, to dates, to lunch with a friend, to being among strangers at a bar. After a while, this last mode of socializing begins to replace the others. Over the course of a few months' time, slowly but surely, John's happiness has eroded. Drinking has changed from a pleasure to a means of escaping pain (technically, from positive to negative reinforcement). John is once more an alcoholic.

g. *A second recovery.* But now John knows exactly what to do. Before hitting rock bottom, he begins to attend AA meetings again, he calls Walter (whom he has been neglecting), he goes through the pain of not drinking. He becomes a teetotaler again. Gradually his life improves. But with that improvement comes the knowledge that drinking, if he were to drink, would be a pleasure. The possibility of becoming a social drinker again seems realizable.

At this point there are at least four ways to go:

1. He may succeed this time in establishing a relatively complex pattern of social drinking.
2. He may stick to the simple pattern of never drinking (being a teetotaler), as AA recommends, telling himself that he is an incurable alcoholic who can never be a social drinker.
3. He may keep cycling forever from long stretches of alcoholism to relatively shorter stretches of teetotalism and back again.
4. He may remain an alcoholic for the rest of his life.

One purpose of this book is to study the characteristics of such alternatives, to ask how our behavior can come to follow rules and exhibit desired patterns, even when each individual act that the pattern comprises is something we prefer not to do at the time. This is nothing other than the study of the concept of *habit* as William James (1890/1981) conceived it: "Habit is . . . the enormous flywheel of society, its most precious conservative agent. It alone is what keeps us all within the bounds of ordinance" (p. 125).

Habit, then, functions in human life as a flywheel functions in a machine, to overcome temporary opposing forces, to keep us behaving for a time in a particular way, according to a predetermined pattern, a general rule. Once a flywheel gets going, the machine is in a sense committed to keep on running, come what may. Similarly, in self-control situations, habits function to help us *avoid* making decisions on a case-by-case basis, to commit us to decisions made earlier, and to reap the benefits of following abstract rules rather than particular impulses. I will argue for looking at self-control this way, and against looking at self-control (in the more usual way) as a wholly *internal* battle.

Finally, I will claim that human happiness is inseparable from self-control. This claim is hardly original. Philosophers and religious leaders have been touting it since ancient times. But rarely have they gone so far as to say that while psychology itself is the science of the mind, the human *function* of psychology is to achieve human happiness in the most direct possible way—by forming our behavior into harmonious patterns—that is, by developing good habits.

This is not a self-help book; it contains principles, not prescriptions. Self-control problems, as problems, are always specific. A person seems to have trouble with drinking, or gambling, or overeating, or some other *specific* bad habit, not with self-control *in general;* but self-control in general is the subject of this book. Although, as we go along, the general problem will be illustrated with particular examples, especially that of alcoholism, how to apply self-control principles to your own specific problem will not be im-mediately obvious. In the case of alcoholism, whole books, whole journals, whole branches of the National Institutes of Health are devoted to the topic. The subject, especially its physiological aspect, is much too extensive to be treated here with any degree of completeness. The same holds for other individual kinds of self-control problems. Although this is not a self-help book, it may serve as a how-to book for reading self-help books—for weeding out from the advice given in those books what is and is not con-sistent with the basic principles of self-control.

1

Habit and Willpower

You are a smoker—two packs a day. You have just finished a fine dinner and are ready for your usual postdinner cigarette. You stop a moment to consider. Maybe you shouldn't smoke it. All the powerful reasons not to smoke come to mind: the bad health—cancer, emphysema, heart disease—the social disapproval, the ever-increasing inconvenience and expense, the loss of power over your own behavior. Balanced against these reasons are the certain and immediate kick of that first puff, the aroma, the feel of the filter in your lips, the familiar glow of the burning ash, the easy movement of your hands as you light up and hold the cigarette and flick the ashes away, punctuating your after-dinner conversation. By smoking the cigarette you will also avoid immediate deprivation, a mixture of feelings of distraction, loss of concentration, and nervousness.

Weighing all the competing forces, you consider two questions, one important, one relatively trivial:

a. Whether to resolve to stop smoking for the rest of your life.
b. Whether to smoke a cigarette right now.

Suppose you respond to the first in the affirmative; you decide to stop smoking for the rest of your life. Then there are only two possibilities. On the one hand, you may keep the resolution and never smoke again. If you do, it hardly matters whether you have one last cigarette tonight; smoking that last cigarette would give you immediate pleasure. After that, if you never smoke again, you will derive all the long-term benefits as well.

On the other hand, it is also possible to make the resolution but fail to keep it. If this second possibility comes to pass, if you are simply making one more empty promise to yourself, then does it really matter whether you smoke this cigarette tonight? Why suffer the pain of abstinence tonight if tomorrow you are going to smoke anyway? In either case—whether you keep the resolution or not—it makes sense to smoke this cigarette tonight. Secure in your reasoning you light your cigarette.

What is wrong with this argument? The problem is that the two questions are not independent of each other. A person could begin acting on a resolution tomorrow or today. But while the physical independence of today and tomorrow is real enough, the fact remains that actions today affect actions tomorrow. Not smoking tonight makes it easier not to smoke tomorrow, and not smoking tomorrow makes it easier not to smoke the next day, and so on.

There is another fault in the logic that views the questions as independent. In twenty-four hours tomorrow will be today. If it always makes sense to smoke one last time, we will never stop smoking. To smoke the "last" cigarette tonight (or eat one more steak dinner, or drink one last scotch and soda) is to fail to perceive the degree to which tonight's act is embedded in a pattern of acts over many nights and days. The decision to stop smoking is in effect a decision to begin a pattern of behavior. The decision to smoke one last time is in effect a decision to maintain a different pattern of behavior—that of smoking. "Shall I begin a new pattern tomorrow or today?" is a psychologically false question. The real issue is whether to begin a new pattern at all or to keep following an already existing one.

To smoke the cigarette tonight (or eat the second dessert, or drink the fourth scotch) is to fail to perceive the connection between tonight's act and the pattern of acts over many nights and days—to be "shortsighted" (or "myopic") about both past and future behavior.

Aristotle drew the following analogy between the pattern of acts of an individual person over time and the pattern of acts of a group of people. In *Posterior Analytics* he said that the pattern of acts (the universal) comes about through individual actions (the particulars) "like a rout in battle stopped by first one man making a stand and then another, until the original formation has been restored" (II ch. 19, 100a, 11). In a battle, one soldier alone knows he cannot possibly survive the onslaught of a pursuing army. That soldier also knows that his action can potentially influence the actions of others and therefore establish a pattern of resistance. Similarly, in life, one night's abstinence from a bad habit would be futile against a pursuing army of temptations. It would be futile, that is, were it not for the connections in our behavior between one night and the next—were it not for our ability to organize our behavior into patterns extending over time (as a military formation extends over space).

In this book I propose to show how patterns of behavior lead to self-control, to explore how behavioral patterns may be established, how they persist over time, how they may be destroyed, and how they may be reconstituted. I will argue that imposition of patterning in our overt behavior is the way in which we can best achieve self-control. In order to make this argument, I must first discuss certain other conceptions of self-control and explain how they fail to lead to useful methods. I begin with an explanation of self-control that is both classic and currently popular—willpower.

Willpower

Let us consider three views of what it means to exert willpower: first, a religious view, originating in the ancient East but popularized in the West by Saint Augustine at about the time of the fall of the Roman Empire; second, the Cartesian view, put forth by René Descartes, the French Renaissance philosopher; third, a modern view, that of modern cognitive neuroscience. (We are going to reject all three views but at the same time borrow something from each of them.)

THE RELIGIOUS VIEW OF WILLPOWER.   The religious view (the view of some religions) is illustrated in Figure 1.1. The circle represents the human body, a veritable arena of battle between good (the angel) and evil (the devil). The good in us is aided by outside social influences, the church or the Bible, while the evil in us is aided by outside individual influences, bodily pleasures, or temptations. According to Saint Augustine, God is supremely powerful and could, if He wished, completely banish evil. If He did, we would be compelled to be good, we would *be* angels, we would never succumb to temptation. For us, as for the squirrel that "saves" nuts, our natural instinct would be to do what is good for us in the long run, and self-control would be pointless. However, as a measure of respect for human beings, God does not compel us to be good; instead, we are allowed to choose between good and evil by means of our own free will. This free will is a gift from God (according to Saint Augustine) because it represents a ceding of power from God to us; it is a little piece of godliness that each of us carries inside. How does it work?

In Figure 1.1 free will is represented by the thick black arrow pointing outward to the left. We are free, from the religious point of view, not to do anything we want, but rather to choose which of the two forces, good or evil, will control our behavior. Will, from the religious viewpoint, is not how we generate behavior, but rather like a toggle switch, flipping back and forth—one moment giving our behavior over to control by the angel, the other moment to control by the devil. Self-control thus consists in keeping that toggle facing upward; impulsiveness consists in keeping it downward. Different religions may have different views of how this switch works. Various Protestant sects, for instance, will emphasize the Bible more than the church as an outside influence; deterministic believers (Calvinists, for example) see the toggle frozen in one position or the other, never to be flipped; others allow one or two flips during a lifetime; still others conceive of repeated flipping as we behave well or poorly.

Willpower, from the religious viewpoint, does not control behavior directly but rather enables good or evil to control behavior. From the religious viewpoint, the willpower that enables you to cover your glass at a dinner party and refuse a drink does not act directly on the muscles that move your hand. Willpower just permits your hand's motion to be guided

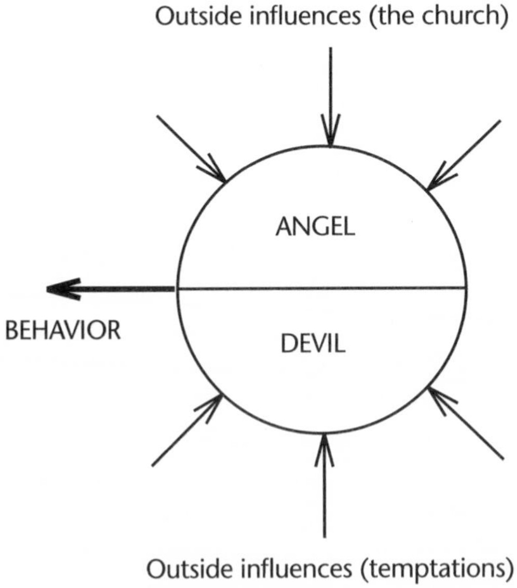

Figure 1.1. The religious view of willpower.

by your desire to do the right thing rather than your desire to enjoy the pleasure of the drink. The warring parties in the diagram are fighting not for your muscles, your brain, your liver or kidneys, but directly for your soul—which is then revealed in the behavior of your whole body. What counts, from the religious point of view, is *why* you placed your hand over the drink—to refuse the drink—not *how* your placed your hand over the drink—the nerves and muscles you used.

The great advantage of the religious point of view is that it offers a way to achieve self-control. Buddhism, for instance, suggests certain mental and physical exercises; Judaism and Christianity suggest study of sacred texts. All suggest prayer. The end result of self-control from the religious point of view is a body under the control of the best part of the soul. What this is exactly, and how it may be achieved, depends on the religion. While the particular advice that religions prescribe may not be accepted by every person in every modern culture, religions at least offer practical access to self-control.[1] Oddly enough, modern cognitive and physiological psychology, with all its scientific regalia, scarcely attempts to find practical methods of self-control.

Many people feel that they do not save enough, do not study hard enough, smoke too much, drink too much, gamble too much, have too much unsafe sex, and so forth. These are important practical problems. They are behavioral problems and are best approached with behavioral (rather than medical) tools. (Taking drugs to control a drug addiction is like swallowing a spider to catch a fly.) This book will help the reader to understand and reformulate such practical problems. But first let us see how psychology got to where it is now via Descartes and his attempt to reconcile the religious view of willpower with Renaissance science.

THE CARTESIAN VIEW OF WILLPOWER.   The natural philosophers of the Renaissance abandoned the religious view of the motion of objects in space, the view that sees all movement as centered on human beings and human concerns. These philosophers took a more objective stance, viewing objects as not just relative to us and our earth, but as tracing a path, along with the earth, through space. When they did so, an elegant picture of the universe emerged; with it, the motion of physical objects could be predicted and even controlled.

Descartes himself was a major contributor to this movement. His analytic geometry had shown that points in space could be expressed in terms of mathematical coordinates; trajectories of objects in space could be converted to abstract algebraic expressions. The powerful tools of mathematics could thus be brought to bear, not just on static things like circles and triangles and plots of land, but on moving objects. Moving objects (thrown, dropped, or shot) could be described and their future positions neatly predicted; machines could be constructed with reciprocating or rotating parts, one part impinging on the other. And the behavior of these machines could in principle be predicted.

Despite all of this progress, one class of objects on earth—animals—appeared not to behave as machines behaved; the very essence of animal movement (human and nonhuman) seemed to be beyond prediction. Whereas stones and blocks of wood are moved by outside forces, the movement of animals apparently originates inside them. To move, cannonballs require a trigger pull and an explosion of gunpowder; clocks, a wound spring or pendulum; fountains, an external source of water pressure and a twist of a valve. What are the motive and controlling forces of animal movement?

Descartes reasoned as follows. If he could conceive of animals as machines, what was known about machines could then be applied to animals. The English physician William Harvey had shown that the heart works like a pump, circulating the blood. The science of anatomy had progressed to the point where muscular movement could be seen as causing limb movement, and it seemed to Descartes that the nerves must somehow transfer signals from the brain to the muscles. Descartes's idea was that a substance called *animal spirits* is distilled in our brains from our blood (much as alcoholic spirits are distilled) and travels down our nerves to our muscles, which then contract in length (by blowing up in width like a balloon) and move the limbs to which they are attached. This mechanism is illustrated schematically in the lower part of Figure 1.2. An outer stimulus enters the body through the sense organs and opens a valve that allows animal spirits to flow into the muscles, causing movement (labeled "behavior"). Behavior of nonhuman animals is entirely determined by this stimulation and response. But we humans have another way to move. Inside each human being is a soul containing concepts, reason, and will. The soul is subject to outside influence, not directly by contact with the world (as in the religious conception), but only indirectly by sensing the flow of animal spirits as it is varied by outer stimulation.

How then can a nonphysical soul (which should really be a non-

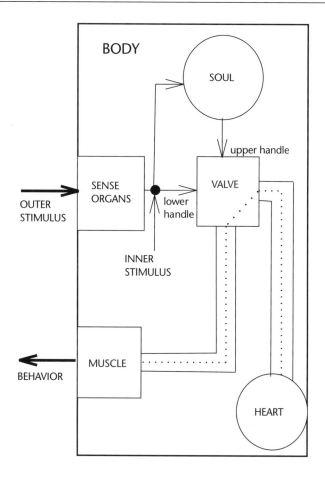

········· flow of animal spirits

Figure 1.2. Descartes's mechanistic view of willpower.

dimensional point in the diagram) get the idea of, say, a rose, from the physical movement of animal spirits? The answer, according to Descartes, is that a soul does not really get the idea of a rose from a rose. Rather it already *has* the idea of a rose. Your soul, according to Descartes, already has all of the ideas it is ever going to have. However, these ideas are, as it were, sleeping. What the real rose does (or rather what the smell, sight, and touch of the real rose does) is awaken the idea of the rose in your soul.

The two handles of Figure 1.2, one controlled by outer stimulation, one controlled by the soul, act on the same valve. These two handles represent the two sources of control of behavior, *external* control, and *self* control. Mr. Jones, saving part of his pay for retirement, has something that the squirrel, saving nuts, does not have—the power to reason. Outer stimuli, such as roses, and inner stimuli, such as stomach contractions, act on Mr. Jones in two ways. They exert a force on the lower handle, tending to make him spend his money. But they also awaken his reason, which may then influence his will to turn the upper handle so as to countermand the effect of the lower handle.

Nonhuman animals have no willpower, according to Descartes, but they need none. The mechanical action of their animal spirits serves them in the context of their natural environments. A nonhuman animal can never be "tempted," according to Descartes, because what it wants to do at the moment is exactly what it should do. Some people feel that such a state would be ideal for human beings too, a return to Eden. But, as philosophers have pointed out since ancient times, the first function of the human power to reason is to help us resist temptation. Without that function our reason would never have evolved (or been given to us by God).

To return to your dinner party, we can say that the host with the wine is turning your lower handle. If left to itself, the hydraulic mechanism inside you will move your hand with the glass out to receive the wine, will lift the glass to your lips, and will move your tongue to swallow the wine, perhaps even without your soul's knowing it. But when you move your other hand to cover the glass, the power of your *will* is doing the moving, not directly as was the case in the religious conception but indirectly by controlling the flow of animal spirits through your nerves and muscles. Descartes (who did most of his thinking in bed) leaves us with this picture: our souls, sitting in the control room of our brains (in our pineal glands, to be precise), isolated from the outside world (but helped by a vast store of innate ideas, together with an innate rationality) read the eddies and swirls of our animal spirits for signs of what is going on in the outside world. Once they have developed a picture of that world, our souls get our bodies into motion by reaching down and, for good or evil, countermanding the valve settings caused by bodily stimuli and environmental stimuli acting through our sense organs. When our souls fail to exert control (when self-control fails) we act impulsively, under the sway of the immediate stimulus.

Willpower thus has a literal interpretation in Descartes's model—the power of our souls to wrest control of our behavior from the outside world. This is how Descartes tried to reconcile the religious view of the soul as an immortal spiritual entity, a repository of good and evil, with a mechanical vision of bodily movement. How successful is this reconciliation?

Descartes was very specific (although wrong, we believe now) about *where* our wills act, and once our wills have acted, he was very specific (and still wrong) about *how* the message gets to our muscles. He was vague, however, about the development and cultivation of the will. The *why* of behavior has become lost, in Descartes's model, in the *how* of behavior. To the extent that the soul has purposes, and power to put those purposes into action, the soul has these purposes and powers, Descartes claimed, innately. Stimulation from outside, including stimulation from the consequences of our actions, are merely disturbances of reason. Our thoughts are coherent, according to Descartes, not because the world is coherent, but because of the innate structure of our minds. Our dreams are incoherent during sleep, not because of lack of sensory input, but because our reason is then asleep. If we could only think "clearly and distinctly" without any disturbance from the outside world we would think true thoughts. The only advice Descartes has for us in trying to control ourselves and behave rationally is to do what he did, to stay in bed and spend time thinking rather than acting.

THE MODERN NEUROCOGNITIVE VIEW OF WILLPOWER. The way modern physiological and cognitive psychology (that is to say, nonbehavioral psychology) views the action of the will is a great improvement over Descartes's conception, especially in terms of how messages get from our brains to our muscles and *where* in our brains various messages go to and come from. Descartes's view that all ideas are innate has been dropped by modern psychology, which has otherwise been guided by his mechanistic model. Figure 1.3 outlines the state of that development in a highly schematic way.

In Figure 1.3, information (arrow 1) coming into the cognitive system, located in the upper brain, combines with "declarative memory," located in the midbrain (perhaps the hippocampus), and forms ideas about the world. These ideas combine in turn with messages coming from the lower brain, where emotions are being processed, and form purposes. The purposes then travel back down, countermanding or augmenting stimuli entering the lower brain (arrow 3), and finally result in behavior (arrow 2). The problem with this model is that it provides no mechanism by which abstract purposes may be translated into specific actions.

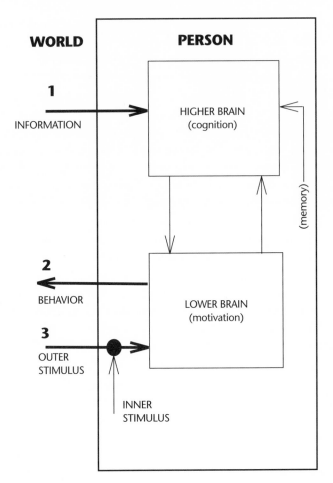

Figure 1.3. Self-control as an internal process (the viewpoint of modern cognitive neuroscience).

The concept of willpower as the exercise of the moral weight of the soul on our lives was undoubtedly too unscientific to survive in modern psychology. But physiological and cognitive psychology have found nothing to replace the concept of the will as the source of our purposes in everyday life. Modern psychology has followed Descartes in pursuit of the *how* of behavior. Like Descartes, it has lost sight of the *why*. So we are as much at sea as we ever were when it comes to developing methods to bring our own behavior under control.

Succeeding chapters will attempt to formulate a different approach, a behavioral approach, to this problem. But first let us go back to the religious view to see why it has had the success that it has. Then perhaps we can develop that view with the object of controlling behavior intelligently.

A Teleological View of Behavior

The viewpoint of this book is called teleological behaviorism. Understanding it requires suspension of the conception of an *inner life* as distinct from *life*. It requires adoption of a view of one life, life as it is acted out, life as overt behavior. If other people with all their senses functioning were present, if the lights were on, and if they still could not see or hear you do something, then (according to teleological behaviorism) you have not done it. You could not think or wish or hope anything without those thoughts, wishes, or hopes being known by a hypothetical person who could follow you around wherever you went and see, hear, smell, touch, and taste you. Our mental lives, says the teleologist, are our patterns of overt behavior extending, perhaps very far, into our pasts and futures. We do indeed have thoughts, wishes, and hopes; but they are not events taking place on some heavenly stage, nor are they the swishing and surging of animal spirits, blood, hormones, electrons, or other physiological entities in our heads or hearts. Mental events are, rather, perceptible patterns in our overt behavior. They are like symphonies or ballets. A thought is one theme within the pattern, a wish is another, a hope is another.

There are many objections to this teleological conception of mental life. The main one comes from modern psychologists and philosophers of various stripes.[2] Their argument runs as follows. It must be possible for two people to do the same thing but do it for different reasons. Since the two people are doing the same thing, their actions must be the same. Yet we have just supposed that their reasons are different. Therefore, reasons (as well as thoughts, wishes, and hopes) cannot be the same thing as actions. Here is the same objection rephrased as a question by the British neuroscientist Jeffrey Grey: "I once asked [the author of this book] what, in his view, is the difference between two awake individuals, one of them stone deaf, who are both sitting immobile in a room in which a record-player is playing a Mozart string quartet" (quoted by Staddon, 1993, p. 123). Grey was implying that there must be a difference—which could lie only in what went on inside their heads. But it is possible to answer Grey's question without resorting to internal unobserved events (without resorting to the dualistic models of Figures 1.2 or 1.3).

Let us call the awake hearing person Adam and the awake deaf person Eve. And first let us ask what it means for Adam to be able to hear and what it means for Eve to be stone deaf. One answer is that a certain pattern of activity is occurring in Adam's brain that is absent in Eve's brain. However, for the teleological behaviorist, the difference between Adam and Eve is that Adam generally does different things when sounds are present than when they are absent, whereas Eve generally does the same sorts of things in the presence and absence of sounds.

As illustrated in Figure 1.4, you could take all of Adam's actions and divide them into two classes, one class for sounds and one class for no

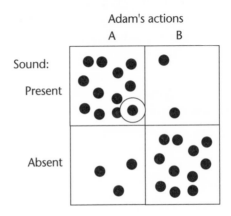

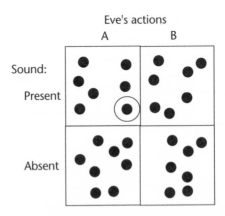

Figure 1.4. The fundamental distinction between a hearing person (Adam) and a deaf person (Eve) in terms of actions (black dots) discriminating between the presence and absence of sounds.

sounds. You could further parse Adam's actions into subclasses for different sorts of sounds. You could not do this for Eve. Figure 1.4 illustrates each action as a point in a 2 × 2 grid. For Adam (who by assumption can hear) there will be some actions (in the category labeled A) that are much more likely in the presence or expectation of sounds than in their absence. Examples would be buying tickets to a concert or engaging in an oral conversation. Similarly, there will be some actions (in the category labeled B) that are more likely in the absence of sounds than in their presence. An example might be Adam's saying, "Gee, it's awfully quiet here." For Eve (by assumption deaf) no matter how hard you tried, there would be no way to separate A-actions from B-actions. She would be equally likely to do any act in the presence or absence of sounds. Eve rarely says, "I hear a strange noise," and she is just as unlikely to say it in the absence of strange noises as in their presence. That is what it *means* to say Adam can hear while Eve cannot.

Although there certainly must be differences between the internal auditory mechanisms of Adam and Eve—physiological differences, underlying the psychological differences between them—the *psychological* difference itself (hearing versus not hearing) rests in Adam's actual behavior over time (his discrimination) and Eve's actual behavior over time (her failure to discriminate) diagrammed in Figure 1.4. It would not matter (in terms of what it *means* for Adam to hear and for Eve to be deaf) if you opened up their heads and found jello in Adam's and chocolate pudding in Eve's. At this very moment (in Grey's question) Adam and Eve happen to be doing the same thing. (Figure 1.4 represents this by the circled points in the two grids.) But their actions at this very moment are merely one corresponding step, as it were, in two entirely different dances.

Identifying a mental event with an act at a single moment in time is like identifying a spot of color with a painting. Asking Grey's question is like asking the difference between a Picasso painting and a painting by a kindergarten child, both of which have a yellow spot in the upper-left corner, or asking the difference between the quartet playing the Mozart piece at the moment between movements, when all four members are stock still, and a painted statue of a quartet. On a trivial level, there is no difference. Looked at another way, there is all the difference in the world. You do not have to refer to either spiritual or physiological states to distinguish between mental states, especially when in everyday life we distinguish among mental states all the time on the basis of actions alone.

What sort of actions? Patterns over time. In the case of Adam and Eve, a series of acts correlated or uncorrelated with sounds. If Adam and Eve were both created at the moment when the Mozart quartet began, both sat unmoving while it was playing, and then, when the quartet ended, both suddenly died, it would not mean *anything* to say that Adam heard the music while Eve did not—even if an autopsy should reveal that Adam's brain was perfectly normal but Eve's was chocolate pudding.

Teleological Behaviorism and Self-Control

The floor above my Manhattan apartment has an indoor swimming pool. I have paid for the use of this pool and I would like to swim for about twenty minutes a day on days when I am there. Swimming is a healthful and generally enjoyable exercise for me. Moreover, once I have done it, my mood improves and I feel better. But I find it exceedingly difficult to actually do it. It takes me about four minutes to get undressed, put on my bathing suit and slippers, collect my towel, goggles, nose clip, and keys, lock the door, go up one flight of stairs, wave to the lifeguard, sign in, get into the shallow end of the pool, put on my goggles and nose clip, and start swimming. Those four minutes, which involve getting chilly and wet, are rather unpleasant—painful, I would say—especially in the winter. Although once I start swimming, I am not even remotely tempted to stop before the twenty minutes are up (and when I finish, I always feel good), I often "forget" to go or I put off going until something comes along to take up my time. What's my problem?

The problem, of course, is getting over those first four minutes. For one thing, they have to come before rather than after the swimming. And, just as crucially, during the twenty minutes of the swim, and even afterward, there exists no four-minute period that comes close to being enjoyable enough to balance the four minutes of chill and wetness I have to go through beforehand. In fact, if I add up the positive values of all the four-minute periods that constitute the swim and its immediate aftereffects, they still do not counterbalance the pain of the four minutes of preparation. The thing about swimming that can tip the scales in its favor is not to be found in any four-minute period, but rather in the pattern of the swim as a whole (in its *gestalt,* or form) and, more globally, in my habit of swimming. In general, I will be a happier person if I swim two or three times a week.

It is important to distinguish two senses in which swimming makes me happy. I have said that it improves my mood; it creates a feeling of well-being. But this is not enough. From the viewpoint of teleological behaviorism, my swimming is a component of my happiness. The relation between my happiness (such as it is) and swimming is not simply instrumental—it is not like that between my salary and my teaching. My teaching and my salary are two separate things. But my swimming is not separate from my happiness, it is a component of my happiness—something that far outweighs a brief chilly and wet experience.

What holds for swimming (in my case) holds even more strongly for what Freud claimed are the essential components of a happy life—work and love. My teaching is reinforced by my salary. But it is also reinforced "intrinsically" by its pattern and its role in the pattern of my life. Writer's block, the apparently insurmountable difficulty of many writers, is nothing but my difficulty in starting to swim writ large. A writer who once begins to write can keep going. Yet the first hour of writing is hard work. Something must be created out of nothing. There is no pleasure to be found in any single hour of writing that can compensate for the pain of getting started. So pencils are sharpened, the desk is cleared, and the writing never gets done. The essential rewards of writing (like those of any meaningful work) lie not in the accumulated instants of writing—but in the pattern of writing itself and in the role of writing in the pattern of the writer's life.

To say that over a certain period or in a certain context (1) John is behaving rationally (or his mind is in control of his behavior) and (2) John's pattern of behavior is valuable or desirable, is to say the very same thing in two ways. Just as what seems rational over a short period or in one context may seem totally irrational in another, so a relatively valuable pattern of behavior over one period or in one context may be relatively worthless in another. The next two chapters are essentially illustrations of this point.

Behavioral Theory and Cognitive Theory

The three heavy arrows of Figure 1.3 represent the data that the cognitive psychologist uses to construct a theory. The psychologist manipulates and observes arrows 1, 2, and 3. From these manipulations and observations a cognitive system is hypothesized. The system consists of a set of internal operations and transformations, often a computer-like information processing system which, given inputs 1 and 3, would produce the observed behavioral output, 2. The system is tested by altering the inputs and predicting new outputs. If the actual outputs differ from those predicted, the theory is revised. Then the revised system is again tested in a new domain, again revised, tested yet again, and so forth. Each revision improves the system, making it better and better as the process continues.[3]

Behavioral theory, illustrated in Figure 1.5, uses the same data as cognitive theory and works in the same way with regard to the construction and testing of theory. The difference is that the systems used by the behavioral psychologist to predict behavior have their existence not inside the person but outside, in the world. The person is seen not as a repository of mental states, but as a whole organism interacting with other organisms and with objects in the world. The person's mental states may be interpreted in terms of these interactions.

It is generally agreed among behaviorists that behavior is determined by two kinds of relationships between the inputs and outputs of Figure 1.5. These relationships are represented by the two boxes labeled "interenvironmental contingency" and "behavior-environment contingency."[4] Interenvironmental contingencies are the kind studied most famously by

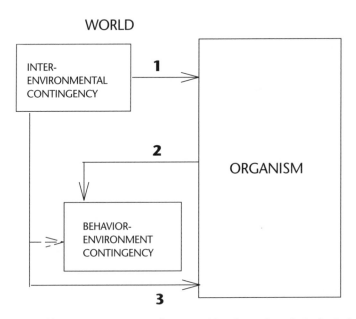

Figure 1.5. Self-control as an external process (the viewpoint of teleological behaviorism).

I. P. Pavlov. A dog is placed in a harness. (Substitute "dog" for "organism" in Figure 1.5.) A bell (1) is sounded just prior to the delivery of food (3) to the dog. The dog eats the food and salivates (2). After this process is repeated a number of times (making the food contingent on the bell) the dog will salivate (2) at the sound of the bell (1) even if the food is not delivered. The dog's behavior depends crucially on the parameters of the contingency—the temporal relationships between the signal and the significant event, their intensities, their frequencies, and the dog's past experience with them.

People, like dogs, will react to signals of significant events as they do to the events themselves. An aspiring corporate lawyer has been called several times to the senior partner's office (1) and bawled out (3). Now she has to enter that office to get a file. Even though the partner is not there at the moment, she behaves in the same way (her heart beats, her palms sweat) that she did before in that place.

Behavior-environmental contingencies are the kind studied most famously by B. F. Skinner. Each time a hungry rat presses a lever (2), a foodpellet is delivered (3). (The food is contingent on the lever's being pressed.) The rat begins to press faster. Again, the properties of the behavior (its rate and its pattern over time) depend crucially on the parameters of the contingency. Behavior-environment contingencies are ubiquitous in human life and their effects are everywhere. Most behavioral research consists of the examination of these effects. The study of self-control is essentially the study of how behavior due to one sort of environmental event (larger distant or abstract rewards) may come to dominate behavior due to another sort (smaller immediate or particular rewards).

The dashed arrow of Figure 1.5 represents a crucial behavioral relationship—that of a discriminative stimulus. Such a stimulus signals not another stimulus, not a specific response, but an entire behavior-environmental contingency. The open/closed signs on a shop door and the occupied/vacant signs on the door of an airplane lavatory are examples. The occupied sign is not specifically paired with any behavior. It says that *if* you try the door, it will not open. Whether or not you do try the door is up to you. Discriminative stimuli are what we use to guide ourselves through life. Much of our language consists of discriminative stimuli and functions to guide the future behavior (linguistic as well as nonlinguistic) of others and of ourselves. Different sentences, different tones of voice, stand for different contingencies. Hearing or reading them, we act accordingly. The red and green lights of a traffic signal, the words *stop* or *go*, and the sentences, "If you cross this intersection now you're likely to have an accident or get a ticket" and "If you cross this intersection now you're unlikely to have an accident or get a ticket" all stand for the same set of contingencies, all have the same meaning, all are equivalent discriminative stimuli. These stimuli play a major role in self-control and its lack. We need to avoid discriminative stimuli that signal reward for undesirable behavior (as an alcoholic should avoid a bar). We need to avoid the establishment of certain common stimuli as discriminative stimuli for undesirable behavior (television watching should not become a discriminative stimulus for eating). And, we need to establish useful general rules as discriminative stimuli for desirable behavior. These topics will be discussed in later chapters. First it is necessary to define precisely what is meant by self-control and its lack.

2

Simple Ambivalence

Ambivalence, says my dictionary, is "the coexistence in one person's mind of opposing feelings in a single context." For a teleological behaviorist a person's mind is that person's pattern of choices over a period of time; the opposing feelings are opposing choices. A person is ambivalent who shifts from moment to moment, choosing now one alternative, now another. Hesitation and vacillation are signs of underlying ambivalence. But the ambivalence itself is manifested only by actually choosing both alternatives, one at one time, the other at another time. If despite hesitation or vacillation at a particular moment a person always chooses A rather than B, the person cannot be ambivalent between A and B—although he might be ambivalent between A and C. If, choosing between buying a brown or a blue coat, I have always opted for brown in the past, I opt for brown now, and I always opt for brown in the future, then no matter what I say to myself or others, I strongly prefer brown. My present hesitation, if any, must be a sign of some other ambivalence—perhaps a reluctance to spend the money.

Mild ambivalence (say, whether to buy a chocolate or a vanilla ice-cream cone) is common to us all, and not a problem of self-control. Still there are two kinds of ambivalence that do map onto everyday self-control problems. The first is the sudden switch from a strong preference for one alternative to a strong preference for another. A typical case is the lament of Archie Goodwin (Nero Wolfe's sidekick in Rex Stout's series of detective stories): "The trouble with an alarm clock is that what seems sensible when you set it seems absurd when it goes off" (from *The Rodeo Murders*). Goodwin's lament exemplifies simple ambivalence—simple, since there are clearly predictable periods when he prefers one alternative (waking up early) and when he prefers the other (staying in bed). The next chapter will analyze complex ambivalence, in which preferences shift unpredictably. For now, however, let us return to Goodwin's lament and analyze this simpler form of ambivalence. It will serve as a paradigm both of how preferences suddenly shift from one period to another, and of how we may cope with such shifts.

Figure 2.1 shows two patterns of behavior—two alternative sleep-wake cycles—that Goodwin might have considered when he set his alarm clock at midnight to wake up at 7:00 A.M. the next day. At midnight (t_A) it "seems sensible" to Goodwin to sleep seven hours, get up at 7:00 A.M. and put in a full day of legwork for his boss, Nero Wolfe. But when the alarm goes off the next morning (t_B), the remainders of the patterns between which he had chosen have suddenly reversed in value. What was chosen the night before is now rejected and what was rejected before would now be chosen. At this point, when the alarm rings, the choice Goodwin made last night "seems absurd."

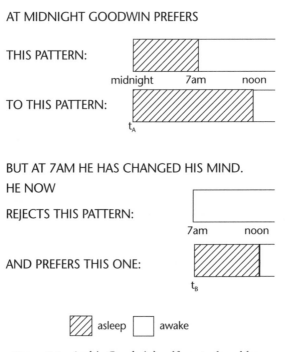

Figure 2.1. Archie Goodwin's self-control problem.

Having set the alarm clock the night before allows Goodwin to choose again, the next morning, whether to get up or to go back to sleep. If Goodwin had placed the clock across the room from his bed, he would have been committing himself to some extent to his earlier choice. Why do people sometimes commit themselves in this manner? What is it about Goodwin's midnight choice that makes it superior to his 7:00 A.M. choice? Clearly his lament is not serious. If we agree with Goodwin that his choice at midnight is sensible we cannot also agree with him that this very choice is absurd at seven the next morning. What is or is not sensible should not change from one moment to another. The reason why Goodwin's midnight choice is more sensible than his 7:00 A.M. choice is (as the reader of *The Rodeo Murders* knows) that Goodwin has many things to do the next morning. The pattern preferred at midnight fits well into its context—Goodwin's life.

As a general rule of thumb, when they conflict, the preferred longer-duration pattern is better than the preferred shorter-duration pattern. But we have to be careful that the shorter-duration pattern is not part of some still-longer, still-more-rational, still-more-preferred pattern. Taking a day off from work, for example, would be an impulsive act in a person (like Goodwin) who habitually shirks work but an act of self-control in someone who works too hard (a "workaholic"). If all we knew about Goodwin were the fact that he took today off, we would know nothing about the degree of impulsiveness or self-control that this fact exemplified. Information about Goodwin's conscious state would not help. What we say to ourselves is notorious for its easy rationalizations, false justifications, and biases. The definitive motive of any act lies in its temporal context—the pattern of past and future acts into which the current act fits. Because a current act may fit into any number of patterns (as a single note in a fugue may be part of more than one overlapping melody), and because these patterns lie in the future as well as the past, a person's *ultimate* motives can never be completely known (even by the person himself). It takes time to observe a motive—the more time, the better known the motive can be. But no motive can be 100 percent known.[1]

Which of several overlapping patterns is the appropriate context for a given bit of behavior, is a crucial question in the study of self-control and I shall discuss it in detail later. For now let us return to the key issue of the present chapter, the reversal of preferences over time.

Time Discount Functions

A time discount function is a mathematical expression of the reduction in value of some commodity due to its delay. For example, if you owned a government bond promising to pay the bearer $1,000 one year from now, you could not sell the bond now for its full value—you would have to sell it at a discount, a reduction representing the fact that the $1,000 will be delayed by a year. For delays shorter than a year, the discount would be less; for longer delays, more. In commerce, discounting is usually expressed as interest. The amount of interest paid on a loan is essentially a discount offered by the borrower to the lender on the total amount (principal plus interest) that the borrower will pay in return. When you deposit money in a savings account, you are essentially buying future money from the bank at a discount. You get a discount because you are paying the bank now while the bank is paying you later.

When a given amount of money is lent to be paid back after a fixed time, interest (hence, the discount) may be determined in advance as a certain percentage of principal (the interest rate) per year of delay. This is simple interest. When, as with a savings account, the duration of the loan is not fixed, simple interest is not practical. Why not? Suppose savings banks did offer simple interest at a rate of, say, 5 percent. If you deposited $100 and withdrew it after two years you would collect $110. But you could have withdrawn $105 after one year, immediately deposited it in another bank paying the same simple interest rate as the first, and collected $110.25 instead of $110 after the second year. Although the difference for a $100 deposit is small (25 cents) it would grow proportionally larger for larger deposits. Bank depositors would therefore have an incentive to withdraw their money (and deposit it elsewhere) as soon as any appreciable interest had accumulated in their accounts. To prevent this, savings banks offer compound interest. They calculate interest frequently, add it to principal, and recalculate the next period's interest based on the total (just as if the money had been withdrawn and deposited in another bank). For a given interest rate, as the frequency of compounding increases, actual interest approaches a maximum, expressed by the following (exponential) discount function:

$$v = Ve^{-rD}, \tag{2.1}$$

where v is the amount originally deposited, V is the amount ultimately collected, r is the interest rate, D is the delay (the time between depositing and withdrawing the money) and e is the base of natural logarithms (about 2.72). If, for example, the interest rate were 5 percent per year and the money were left in the bank for two years, rD would equal 0.10. In psychological terms, V is the actual value of a future reward delayed by D units of time and v is the present (or the discounted) value of that reward.

Equation 2.1 satisfies three criteria for a discount function, with constant future reward V and interest rate r:

1. If there is no delay, there is no discounting (at $D = 0$, $v = V$).
2. As delay increases from zero, present value decreases monotonically (as D increases, v decreases).
3. As delay approaches infinity, present value approaches zero (as $D \rightarrow \infty$, $v \rightarrow 0$).

Equation 2.1 has a fourth property, very important with respect to self-control. It implies that two discount functions with the same interest rate r cannot cross.

At the savings bank, compound interest is always based on the total amount in an account at the time the interest is calculated. In calculating compound interest, the bank can ignore how much was originally deposited and when it was deposited. All it cares about is how much money is on deposit right now. If right now John has more money in the bank than Mary, John gets more interest than Mary, and as long as neither of them deposits or withdraws any money, John will always have more money in the bank than Mary. It should not matter if John's deposit, made long ago (and doubled by compound interest), was originally smaller than Mary's deposit, made yesterday. If John currently has more money in his account than Mary has in her account, John should get more interest than Mary. The exponential form of Equation 2.1 produces noncrossing discount functions and implies intertemporal consistency. Anything else would be irrational. Indeed, economists call Equation 2.1 a "rational" discount function.

It is important to note that, for an economist, rationality resides in the form of the discount function and not in the interest rate itself. A person who discounted future rewards extremely, who preferred $10 today to $100 tomorrow, would be deemed myopic (shortsighted) by an economist. But if preference were consistent (if the person also preferred $10 tomorrow to $100 the day after tomorrow, $10 in ten days to $100 in eleven days; in general, $10 in x days to $100 in $x + 1$ days), the economist would consider that person's preferences to be perfectly rational.

Figure 2.2a shows a set of discount functions given by Equation 2.1. The horizontal axis shows time, where t_A is present time. The vertical axis shows current discounted value (v) of two delayed rewards, a smaller-sooner reward (V_1 to be obtained later, at t_B) and a larger-later reward (V_2 to be obtained after further delay). As time passes, current time (t) moves along the horizontal axis and approaches t_B (delay to both rewards diminishes). The dotted and solid lines descending to the left from V_1 and V_2 are discount functions given by Equation 2.1 with a relatively high discount rate ($r = 0.1$). In Figure 2.2a the current value of the smaller-sooner reward (v_1) is greater than that of the larger-later reward (v_2) at all times between t_A and t_B.

Figure 2.2b shows a set of discount functions given by Equation 2.1 with a relatively low discount rate ($r = 0.02$). Here the current value of the larger-later reward (v_2) is greater than that of the smaller-sooner reward (v_1) at all times between t_A and t_B. Note that for a given r the discount functions do not cross, representing the fact that, with a constant discount rate, preference either way is consistent over time. A person whose subjective discount rate is relatively high (as in Figure 2.2a) would be labeled myopic by an economist for consistently preferring the smaller-sooner to the larger-later reward. But the economist would judge that person to be no less "rational" than another whose subjective discount rate is relatively low (as in Figure 2.2b), who consistently prefers the larger-later to the smaller-sooner reward. According to the economist, rational discounting consists only in obeying Equation 2.1, thereby exhibiting consistent preferences, and not in what those preferences are.

The economist's identification of inconsistency of choice with irrationality goes against both common sense and philosophical thought. Superior rationality is normally supposed to differentiate humans from other animals. In their natural environments, however, other animals are no less consistent than humans are in theirs. The crucial distinction between humans and other animals, the distinction underlying that between rationality and irrationality, is farsightedness versus myopia. Inconsistent behavior that can be traced to myopia, as in the case of Goodwin and the alarm clock, is generally thought to be irrational. But inconsistent behavior per se

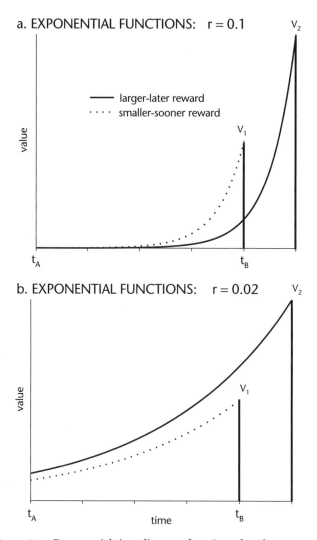

Figure 2.2. Exponential time discount functions that do not cross.

(going to the mountains one summer and to the beach the next) is just variable behavior.

A hungry pigeon prefers 1 ounce of food now to 4 ounces delayed by a few *seconds*. Corresponding disparities in preference by humans are obtainable only when delay is measured in *days, months,* and *years*. In Plato's metaphor for the human soul, a two-horse chariot, the charioteer stands for reason because he is raised above the horses and can see farther than they can (*Phaedrus*, 253*e*). The horses (standing for pleasure-seeking and success-seeking aspects of the soul) are myopic, whereas the charioteer is farsighted. A person as a whole may behave consistently over time *because* of that farsightedness—and because the charioteer has control of the horses. Obedience to Equation 2.1 (the exponential discount function) indeed guarantees consistency of behavior over time. But when that obedience is accompanied by a high degree of discounting (myopia), the consistency observed may be a foolish consistency ("the hobgoblin of little minds") and not rational in any sense.

In summary, the exponential discount function implies that the rank order of the present values of all future rewards is preserved as time passes (and the delay to all of them diminishes equally). A person who lives only in the present, who consistently prefers any sooner reward, regardless of how small it may be, to any later reward, regardless of how large it may be, is (according to Equation 2.1) choosing rationally—because his preferences are consistent over time.

All the same, people often reverse the present values of future rewards as time passes. At midnight Goodwin valued being awake at 7:00 A.M. more than sleeping at 7:00 A.M. But at 7:00 A.M. he valued sleeping more than being awake. Reversals of preference like Goodwin's are prevalent in all human choice. Exponential discounting was presented to serve as a benchmark for temporally consistent behavior. Equation 2.1 was devised to guide the behavior of banks and other financial institutions; it does not describe, and was not intended to describe, the everyday choices of humans or other animals. The next section will present a discount function that does describe human and nonhuman behavior, including preference reversals (inconsistency) over time.

Crossing Discount Functions

Unlike the economist's rational discount function (Equation 2.1), psychological discount functions usually cross. Our subjective evaluation of a reward (our appetite for it) grows much faster when we are closer to the reward than when we are far away. This is especially true of nonhuman animals and human children. It is this uneven (and economically "irrational") growth in our appetites that often causes problems in self-control.

A person choosing between two distant rewards, one just a little more distant than the other, can be "objective" in evaluating them. In other words, their relative values seem about equal to their relative importance in the person's life.

When at midnight Archie Goodwin considers sleeping from seven to noon the next morning versus putting in a full day's work, his subjective view of the values of the alternatives before him is much like our objective view. It seems reasonable both to him and to us that he set his alarm clock for 7:00 A.M. But when both rewards are not distant, when one is almost upon him, the discount function of the closer reward rises rapidly; at that point he is in effect blinded by the sudden increase in the value of the closer reward. Thus at seven, when the alternative of sleeping until noon is almost immediately available and that of putting in a full day's work is still an hour or so away, Goodwin's self-objectivity is overwhelmed by the sooner alternative. His relative evaluation of the two alternatives now deviates both from their objective values (their functions in his life) and from his own veridical perception of those values the night before. Now Goodwin (inconsistently) tends to favor the upcoming, smaller reward. The fact that his relative evaluation of the two alternatives has switched even though the alternatives themselves have not changed means that his subjective (or psychological) discount functions have crossed. Goodwin's inconsistency rests on an illusion that we all experience every day. When we can hold all alternatives at a distance, our evaluation of them remains true to their values in our lives. But when a lesser-valued alternative is virtually dangled in front of our noses, our desire for it suddenly elevates, and unless we have somehow bound ourselves to our previous preferences, we succumb.

Figure 2.3 shows a similar crossing of discount functions, here perception of size rather than value of reward. A person starts at point A. In the near distance is a tree and in the far distance is the moon. The person walks to point B, closer to both tree and moon. The symbols pointed to by dotted arrows show the relative perceived sizes of tree and moon (relative size and distance of the moon drastically curtailed to fit on the page). The person at point A (like Goodwin at midnight) sees the two objects relatively as they are, as reason says they are. At B (like Goodwin the next morning) their apparent relative sizes have reversed and the tree appears much bigger than the moon. Just as value is discounted by time, so size is discounted by distance. In both cases the discount functions cross.

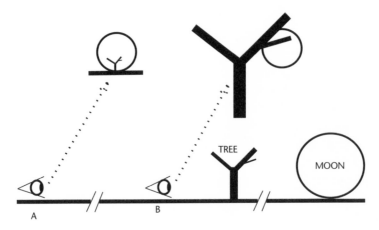

Figure 2.3. Appearance of tree and moon far from tree (A) and close to tree (B).

The perceptual illusion caused by this crossing is so much a part of nature, so common in the experience of all animals, that we are born with
mechanisms (resting on parallax, binaural separation, and other cues) that
prevent us from succumbing to it—from treating the moon at point B as a
shiny grapefruit perhaps. Were we not born with such mechanisms we
would soon acquire them. We would learn to use the available cues to separate truly small objects from large objects at a distance. Still, there is something compelling about the largeness of the moon relative to the tree as
seen from point A and its smallness relative to the tree as seen from point
B. If the moon were instead a large reward in the distant future and the tree
were instead a smaller reward in the nearer future, our preferences would
tend to reverse just as our perceptions tend to reverse.

The rules for truly evaluating alternatives coming at different times are
much more complex than those for judging different-sized objects at different distances. Our natural perceptions may be true and if false may be
corrected. But our preferences are much more susceptible to illusion than
our perceptions, and unless we take special measures to correct them (like
Goodwin's alarm clock), they can destroy our lives.

Nowhere is the discrepancy between perception and preference more
vivid than in the case of nonhuman animals. Thousands of experiments
have been performed to study the preferences of hungry and thirsty animals (rats, guinea pigs, pigeons, crows, starlings, monkeys, horses, cows,
lizards, bees, ants, cockroaches, and a host of others) between various
amounts of food or water delivered after greater or lesser periods of delay

(see Logue, 1988, for a recent review). The results are universal. All animals are highly sensitive to subtle differences in amount of food or water regardless of how far in the distant future the commodities may be delivered.

Consider pigeons. A pigeon is deprived of food (but not water) until it weighs about 80 percent of its normal weight, its weight when it is allowed to eat and drink freely. Then the pigeon is trained to peck at an illuminated button on the wall (like an illuminated elevator button); the experimenter follows each peck with delivery to the pigeon of a small amount of mixed grain—corn, vetch, hemp, wheat. Pigeons soon learn to peck the button.

Then the experimenter puts two illuminated buttons, a red one and a green one, side by side on the wall of the cage.[2] If the pigeon pecks the red button, it gets 2 ounces of food; if it pecks the green button, it gets 1 ounce of food.

As Figure 2.4a illustrates, almost all pigeons soon learn to peck the red button and ignore the green one. This is not very surprising. Pigeons in nature spend their lives making discriminations much more subtle than this between sources of food.

Suppose that instead of delivering the food immediately after each peck on either the green or red button, the experimenter turns off the illumination after the peck and has the pigeon wait 10 seconds before getting the food (still 1 ounce for pecking the green button and 2 ounces for pecking the red button). The pigeon now (Figure 2.4b) waits longer before pecking, discounting the food in 10 seconds even more proportionally than the bank discounts the value of a bond to be paid in 10 years. But (eventually) it still pecks the red button, gets 2 ounces of food 10 seconds later, and ignores the green button. (If you were to switch buttons, following red by 1 ounce and green by 2 ounces, the pigeon would follow your switch and would peck the green button.) The pigeon shows unambiguously by its behavior that it still values the larger amount of food more than the smaller amount.

Now let us consider two more crucial steps. First, extend the larger (2-ounce) food delivery by 4 more seconds (Figure 2.4c), so that a peck on the red button leads to a 14-second delay followed by 2 ounces of food, while a peck on the green button leads to a 10-second delay followed by 1 ounce of food. The pigeon has to balance the extra ounce of food against 4 more seconds of waiting. (The pigeon here is in a situation resembling Archie Goodwin's, when he sets his alarm clock.) Whichever button it pecks, the pigeon will have to wait at least 10 seconds so that the pigeon's choice relates to events in the future (10 seconds is the future for a pigeon just as the

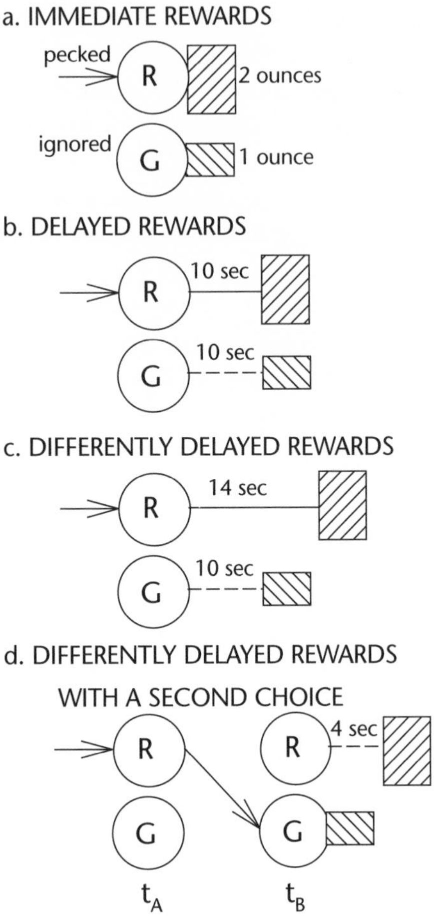

a. IMMEDIATE REWARDS

pecked
⟶ R ▨ 2 ounces

ignored
G ▨ 1 ounce

b. DELAYED REWARDS

⟶ R ——10 sec—— ▨

G ----10 sec---- ▨

c. DIFFERENTLY DELAYED REWARDS

⟶ R ——14 sec—— ▨

G ----10 sec---- ▨

d. DIFFERENTLY DELAYED REWARDS
WITH A SECOND CHOICE

⟶ R   R --4 sec-- ▨

G   G ▨

t_A t_B

Figure 2.4. A typical pigeon's choices (arrow indicates button pecked) between small and large rewards after various delays.

next morning is the future for Goodwin). The pigeon, faced with two distant reward alternatives, chooses the one that is in fact "better" (that would preserve the pigeon's life better in its fiercely competitive environment): it pecks the red button, waits 14 seconds and eats the 2 ounces of food, rejecting the 1-ounce alternative even though the wait for it is briefer.[3]

Now consider the fourth step (Figure 2.4d). It begins (at time t_A) like the previous step with a choice between 1 ounce of food to be delivered in 10 seconds (green button) and 2 ounces to be delivered in 14 seconds (red button). As before, the pigeon pecks the red button and would obtain the 2 ounces of food in 14 seconds. But after 10 seconds have elapsed (time t_B) the two buttons are illuminated again. The pigeon is given a chance to "change its mind." And it does. Virtually all pigeons strongly prefer 1 ounce of food delivered immediately to 2 ounces delayed by only 4 seconds. (What "seemed reasonable" to the pigeon at t_A 10 seconds ago now at t_B "seems absurd.") The pigeon at t_B pecks the green button and obtains only 1 ounce of food, losing the extra ounce. In the space of 10 seconds the pigeon has switched from a preference for one alternative to a preference for the other. This behavior satisfies the definition of simple ambivalence presented at the beginning of this chapter. Between the earlier choice at t_A and the later choice at t_B the pigeon's discount functions have crossed.

Hyperbolic Discounting

The equation used to construct the discount functions of Figure 2.5 is

$$v = \frac{V}{1 + kD} \qquad (2.2)$$

where v is the current discounted value of a reward, V is the undiscounted value of the reward, D is the delay of the reward, and k is a constant representing degree of discounting (corresponding to r in Equation 2.1). The form of Equation 2.2 is hyperbolic, not exponential (as is Equation 2.1); two hyperbolic functions with the same discount rate (k) may cross. In Figure 2.5a, with $k = 0.1$, the larger-later reward (V_2) is preferred at t_A (the solid line is higher), but near t_B, when the smaller-sooner reward is imminent, it is preferred (the dotted line is higher). Thus, unlike the exponential discount function, the hyperbolic discount function describes the preference reversals often found in the behavior of pigeons and people.

The hyperbolic function does not separate preference reversals (economic irrationality) from impulsiveness (myopia). Figure 2.5b shows discount functions for the same rewards and over the same range of delays shown in Figure 2.5a, except that the degree of discounting (k) in Equation 2.2 has been set at 0.02 instead of 0.1. Now, over the range shown, the discount functions do not cross.[4]

Reversals like those found in choices over time (Figure 2.4d) and in perception (Figure 2.3) are found also in other psychological processes and even in physical processes. Recent memories, for example, fade more quickly than distant memories. I may remember what I ate for breakfast

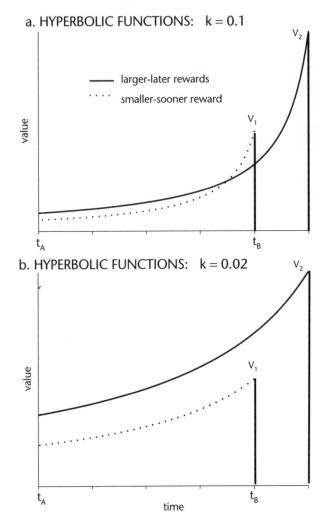

Figure 2.5. Hyperbolic time discount functions that cross between t_A and t_B with high k (Equation 2.2) but not with low k.

this morning better than what I ate at my bar-mitzvah many years ago. But a year from now the memory of this morning's breakfast will have faded to oblivion while that of my bar mitzvah dinner will still be dimly there—the memory-decay functions will have crossed. In physics, the inverse-square law for decay of energy flux with distance from the source is a hyperbolic-like discount function. Energy from a smaller-nearer source decays faster with distance than that from a larger-farther source. Music heard through earphones, for example, may be turned up loud enough to drown out the noise of a subway train. Two feet away from both earphones and train, though, the relative sound energies (actual and perceived) reverse.

Pigeon Discount Functions

Hyperbolic time discounting was first found in experiments with pigeons by Chung and Herrnstein (1967). But the exact form of Equation 2.2 was first proposed and tested in an experiment with pigeons by Mazur (1987). That experiment is worth discussing. As in Figure 2.4, pigeons chose between various amounts and delays of food reward by pecking buttons. Four pigeons (S1, S2, S3, S4) were deprived of food until they weighed 80 percent of their free-feeding weight. Then, each day, each pigeon was taken in turn from its home cage, weighed, and placed in an experimental chamber containing a retractable hopper where access to mixed grain could be made available for a period depending on the pigeon's behavior. Over the course of the experiment each pigeon was presented, in the experimental chamber, with choices between a series of smaller-sooner and larger-later rewards. Choices were made by pecking illuminated buttons (as in Figure 2.4). There were four crucial parameters: the amounts of the two rewards and the delays of the two rewards. Both amounts were held constant throughout the experiment. The smaller-sooner reward always consisted of 2 seconds of access to mixed grain from the hopper; the larger-later reward always consisted of 6 seconds of access. (Amount was varied as seconds of access rather than ounces of grain.)

Mazur fixed the delay to the smaller-sooner reward and varied the delay to the larger-later reward up and down until the pigeon was indifferent between the two rewards. For example, pigeon S1 was indifferent between the smaller reward with delay set at 1 second and the larger reward delayed by about 3 seconds. Then Mazur fixed the delay to the smaller reward at another interval and again varied the delay to the larger reward until he found another indifference point. For example, pigeon S1 was indifferent between the smaller reward with a delay set at 10 seconds and the larger reward delayed by about 26 seconds. This procedure, called a titration procedure, essentially treats a pigeon's choices like a balance scale where the delay to the larger reward acts like a sliding weight. The important datum was the delay to the larger reward at which the two rewards were valued equally.

The procedure was repeated for each pigeon with delays to the smaller reward fixed at 0, 1, 2, 6, 10, 12, and 20 seconds (in random order). Then

Mazur fixed the delay to the larger reward and titrated the delay to the smaller reward, again finding points of indifference. At the end of the experiment he could plot, for each pigeon, the delay to the smaller reward versus the delay to the larger reward at which that pigeon was indifferent between the two rewards.

Equations 2.1 and 2.2 make different predictions about how these functions should look (see the appendix to this chapter). The points in Figure 2.6 represent the actual titrated adjustments at various delays for each pi-

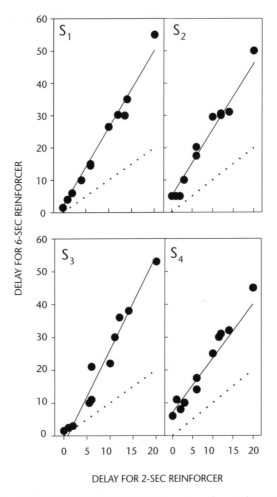

Figure 2.6. The results of Mazur's adjusting procedure for studying delayed reinforcement. (From Mazur, 1987.)

geon. The dotted lines show the predictions of exponential discounting; the solid lines show the predictions of hyperbolic discounting. Clearly the hyperbolic discount function (Equation 2.2) describes the data better than the exponential function (Equation 2.1).

Human Discount Functions

In Mazur's (1987) pigeon experiment, the brief access to food given to very hungry pigeons served as a powerful reward. It is not possible in a psychology experiment to offer human subjects any reward nearly so powerful (because it is unethical to deprive human subjects of necessities such as food or water). Two tactics have been used instead. One is to present real but small rewards (small amounts of money, food, or candy) or tokens exchangeable for small prizes at the end of the experiment. The other is to solicit cooperation in an imaginary exercise, asking subjects to choose among large but hypothetical rewards.

Both tactics have disadvantages. First, discounting of small rewards over an hour-long experimental session may have no relation to discounting of meaningful human rewards (like a desirable job or good health) that in real life may be delayed for years from the acts by which they are obtained. Second, even with the will to cooperate, people may not be able to predict how they would choose between smaller-sooner and larger-later meaningful rewards. Often it is only when a smaller-sooner reward (a temptation) is offered that people appreciate its attractiveness. Third, the desire to please the experimenter, appear intelligent or mature, or finish with the experiment quickly may overwhelm any real-but-small or large-but-hypothetical reward alternative. Despite these obstacles, the discount functions obtained with human subjects, with both tactics, conform to those obtained with pigeons in the sense that they are hyperbolic rather than exponential in form (Green, Fry, and Myerson, 1994; Kirby and Herrnstein, 1995; Logue, 1988; Raineri and Rachlin, 1993; Stevenson, 1986).

Consider an experiment by Green, Fry, and Myerson (1994) using sixth-grade children, college students, and elderly adults (68 years old on average). Each chose between hypothetical rewards stated on pairs of index cards. A delayed-reward card promised a reward of $1,000 to be received after a delay of 1 week, 1 month, 6 months, 1 year, 3 years, 5 years, 10 years, or 25 years. An immediate-reward card announced an amount of money to be received immediately. A single delayed-reward card was kept in front of the subject while a series of immediate-reward cards with amounts varying up and down were shown until the subject was indifferent between the two rewards. (This is a titration procedure with *amount* of a smaller immediate reward titrated rather than *delay* to a larger-later reward, as in Mazur's experiment with pigeons.) Then a new delayed-reward card was placed in front of the subject and the process was repeated. A function was obtained for each subject showing the amount of money available immediately equivalent to $1,000 available with various delays.[5]

Figure 2.7 shows the average results for each age group. The curves show three hyperbolic functions fitting the data with different degrees of discounting (k). Although the fits to the average points were not as good as for individual pigeon subjects in Mazur's experiment, and although there are systematic deviations correctable by using Loewenstein and Prelec's more general formula (see Equation 2.3 in the appendix), the data are described fairly well by Mazur's equation. The percent of data variance ac-

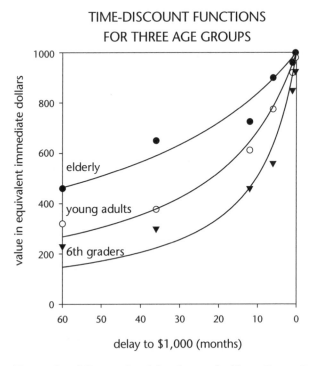

TIME-DISCOUNT FUNCTIONS
FOR THREE AGE GROUPS

Figure 2.7. The results of discounting delayed rewards. (From Green, Fry, and Myerson, 1994.)

counted for is 94, 99, and 95 for children, young adults, and elderly people, respectively. As expected, children discounted money most steeply; older adults, least steeply. Assuming that the amounts of money involved directly measure value, the constant k may be approximated. It was 0.10, 0.05, and 0.02 for children, young adults, and elderly people, respectively. The higher the *k*, the steeper the discounting.

If we make a corresponding assumption with pigeons (that seconds of access to food directly measure value), *k* may be approximated from Mazur's experiment (from the *y*-intercepts of the graphs of Figure 2.6). The average *k* for pigeons calculated by this method is 0.77, apparently comparable to the *k*'s of humans. Delays for pigeons were measured in seconds, however, while those for humans were measured in months. In months the average *k* for pigeons is about 1,000,000. The comforting conclusion for our species—that humans are about a million times less impulsive than pigeons—must be tempered by the fact that the pigeons in Mazur's experiment were deprived of and tempted by food, a "primary reinforcer" (biological necessity), whereas the humans in the Green group's experiment were not explicitly deprived of anything and were only hypothetically tempted by money (a "conditional reinforcer"). When non-humans are tested with conditional reinforcers (Hackenberg and Axtel, 1993; Silberberg, Bauman, and Hursh, 1993), their impulsiveness decreases (although *k* decreases only to about a half, not a millionth, of that with food reward).

In general, *k* depends very strongly on the species tested. It also depends, within a species, on age and experience, on how long it takes to consume the reward once it is obtained—long consumption durations tending to reduce *k*—and on activities during the delay period—anticipatory activities tending to reduce *k* (Loewenstein and Prelec, 1992; Raineri and Rachlin, 1993). With money (a conditional reinforcer), *k* depends on what the money can buy. Ostaszewski, Green, and Myerson (1998), for example, found that Poles discounted both U.S. dollars and Polish zlotys hyperbolically (Equation 2.2 accounting for more than 95 percent of the variance in each case). But *k* for the unstable ("soft") zloty was about 5.5 times higher than that for the stable ("hard") dollar.

A series of experiments by Mischel and his colleagues (summarized in Mischel, Shoda, and Rodriguez, 1989) has studied delay of gratification in children. The procedure is as follows. A boy is seated at a table on which there is a bell. The experimenter puts a less-preferred reward (a pretzel, for example) on the table in front of the child. Then the experimenter tells the boy that she will be leaving the room and will return with a more preferred reward (a marshmallow, perhaps), which the child may obtain provided he does not signal the experimenter to come back into the room (by ringing the bell) before the experimenter does so by herself. If the child makes the signal, he gets the small reward (the pretzel) and forfeits the large one (the marshmallow).[6] If he refrains from signaling until the experimenter comes back, he gets the large reward. (After 15 minutes the experimenter would return, but most children do not wait that long.) The experimenters observe how long each child waits before signaling.

The dependent variable in the experiment, how long the child waits, is remarkably sensitive to several of the variables that affect self-control.[7] Older children, more intelligent children, better-behaved children, children with richer parents, and children from more industrialized countries wait longer than younger children, less intelligent children, children with poorer parents, and children from less industrialized countries. There must be some relation between delay of gratification as studied by Mischel and self-control as studied by Green, Fry, and Myerson. It would not be parsimonious to regard the two highly correlated experimental procedures as separate processes. But what exactly is the relation?

Consider the following dilemma, which I frequently have to face. Several people are waiting for a crosstown bus in New York at eleven o'clock on a cold night. Empty taxis (which cost three times as much as the bus) cruise around the shivering group like sharks around a shipwreck. How long do you wait before giving up and hailing a taxi? It depends on when you estimate that the next bus will come. The bus here represents a larger-later reward (in the sense that its lesser fare subtracts less than the taxi fare from the reward of getting home). The taxi represents a smaller-sooner reward and, as we have defined it, a temptation. If the larger-later reward (the coming of the bus) is not too far in the future, it would not be discounted too much and its current value, even when discounted, would be higher than that of the smaller-sooner reward. In a normal situation, where buses come on a fixed schedule, the time left until the coming of the bus would vary *inversely* with the time elapsed. The longer you waited, the less time you would have to wait. But a New York street corner at eleven o'clock on a cold night is far from normal. A schedule is posted on the bus shelter but, as all the waiting people know, it is useless. There is in fact no way to know when the next bus will come. It may never come—or at least, not until the next morning.

The people waiting for the bus are effectively equivalent to the children in Mischel's experiments. The only possible basis for their estimation of how long they have to wait is how long they have already waited. Where waiting time is completely unpredictable, as at the bus stop and in delay-of-gratification experiments, we would expect estimates of time left to vary *directly* with time elapsed. The longer you have already waited for the bus, the longer you expect to wait. As time goes by, therefore, the larger reward recedes farther and farther into the distance. The steeper the discount function (the higher the k in Equation 2.2), the sooner the current value of the larger reward will sink below the constant smaller-sooner reward, the sooner the person waiting for the bus will hail a taxi, and the sooner the child in the delay-of-gratification experiment will ring the bell. Thus, waiting time in delay-of-gratification experiments depends on delay discount functions. Children with flatter discount functions delay gratification longer than those with steeper discount functions, and people waiting for the bus hail taxis one by one in order of the flatness of their discount functions.[8]

Why are we ambivalent? Why do we animals normally prefer better rewards when all rewards are equally distant in time, but reverse our preference when the lesser reward is available immediately? What is it about the immediacy of an event that blinds us to better alternatives that we might have if we could only wait a little while for them? One conceivable answer lies in our evolutionary heritage (Logue, 1988).

In the supermarket a turkey in the shopping cart is worth just half of two turkeys in the refrigerator case. But before the days of modern social systems, life was much less certain than it is now. If you were out hunting for turkeys to eat, a bird in the hand would be worth two (or more than two) in the bush. In those days it would have paid the hunter to hold onto his catch rather than pursue larger game less probably caught, to be consumed later. In prehistoric times, because of the variability of the environment, obtaining a delayed reward was fraught with chance. Like other animals, humans would survive and reproduce if they had a strong tendency to grab the smaller immediate reward and forgo the larger but delayed reward. Only in some particular and carefully selected cases, such as that of the squirrel's storage of nuts for the winter and the ant's selfless storage of food to feed a queen, did species evolve with neuronal and hormonal mechanisms by which in some circumstances preference for immediate consumption could be overcome. (In the spring, summer, and winter, squirrels save food no more than pigeons do.)

In prehistoric human environments, as in the pigeon's current natural environment, the availability of food was uncertain. It was unlikely that a Cro-Magnon man would become unhealthy if he gorged himself when food was available. Rather, gorging himself would serve to effectively bridge the frequent periods when food was scarce. Evolution therefore has given pigeons, people, and all other animals a strong desire for immediate rewards and an even stronger tendency to avoid immediate pain. A rat for instance will choose to receive a train of 4 or 5 electric shocks delayed by 10 seconds rather than a single shock delivered immediately (Hineline, 1977). At the same time, counter to our tendency for immediate consumption, human reason evolved to predict the future and human society evolved to reduce the improbability of distant rewards.[9] Hence our ambivalence. What can we do about that ambivalence? In future chapters I will examine this question as it applies to complex ambivalence. Below I consider the simpler case where preference among alternative rewards changes suddenly from one extreme to the other.

Commitment

What can we do about simple ambivalence when it occurs in our daily lives? The answer is clear: we can do something at the earlier point t_A to prevent ourselves from changing our minds; we can commit ourselves at t_A to the alternative we have chosen, so that at t_B we will either not be able to change our minds or, if we do, the change will be costly.

When Archie Goodwin set the alarm clock at midnight (t_A) to ring at 7:00 A.M. (t_B), he was simply presenting himself with the alternative of getting up rather than staying asleep. As we have seen, if he had placed the alarm clock across the room from the bed he would have biased his later choice in favor of getting up. To that extent he would have been committing himself to his earlier choice.

A more extreme form of commitment would have taken place if Goodwin physically prevented himself from going back to sleep—say, by arranging some Rube Goldberg contraption to flood his bed with cold water when the alarm rang. Such drastic commitment is obviously rare in everyday human life but it can easily be arranged in the animal laboratory. Figure 2.8 repeats the conditions of Figure 2.4d but adds still another choice: another button, a yellow one, that is illuminated shortly after t_A and well before t_B. Let us call this time $t_{A/B}$.

If the pigeon first pecks the red button (at t_A) and then ignores the yellow button as shown in Figure 2.8a, all will be as before; the conditions of Figure 2.4d will prevail and the pigeon will have a chance to reverse its choice at t_B. (And the pigeon *will* reverse its choice, peck the green button and obtain only 1 ounce of food.) If, however, the pigeon first pecks the red button at t_A and then pecks the yellow button at $t_{A/B}$ as shown in Figure 2.8b, the pigeon will *not* be offered a choice at t_B. At t_B the green button will remain unlit and the pigeon will have only one button, the red one, to peck; the pigeon will peck it and obtain 2 ounces of food 4 seconds later. By pecking the yellow button, the pigeon commits itself to the choice it

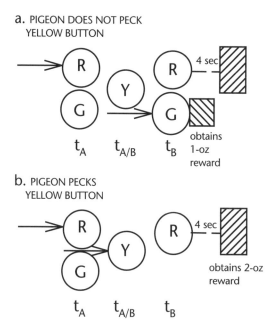

Figure 2.8. Contingencies of strict commitment. With no commitment (a), a typical pigeon will obtain the smaller reward. With commitment (b), the pigeon can only obtain the larger reward.

has just made. The green button at t_B essentially "tempts" the pigeon to peck it by its promise of immediate food. By pecking the yellow button at $t_{A/B}$, the pigeon effectively avoids this temptation[10] and obtains what it preferred at t_A.

Commitment may be defined as a current choice to restrict the range of future choices. In Figure 2.8 a pigeon that chooses *not* to peck the yellow button at $t_{A/B}$ will be able to choose in the future (t_B) between pecking the green or the red button (and obtaining the smaller-sooner or the larger-later reward). A pigeon that pecks the yellow button at $t_{A/B}$ restricts its future choice to the red button only (obtaining the larger-later reward). Pecking the yellow button thereby commits the pigeon to obtaining the larger-later reward.

Assuming that the amount of mixed grain eaten is a direct measure of value, and assuming a degree of discounting ($k = 0.77$) about equal to that obtained by Mazur (1987), Equation 2.2 predicts a reversal of preference depending on when the yellow button is introduced. If the yellow button is presented early in the sequence (say, at $t_B - t_{A/B} = 10$ seconds), the value at that point of the smaller-sooner reward (v_S) and the value of the larger-later reward (v_L) are, according to Equation 2.2,

$$v_S = \frac{V_S}{1+kD_S} = \frac{1}{1+0.77(10)} = 0.11;$$

$$v_L = \frac{V_L}{1+kD_L} = \frac{2}{1+0.77(10+4)} = 0.17 \quad v_S < v_L$$

Ten seconds later, at t_B, when the red and green buttons are presented:

$$v_S = \frac{V_S}{1+kD_S} = \frac{1}{1+0.77(0)} = 1;$$

$$v_L = \frac{V_L}{1+kD_L} = \frac{2}{1+0.77(4)} = 0.49 \quad v_S > v_L$$

Equation 2.2 therefore predicts that at $t_B - t_{A/B} = 10$ seconds, pigeons will peck the yellow button, thereby committing themselves to obtaining the larger reward. The point of equality, where $v_S = v_L$, is at about $t_B - t_{A/B} = 2.7$ seconds. At greater intervals the larger-later reward would be preferred (and the yellow button would be pecked); at lesser intervals the smaller-sooner reward would be preferred (and the yellow button would not be pecked). The pigeon pecks the yellow button not because pigeons are smart but because pecking the yellow button leads to what the pigeon prefers at the time (the larger reward), whereas not pecking it leads to what the pigeon does not prefer (the smaller reward). Superior intelligence would be demonstrated by putting commitment procedures into place, not by commitment itself.

Equation 2.1, exponential discounting, cannot predict preference reversals as long as the discount rate (r) remains constant. Equation 2.1 predicts that pigeons would never make a commitment response. Whichever reward (smaller-sooner or larger-later) they preferred at t_B, they should (according to Equation 2.1) also prefer at $t_{B/A}$.

The choice to peck or not to peck the yellow button is asymmetrical in the sense that pecking and not-pecking have different intrinsic qualities (pecking usually requires more effort than not-pecking, for example). But numerous experiments studying symmetrical as well as asymmetrical choices with various species including rats, monkeys, human children and adults, in addition to pigeons (with rewards altered correspondingly) have found significant rates of commitment.

The experiment closest to the one illustrated in Figure 2.8 was performed by Ainslie (1974) and described by Rachlin (1970). Rachlin and Green (1972) reported a similar study of strict commitment with pigeon subjects using a symmetrical choice procedure. Figure 2.9a diagrams the experiment. Pigeons chose at t_A (by pecking one of two buttons) between a noncommitment sequence (the upper branch in the figure) leading to a second choice at t_B between a smaller-sooner and a larger-later reward, and a commitment sequence (the lower branch in the figure). Choice of the commitment sequence eliminated the smaller-sooner alternative and led at t_B to the larger-later reward only. The time between the earlier and later choices ($t_B - t_A$) was systematically varied. When $t_B - t_A$ was brief (1 or 2 seconds), the pigeons preferred the upper (noncommitment) sequence. When $t_B - t_A$ was longer (9 or 10 seconds), the pigeons preferred the lower (commitment) sequence. The point of indifference between the two sequences was predicted fairly accurately by Mazur's hyperbolic discount equation (Equation 2.2). Similar experiments and results were reported by Ainslie and Herrnstein (1981) and Navarick and Fantino (1976). With appropriate modification of procedure and rewards, corresponding results have also been found with human subjects (Millar and Navarick, 1984; Solnick et al., 1980).

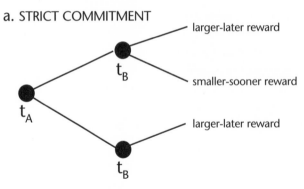

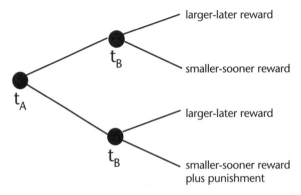

Figure 2.9. Contingencies of strict commitment (a) compared with those of punishment commitment (b). With strict commitment, a commitment response makes the smaller reward unavailable. With punishment commitment, a commitment response makes the smaller reward more costly.

Opportunities for completely removing temptations are rare in everyday life. If the television set is smashed to pieces, a new one can be bought. If the refrigerator is locked, you can go to the delicatessen. If you commit yourself to a sanitarium, you can decommit yourself. Only by performing a criminal act and being deliberately caught and sent to jail, or acting in such a bizarre way that you are committed by others to a mental institution, or by undergoing an operation (such as castration or wiring your jaws shut) that renders you physically incapable of a tempting act, can you commit yourself completely to some predetermined course of action or inaction.

In ordinary life most commitment works not by eliminating a tempting alternative but by attaching a cost to it. Again, a laboratory experiment with pigeons (Green and Rachlin, 1996) illustrates the process. The procedure (shown in Figure 2.9b) mimicked that of Figure 2.9a except the lower sequence led not to strict commitment to the larger-later reward alternative but to a choice between the larger-later reward and a smaller-sooner reward followed by a 30-second blackout in the experimental chamber. The 30-second wait is highly aversive to a hungry pigeon and serves as punishment for choosing the smaller-sooner reward within the lower sequence.

Note that in Figure 2.9b the only difference between the upper and lower sequences is that the lower sequence may lead to punishment. Nevertheless, pigeons did frequently choose the lower sequence, and chose that sequence more frequently as $t_B - t_A$ increased. Punishment essentially diminishes the value of the smaller-sooner alternative (the temptation). By choosing the lower sequence at t_A, the pigeons put themselves into a situation at t_B where the larger-later reward was preferred. This is commitment by punishment. Although not as effective as eliminating the smaller-sooner reward entirely (strict commitment), commitment by punishment is still highly effective.

Unlike strict commitment, commitment by punishment does correspond to many everyday human self-control procedures. We enter into agreements (like marriage) that include penalties for noncompliance. Smashing the TV to keep from watching it does impose the price of a new set on any change of mind we may have. At least part of the reason for subscribing to a concert series or lecture series or joining a health club is the penalty of monetary loss if we fail to show up regularly.

Alcoholics occasionally attempt to control their habit by taking the drug antabuse—which causes severe pain after drinking. For an alcoholic, taking antabuse is like choosing the lower sequence at t_A in Figure 2.9b. An alcoholic may at an earlier time (say, before leaving home for a party) decide not to drink that evening. If he takes antabuse at that point (chooses the lower sequence) and then drinks anyway at the party (chooses the smaller-sooner reward), he will suffer painful consequences (analogous to the 30-second blackout). If he takes the antabuse and then does not drink, he presumably attains the larger-later rewards dependent on sobriety (good health and the like).

In experiments with pigeons like that diagrammed in Figure 2.9b (with $t_B - t_A$ sufficiently large) the typical pigeon will choose the lower sequence at t_A and then choose the larger-later reward at t_B. Interestingly, some pigeons some of the time will choose the lower sequence at t_A and then choose the smaller-sooner reward at t_B thereby undergoing unnecessary punishment (unnecessary in the sense that had they previously chosen the upper sequence these pigeons would have been able to obtain the same smaller-sooner reward without the punishment). This apparently self-defeating behavior is also common in everyday human life. We smash the television set and then sheepishly go out and buy a new one; we subscribe to the concert series or join the health club and then don't go. Occasionally an alcoholic will take antabuse and then drink anyway, undergoing severe pain. Such drastic departure from our best-laid plans is a form of "defection" from our own previous commitment. I shall have a great deal to say about that later. Before doing so, I need to point out that the simple ambivalence exemplified by Archie Goodwin's sudden shift of preference between midnight and 7:00 A.M. or the pigeon's shift between t_A and t_B is rare in everyday human life. Much more common is a virtually continuous ambivalence, less like a tug of war with opposing forces in a neat line than like a game of blind man's buff with pushes, tugs and nudges in all directions at once. Instead of clearly defined points of time where one strong preference gives way to its opposite we generally experience a continuous opposition of forces and apparently random alternation between making and breaking our resolutions. I turn to this more complex form of ambivalence in the next chapter.

Appendix: Indifference Curves
Implied by Various Discount Functions

By finding indifference points, Mazur (1987) experimentally set the current value of the smaller-sooner reward (v_S) equal to that of the larger-later reward (v_L). Exponential discounting (Equation 2.1) predicts that

$$v_S = v_L, \quad V_S e^{-rD_S} = V_L e^{-rD_L}, \quad D_L = \frac{\ln V_L - \ln V_S}{r} + D_S.$$

Because the amounts of the rewards are constant and r is a constant, the term $(\ln V_L - \ln V_S)/r$ must be constant. Thus, the relationship between delays D_L and D_S at indifference is predicted to be a straight line with a slope equal to 1.0 and a positive y-intercept (positive because $V_L > V_S$).

Hyperbolic discounting (Equation 2.2) predicts:

$$v_S = v_L, \quad \frac{V_S}{1 + kD_S} = \frac{V_L}{1 + kD_L}, \quad D_L = \frac{V_L - V_S}{kV_S} + \frac{V_L}{V_S} D_S.$$

Again, because amounts are constant, the relationship between D_L and D_S at indifference is predicted by Equation 2.2 to be a straight line and again (because $V_L > V_S$), the y-intercept is predicted to be positive. But now (also because $V_L > V_S$) the slope of the straight line is predicted to be greater than 1.0. Figure 2.6 shows Mazur's results. The relationship is close to linear for each pigeon (the best-fitting straight lines account for 98.3 percent to 99.7 percent of the variance among the points) and the intercepts are generally positive, as both exponential and hyperbolic discounting predict. But for the four pigeons (S1, S2, S3, S4), the slopes are 2.6, 2.2, 2.7, and 2.0, respectively. These slopes are all significantly greater than 1.0 as hyperbolic discounting (Equation 2.2) predicts. The dotted lines show the slopes of 1.0 predicted by exponential discounting.

A generalized version of Equation 2.2 has been suggested by Loewenstein and Prelec (1992):

$$v = \frac{V}{(1+kD)^b}. \tag{2.3}$$

When $b = 1$, the Loewenstein-Prelec discount function reduces to Equation 2.2.[11]

The data obtained in most studies with humans as well as nonhumans may be described by the simpler (single-constant) Equation 2.2. Occasionally, however, in experiments with human subjects—where data are averaged, rewards are hypothetical, and events during the delay period (also hypothetical) are less well controlled than with nonhumans—the extra parameter of the Loewenstein-Prelec equation becomes necessary.

The matching law, originally proposed by Richard Herrnstein (1961) is an empirical law of choice, confirmed in hundreds of experiments with humans, pigeons, and numerous other species (see the collection of articles in Herrnstein, 1997). A general form of the matching law (Baum and Rachlin, 1969) is

$$\frac{B_1}{B_2} = \frac{v_1}{v_2} = \left(\frac{R_1}{R_2}\right)^s,$$

where B is a measure of behavior and R is the reward rate (value over time) dependent on B. The exponent s is a measure of the discriminability of the choice alternatives (Baum, 1974) or the economic substitutability of the rewards (Rachlin, 1982). When the choice alternatives are perfectly distinct and the rewards perfectly substitutable, the exponent s

equals 1.0. As choice alternatives become less discriminable and rewards less substitutable, s decreases. For completely confused choice alternatives, $s \to 0$ (implying indifference). For alternatives (such as food and water) that are economic complements, s becomes negative (Hursh, 1978), resulting in "antimatching" (behavioral allocation inversely proportional to reward rate).

The "rate" of a single reward is the inverse of its delay. In choosing between two single delayed rewards, as in Mazur's (1987) experiment with pigeons, the matching law implies the hyperbolic discounting Mazur found. The fact that the pigeons in Mazur's experiment chose between alternatives by pecking one of two differently colored (highly discriminable) buttons and that the alternatives (greater or lesser duration of access to mixed grain) were identical in quality, implies a matching exponent of 1.0, as Mazur also found. However, where choice alternatives are not perfectly discriminable and rewards not perfectly substitutable, Loewenstein and Prelec's more general discount function would be expected.

3

Complex Ambivalence

When Goodwin sets his alarm clock at night for 7:00 A.M., he is not at that point tempted to sleep to noon.[1] He in effect stands outside of his next morning's self. He has a platform from which he can launch his commitment. But the alcoholic has no platform; he is always tempted. The alcoholic is never free of the desire for a drink, except perhaps for a brief period after a binge; even then, he is eager to cure his hangover with another drink. The alcoholic is continuously beset by ambivalence; he drinks for a period and abstains for a period, but even when he abstains he is tempted to drink. This pattern is complex ambivalence. Unlike simple ambivalence, it is not easily avoided with simple commitment devices. Commitment would be effective only if initiated immediately and maintained indefinitely. A later chapter will discuss how commitment may apply to complex ambivalence. First we have to see precisely what it is that distinguishes complex from simple ambivalence.

Figure 3.1 illustrates the difference between the two types. They are alike in the sense that one alternative (the temptation) is always an immediately available but lesser-valued reward. A child, offered the alternatives—one candy bar right now versus two candy bars tomorrow—and tempted to choose the one candy bar now, is in principle like the alcoholic tempted to drink now. But the child who chooses two candy bars tomorrow is in no way like the alcoholic who (at last) chooses sobriety. Two candy bars are commensurable with one candy bar, and the time of delivery of the two candy bars may be specified. Sobriety, by contrast, is not commensurable with having a drink and does not arrive or depart at specific times. The borderline between alcoholism and sobriety is very fuzzy. It seems (and often is) possible to be sober and still have a drink. The relationship of sobriety to having a drink is that of a temporally extended event to a temporally

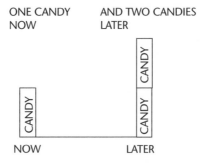

a. A CHILD CHOOSING BETWEEN

ONE CANDY   AND TWO CANDIES
NOW   LATER

NOW   LATER

IS CHOOSING BETWEEN
TWO CLEARLY DEFINED
ALTERNATIVES

b. BUT AN ALCOHOLIC CHOOSING BETWEEN

A DRINK

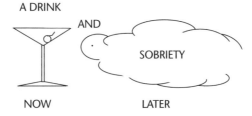

AND

SOBRIETY

NOW   LATER

IS CHOOSING BETWEEN ONE
CLEARLY DEFINED ALTERNATIVE
AND A VAGUELY DEFINED,
ABSTRACT STATE

Figure 3.1. Examples of (a) simple ambivalence and (b) complex ambivalence.

discrete event—of an abstract pattern of behavior to a specific act. This sort of conflict—between abstract and specific—is difficult to grasp. What is the nature of the conflict and what does it imply about self-control?

Imagine that you see a snippet of film that shows a man swinging a hammer. But what is he *actually* doing? Consider the following alternative descriptions. He is

a. swinging a hammer
b. hammering a nail

c. joining one piece of wood to another

d. laying a floor

e. building a house

f. providing shelter for his family

g. supporting his family

h. being a good husband and father

i. being a good person

All of these may be valid descriptions of his behavior. Based on the snippet of film you saw, all you can say is that he is swinging the hammer. He might have been swinging it at someone's head. But if you said, "He's just swinging the hammer," someone else who saw more of the film might with justice say, "Yes, he's doing that, but what he's *really* doing is hammering a nail." A third person who has seen still more of the film might then correct the second in a similar way: "Yes, he's hammering a nail, but what he's *really* doing is laying a floor." And so forth until we get to a Godlike observer who has sat through a film of virtually this man's entire life and can make the final judgment: "He's being a good person."

The important point is that all nine descriptions, are descriptions of the man's behavior. As you go down the list, more and more context is incorporated into the description, but that context is always behavioral. The final Godlike observer need not look into the man's heart as long as he has looked at the complete film of the man's life. Then the observer can say "He is a good person" without fear of contradiction—regardless of the state of the man's heart. The validity of any of the above descriptions may be settled by moving the camera back or showing more film—earlier and later.

This teleological and behavioristic way of talking is different from the usual way. Usually, as you go down the list, you are supposedly going deeper and deeper into the man himself. Deeper and deeper into his internal intentions, his internal consciousness, his nervous system, or his soul (where the soul is considered to be some nonmaterial internal entity). In a sense, the usual conception has to be true. If the man is building a house, some internal mechanism must be causing his movements. Correspondingly, if a sound system is playing Beethoven's Fifth Symphony there must be some mechanism that does the job—AM, FM, LP, CD, or tape. But the mechanism is not the thing we are describing. For a sound system to be playing Beethoven's Fifth, that symphony must be coming out of the system regardless of the mechanism. Similarly, for a man to support his family, he must support his family regardless of the mechanism that allows him to behave.

You might say that there is a difference between the man who intentionally swings a hammer and the man who accidentally swings a hammer—even though the two men are behaving alike. And, you might add, the difference lies inside them. Again, while it is true that something inside people must mediate behavioral differences, the difference between intention and accident *is* behavioral. The difference between a man purposely swinging a hammer and a man accidentally swinging a hammer can be resolved not by looking inside him but by looking at more of his behavior. A man accidentally swinging a hammer will not be hammering a nail or laying a floor.

Behavioral Context and Self-Control

What implications does this point of view have for self-control? The answer is that no particular act or pattern of acts can be judged by itself. An act or pattern of acts may be impulsive or self-controlled, depending on the behavioral context in which it is embedded. No single act or pattern of acts can be understood outside its context. A person having a single drink is just having a single drink until we have, as it were, seen the rest of the film—until we have seen the context (alcoholism, almost complete abstaining, or social drinking) into which this act or pattern of acts fits.

Imagine the following: You enjoy both popular and classical music and you like to listen to music on the compact-disc player in your car. Because a popular song lasts about three minutes and a symphony lasts about an hour, on short trips of less than an hour you listen to popular songs. On long trips, trips of several hours, you have a difficult choice. How can you weigh the two alternatives (a popular song versus a symphony) and come up with a single value for each? If we compare a three-minute song with any given three-minute period in a symphony, the song is always more valuable, more pleasurable, of higher utility. Yet the sum of an hour's worth of three-minute songs is worth less to you (I am assuming here) than listening to the whole symphony.[2]

Figure 3.2 illustrates the problem. The left-right distance represents time passing; the heights of the horizontal bars above the thin line represent the relative values of three events. The one-hour symphony (the long hatched

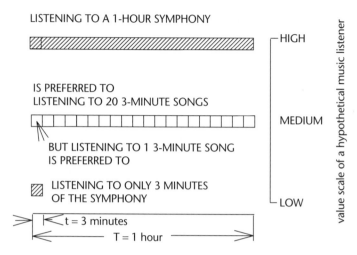

Figure 3.2. Example of the dilemma of complex ambivalence. The longer, more complex activity is preferred to the simpler act, but the simpler act is preferred to a portion of the longer, more complex activity.

bar) has the highest value; the three-minute song (a section of the white bar) has the next-highest value; the first three-minute section of the symphony heard alone (the short hatched bar) has the least value. Ambivalence arises because you have to listen to the first three minutes of the symphony in order to hear the rest. Thus you have to choose the presently lower-valued music in order to hear the ultimately higher-valued music.

Our usual tendency to analyze each alternative into its elements and to evaluate those elements one by one will not work here. Suppose that the trip is a very long one (the beginning of a cross-country trip, say). You might prefer to listen to one popular song and then switch to the symphony, having the best of both worlds, so to speak. But *after* you have listened to that song you will be in the same position as you were at the beginning (assuming you haven't tired of the songs) and will now prefer to listen to one *more* song and *then* to the symphony. Then, one more, and one more, and one more, until at last you reach California without ever having played the symphony—even though if you had played it, you would have enjoyed it more than the songs that occupied the same period.

The core of your dilemma is that the pleasure you get from a symphony is of a different kind and not precisely commensurable with the pleasure you get from a popular song. It is just not possible to add the momentary pleasures of each three-minute period of the symphony and come up with a sum that represents the value of the whole event.

We call the feeling we get from listening to a symphony, *pleasure,* just as we call the feeling we get from listening to a song *pleasure.* These two so-called pleasures cannot be put on a scale, weighed, and compared, how-ever. The pleasure of listening to any particular three-minute section of a symphony depends strongly on also listening to the rest of the musical piece. If you listen to the first fifty-seven minutes of the symphony but miss the last three, you are likely to feel that the whole experience was ru-ined. How can that final three minutes reach back in time and ruin the ini-tial three minutes of pleasure that you presumably *already* experienced? It is as if the initial moments of the symphony are some sort of investment that pays off only when it is finished.

Yet we do truly enjoy the symphony while it is going on. The investment lies not in an absolute negative feeling (dysphoria) at the beginning of such activities but in the more pleasurable but more brief activities that we forgo. (I am assuming that the value of the whole one-hour symphony is greater than the sum of the values of twenty three-minute songs.) But the value of a one-hour symphony cut off after fifty-seven minutes might well be less than that of the sum of the values of nineteen three-minute songs. In that sense—when the symphony is cut off after fifty-seven minutes— our investment in it has not paid off.

On a more compressed level, the same is true of a popular song. Inter-ruption can spoil the value of a song as much as or more than that of a symphony. Who among us has not sat in the parking lot waiting for a song to be over before leaving our car? Just as a song is shorter than a symphony, a joke is (usually) shorter than a song. A song lasts three minutes but a joke may take fifteen seconds to tell. Instead of listening to the song, we could (let us suppose) have tuned in to a comedy station and heard a stand-up comic delivering rapid-fire fifteen-second jokes. Let us assume that any of the twelve fifteen-second jokes that it takes to occupy three minutes would have been more emotionally satisfying than any fifteen-second portion of the three-minute song. Yet the song as a whole is more valuable to us (I am assuming) than the twelve jokes as a whole. This is the essence of complex ambivalence. The value of any activity has a unitary or molar quality that cannot be broken into pieces and separately weighed.

The gestalt psychologists, referring to perception, said that the whole is greater than the sum of its parts. We do not say, "His nose is like my father's nose, his mouth is like my father's mouth, his eyes are like my father's eyes, therefore he is my father." Rather, we recognize our father's face, as a whole, as a certain abstract relationship of its elements. The *essence* of our recognition is not the parts but the relationship of the parts. We recognize a song, the gestalt psychologists said, not as the sum of a series of notes, but as a relationship of the notes. When a song is transposed to a different key or played by a different instrument, it remains the same song—and we recognize it—even though the underlying physical sounds may be entirely different from any we have previously heard.

The point here is that not just our recognition of songs, but also the pleasure we get from them, has a molar, unitary quality. If you break a song or symphony into its component pieces and rearrange them, you not only destroy the listener's recognition, you also destroy the listener's enjoyment.[3]

There is nothing unique about songs in this respect. Watching a half-hour TV program may provide us with immediate excitement, not nearly approached by any given half-hour of novel reading. Yet the ten or twelve hours that it takes to read a novel may well be more satisfying if spent actually reading it than if spent watching twenty half-hour TV programs. The choice between beginning to read the book for a half-hour and watching a half-hour program is easily resolved in favor of the television. After the TV show is over, we have the same choice to make all over again—watch another program or pick up the book. If we resolve the choice in the same way, again and again and again we will end up (as we often do) spending our leisure time watching television instead of reading the book, despite the fact that when all is said and done we would have enjoyed reading the book more than watching TV.

Let me formalize these examples of complex ambivalence. Suppose two alternative activities are available, a relatively brief activity lasting t units of time and a longer activity lasting T units of time, where $T = nt$ and n is a positive number greater than one. In other words, the duration of t is less than that of T, and n of the smaller t's can fit into a single T. Complex ambivalence then depends on two conditions:

1. The whole longer activity is preferred to n repetitions of the brief activity.
2. The brief activity is preferred to any t-length fraction of the longer activity.

Cases that satisfy conditions 1 and 2 constitute most of our everyday self-control problems. Suppose you charge $100 every month on your credit card. If you consider this month only, paying the minimum is preferred to paying the full amount. The minimum payment is *always* much less than the full amount. Yet if you continue to charge $100 a month and continue to pay the minimum, you will soon be paying more than $100 per month, mostly in interest, until you reach your limit. If you look at several years as a whole, the total paid by paying the minimum is much much larger than the total paid by paying the full amount each month. Ambivalence as to whether to pay the minimum or the full amount on a credit card bill is therefore a case (a paradigm) of complex ambivalence.

The deluge of credit card offers that most of us receive in the mail does not appear as insidious as if we were to receive cocaine samples in the mail—but the tragedy that easy credit may generate in people's lives is of the same kind.

In general, living a healthy life for a period of ten years, say, is intrinsically satisfying. You feel better, you eat and drink moderately, you don't smoke, you get sufficient exercise, and so forth. Over a ten-year period, virtually all of us would prefer living a healthy life to being an alcoholic, being a glutton, being a smoker, being a couch potato. Yet we also (more or less) prefer to drink this drink than not to drink it, to eat this chocolate sundae than to forgo it, to smoke this cigarette than not to smoke it, to watch this TV program than to spend a half-hour exercising. The ambivalence is very real. Looked at narrowly, the shorter activity is better than the longer one (it is better to drink now than to be sober now); looked at widely, the longer activity is better than the shorter one (it is better to be sober generally than to be an alcoholic). The alcoholic's dilemma is an ambiguity in time that has no intrinsically correct resolution. Which alternative is better depends on whether the alcoholic's focus is narrow or wide.

Figure 3.3 takes the music example shown in Figure 3.2, magnifies the time periods, and applies it to alcoholism.(Chapters 4 and 5 will be more precise.) Almost all alcoholics prefer to be sober (or to drink moderately) than to be alcoholics. But they also strongly prefer to drink today than to abstain today; and since it is always today, they drink.

Of course the physiological underpinnings of alcoholism differ entirely from the physiological underpinnings of listening to a song. But (assuming a symphony is actually preferred) the behavioral structures of the two dilemmas are analogous. And, as we shall see later, the methods by which we

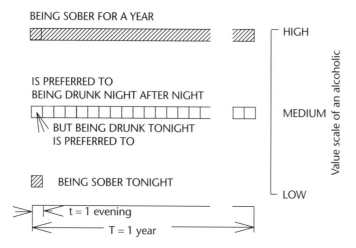

BEING SOBER FOR A YEAR

IS PREFERRED TO
BEING DRUNK NIGHT AFTER NIGHT

BUT BEING DRUNK TONIGHT
IS PREFERRED TO

BEING SOBER TONIGHT

t = 1 evening

T = 1 year

HIGH

MEDIUM

LOW

Value scale of an alcoholic

Figure 3.3. The dilemma of complex ambivalence illustrated by alcoholism. Being sober for a year is preferred to being drunk for a year, but being drunk tonight is preferred to being sober tonight.

may avoid alcoholism, escape alcoholism, and avoid relapse to alcoholism are also analogous to those by which we may get ourselves to listen to symphonies (when we actually prefer them) rather than songs.

Levels of Value

Figure 3.3 presents a stark and depressing picture. It is as if the alcoholic's only choice is either to give in to alcoholism (be drunk all the time) or by managing to avoid alcoholism (in ways not yet discussed) to be a teetotaler, to abstain completely, to miss out on parties, to become a social stick-in-the-mud, perhaps even to be less healthy (if we believe recent studies showing that moderate drinkers live longer than teetotalers). Let us assume for the moment that moderate drinking—social drinking, or one glass of wine with dinner—is better for you than teetotaling in the context of your social life or your overall health.

Figure 3.4 adds this further level. It diagrams three hypothetical patterns of behavior over time. Let us say the alcoholic has become a teetotaler—he has abstained from drinking for a year. He is now reaping the benefits of his abstention. His life as a whole is clearly better than it was before. His re-

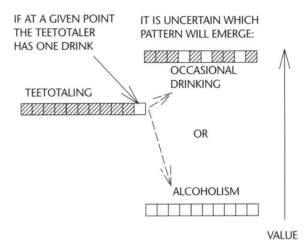

Figure 3.4. An example of how a single instance of an act may (in retrospect) be part of a higher-valued pattern or a lower-valued pattern.

lations with his family are certainly better, his performance in his job is better, and the satisfaction he extracts from these changes has made him a better person than before. Sobriety fits better than alcoholism into the larger pattern of his life. Figure 3.4 indicates this by placing the bar labeled "teetotaling" far above that labeled "alcoholism."

However, from his present vantage point, the reformed alcoholic sees the possibility of a still better way of living. He sees others who can enjoy a drink at a party, even occasionally get drunk, yet maintain satisfactory relationships with family and friends and function well at their jobs. This is the alcoholic's view from the position of teetotaling. So one evening he has a glass of wine with dinner. Now what? There is no way of knowing. He could easily proceed once again toward alcoholism or he could have taken the first step toward a new and better life. Which will it be? How can we predict which it will be? If we ask him, of course he will say that this drink is the first step upward toward social drinking; otherwise he would not have taken the drink. He sincerely believes that he has taken that first step. But has he?

The truth of the matter lies not in the current state of his consciousness or his nervous system but in the future patterns of his behavior. The best predictor of those patterns is not the man's own introspection (no matter how honest), not his deepest intentions, but someone's actual observations of the patterns of his past behavior. That someone could be the man himself; remember the assumption that he has been abstaining for a year and has just taken a drink. He quite naturally feels that his current resolution to change (from teetotaling to social drinking) outweighs the actual outcomes of his past resolutions. Yet his close friends and relatives are not apt to be so influenced. If they have observed (and suffered through) many previous periods of teetotaling followed by gradual relapse back to alcoholism, they are less likely than the man himself to see this time as different from the rest.

Our friends and relatives are essential mirrors of the patterns of our behavior over long periods—mirrors of our souls. They are the magic "mirrors on the wall" who can tell us whether this drink, this cigarette, this ice-cream sundae, this line of cocaine, is more likely to be part of a new future or an old past. We dispense with these individuals at a terrible risk to our self-control. The temptation to dispense with them is great in proportion to the temptation to have the one drink or one cigarette. We may try to bully them into lying to us, but to the extent that our bullying succeeds, we befog our own self-perception. The ex-alcoholic should be careful to take that single drink only under the close supervision and in collusion with the person closest to him, the person who will suffer most if he slips into alcoholism.

Revolt against Indulgence

Let us take a step back. The alcoholic has gone a year without drinking and he is at a dinner party. The hostess, not knowing that he is a reformed alcoholic, offers him a glass of wine. He has previously considered becoming a social drinker rather than a teetotaler. This is his chance. With a wildly beating heart, however, he puts his hand over the glass and says, "No, thanks." Maybe he will start drinking next time.

The teetotaler's ambivalence in choosing between continuing the pattern of teetotaling and starting on a pattern of social drinking is a transposed version of the alcoholic's ambivalence in choosing between continuing to drink and starting on a pattern of teetotaling. The alcoholic continues his present pattern by having this drink; the teetotaler continues his present pattern by not having this drink. The alcoholic would exhibit self-control by not drinking for a time; the teetotaler would exhibit self-control by drinking moderately for a time. In other words, social drinking is to teetotaling as teetotaling is to alcoholism. In terms of amount of alcohol consumed, social drinking stands between alcoholism and sobriety. But in terms of self-control, social drinking is the most complex and difficult to maintain of the three behavioral patterns. Everything we have said about how easy it is to be an alcoholic relative to being a teetotaler may be said about how easy it is to be a teetotaler relative to being a social drinker. The alcoholic who has abstained from drink for a year (and is contemplating becoming a social drinker) is as ambivalent about having this drink as is the current alcoholic. It is just that the ambivalence goes in a different direction.

In terms of its effect on love and work and health, the harm of being a rigid teetotaler (relative to social drinking) is minuscule as compared with the harm of being an alcoholic (relative to teetotaling). This is why Alcoholics Anonymous insists that reformed alcoholics "put the cork in the bottle" and never even contemplate having a drink. Teetotaling is a revolt against indulgence.

It is important to note that the order of values diagrammed in Figure 3.4 does not apply in every case. Recall that no act or pattern of acts can be judged outside its context. Once, after a public lecture in which I argued that social drinking was usually a more difficult but ultimately better pattern of behavior than teetotalism, a young woman came up to me and said that although she had enjoyed the lecture she disagreed strongly with its final conclusion about teetotalism. She was, she said, the fifth child among eight brothers and sisters. The older four were all alcoholics; she herself was a teetotaler; the younger three were social drinkers. She felt that her example served as a sort of barrier against alcoholism for her younger siblings. They had to have some model, she felt, to balance against the vision that fate (or genetics) had doomed them to alcoholism. She was that model.

Whether or not she was correct about her particular case, she had put her finger on a critical point. The meaning of any action is given by its behavioral context. Teetotalism, for her, was not a rigid reaction to alcoholism but part of a highly complex pattern of acts constituting care for and responsibility for her family. She was setting an example, not simply revolting against indulgence. Just as a single drink may be elevated in ultimate value when it is part of a pattern of social drinking, so teetotalism may be elevated in value when it is part of a pattern of social responsibility. What counts ultimately is not the acts or patterns of acts themselves but the wider context into which they may fit.

Nevertheless, for most of us teetotaling is a kind of lack of self-control. If teetotaling does no serious harm, corresponding revolts against indulgence in other areas of life may do harm. The misnamed "workaholism," for example, corresponds more closely to teetotaling than it does to alcoholism. The workaholic does not even consider taking a day off for the same reason that the teetotaler does not even consider having a drink. The workaholic who takes one day off is like the teetotaler who has one drink. At that point the workaholic is in a state of complete uncertainty about future patterns of behavior. This day off could be the first day of a more balanced life or the first step down the path leading to complete laziness and indifference. Just as the reformed alcoholic having one drink is the last person you should ask about which pattern will develop—social drinking or alcoholism—so the workaholic taking one day off is the last person you should ask about which pattern will develop—a balanced life or slothfulness.

Workaholism, like teetotalism, is a problem of secondary self-control. Both are reactions at one extreme against a still more damaging pattern at the other extreme. Both are revolts against indulgence. In most cases such revolts are less damaging than indulgence itself, but in some cases they can be worse than indulgence. The workaholic who sacrifices her own life to her career may also be sacrificing her family's lives. Modern literature is full of stories of women and men who have unwittingly made such sacrifices. These cases have in common the adoption of a relatively simple behavioral pattern (teetotaling, workaholism) in the face of the complexities of modern life (where moderate drinking and moderate industriousness are rewarded). Although the simple pattern adopted may be less harmful than the simple pattern at the other extreme, it is still harmful relative to the complex abstract pattern that constitutes a balanced (happy) life.

Internal Commitment

The kinds of commitment discussed in Chapter 2 require a period when a larger-later reward is clearly preferred, followed by a period when a smaller but immediately available alternative (a temptation) is clearly preferred. During the former period, the temptation can be avoided by instituting a commitment procedure that either makes it entirely unavailable (as Figure

2.9a illustrates) or loads it down with punishment (Figure 2.9b). Commitment works well in cases of simple ambivalence, where there is a distinct reversal of choice from one time to the next: at midnight Archie Goodwin prefers to get up at 7:00 A.M.; at 7:00 A.M. he prefers to get up at noon. In cases of complex ambivalence, such as an alcoholic's ambivalence about whether or not to have a drink, commitment is difficult to institute: there is no clear period when the alcoholic reliably prefers to be sober and no clear period when he reliably prefers to have a drink. He *always* prefers to be sober and he *always* prefers to have a drink.

The history of the use of the drug antabuse illustrates the problem (Davison and Neale, 1994). If you take antabuse and then have a drink, you will undergo severe pain. Most people, most hard-core alcoholics who take antabuse, cannot and do not drink during the period when antabuse is in their bloodstreams. But not always. It is possible to sip alcohol so slowly that the antabuse never kicks in. Alcoholics forced to take antabuse may learn this skill. Some alcoholics will even voluntarily take antabuse and then drink anyway, thereby undergoing the pain unnecessarily. This resembles the behavior of some of the pigeons in the experiment of Figure 2.9b. The pigeons committed themselves by pecking a button that would impose a penalty if they later chose a small, immediate ("tempting") food reward; some pigeons would commit themselves and then go ahead anyway to chose the tempting reward, thereby undergoing the penalty (a relatively long blackout period) unnecessarily.

The main problem with antabuse, however, is not that it does not work but that alcoholics generally refuse to take it. Why? Because there is no time, even during a hangover, when the alcoholic would not feel better with a drink than without one. The same goes for heroin. As a character in Linda Yablonski's recent novel *Junk* says, "However good or bad you feel, heroin makes you feel better" (as quoted in the *New York Review of Books*, Sept. 25, 1997, p. 13.)

Because complex ambivalence is virtually continuous, commitment must be correspondingly continuous. Alcoholics will occasionally (if they have not impoverished themselves by their drinking) commit themselves to an institution such as the Betty Ford Clinic, where they will be prevented from drinking for a time. Or they may be committed by someone else. Such an institution offers the alcoholic the chance to choose between alcoholism and sobriety. (Still, *this* drink is preferred. Some commit themselves and at the same time try to smuggle in a bottle of whiskey.) But it is not possible to live in such an institution and still have a normal life. While there is no alcohol in such institutions, neither is there family or work. The effectiveness of an institution for self-control depends not on commitment in the sense of an alarm clock on the other side of the room (which can fit easily into everyday life) but on its effectiveness in changing habits—in altering patterns of behavior.

That much is generally understood. Realizing that no commitment device can effectively control complex ambivalence and at the same time allow people to live ordinary lives, theorists have speculated that when faced with complex ambivalence, people may *internalize* commitment. The basic mechanism of internal commitment, these theorists speculate, is guilt. Internal guilt is the feeling of having committed some sort of offense. It is a negative feeling and most of us would rather not feel it. The alcoholic who does not take antabuse is thus, according to these theorists, much like the one who does—except instead of feeling pain after drinking, this alcoholic feels guilt. Just as the antabuse taker is punished for drinking by pain, the non–antabuse taker is punished by guilt. Or so it would seem in theory. While there is no question that in cases of ambivalence people who do things they believe they should not do feel guilt, and there is no question that guilt is an unpleasant feeling, there is reason to doubt that guilt can serve as effective punishment in cases of complex ambivalence such as alcoholism.

The difference between guilt and the pain from antabuse is that guilt is self-imposed in a way that the pain from antabuse is not. The pain from the antabuse is caused by a bodily interaction between antabuse and alcohol. The pain from the guilt is indistinguishable from the guilt itself. When antabuse is self-imposed, the self-imposition comes *before* the drink and the pain comes after. However, the self-imposition of the guilt and the pain of that guilt both come *after* the drink (and, unlike the pain from antabuse, guilt may be relieved by having yet another drink).

Feeling guilty may work in very mild cases of complex ambivalence, much like slapping oneself on the hand may work after having the drink— mainly as a method of relatively neutral feedback. You could say to yourself, "Yes I just did that and I shouldn't have," or you could slap yourself, or you could hit yourself on the head with the heel of your hand while cursing under your breath. Or you could feel guilt. All may have a slight effect on your behavior; none can have any permanent effect or even any strong effect.

Trying to punish yourself after the fact is like trying to lift yourself by your own bootstraps. To control an act you need an outside link, some external force (a reward or punishment) or some force set in motion prior to the act (a commitment). Otherwise you are doing no more than underlining or recording the act. Although recording instances of an act may indeed help in controlling it (see Chapter 6), except in very mild cases of complex ambivalence, it is not enough.

Moreover, even if guilt were effective in controlling our own behavior (for which there is no evidence), we would still have to ask, How do we control our guilt? Then we would have to ask, How does our guilt in turn control our behavior? It is far better, far simpler, far more effective, to ask directly, How do we control our behavior? That last question is the principal concern of this book.

The Primrose Path

Herrnstein and Prelec (1992) have proposed a process, called the primrose path, for the development of addiction under conditions of complex ambivalence. A highly simplified version is illustrated in Figure 3.5. The question that the primrose-path process tries to answer is, How can you always choose the best among all available alternatives and still end up in a worse state than when you started?

Again, let us follow along with the example of alcoholism. Sobriety is represented in Figure 3.5, as in Figure 3.3, by a shaded bar at a moderately high value (see scale at the right of the figure). Also as in Figure 3.3, alcoholism is represented by an open bar at a moderately low value. These extended bars represent steady states. Figure 3.5 shows the process of transition from one to the other. People simply choosing between the two extended bars would always choose the higher (sobriety) over the lower (alcoholism). However, although a T-length unit of not drinking is worth more than a T-length unit of drinking, a t-length unit of drinking is worth more than a t-length unit of not drinking. For a person who chooses not between extended states but only between brief units of short duration (t), the very highest valued alternative would be a unit of drinking. Choice of that alternative is represented in Figure 3.5 by the arrow AB.

Each small box in Figure 3.5 represents one of a pair of outcomes of a single choice. The outcomes of a given choice (to drink or to refuse a drink) are paired along a line tilted slightly to the right of the vertical. For

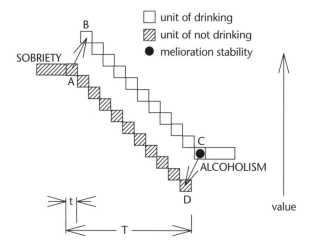

Figure 3.5. The primrose path from sobriety to alcoholism (ABC) and the straight and narrow path from alcoholism to sobriety (CDA).

example, A and B are the pair of outcomes of not drinking and drinking in the state of total sobriety; the pair of boxes just to the right and down one step from A and B are the pair of outcomes just after a single drink has been chosen; the pair down one more step are the outcomes just after two drinks have been chosen, and so forth, running down to boxes D and C, the outcomes after drinking has been continuously chosen—in the state of complete alcoholism. Each open box (representing the outcome of a choice to drink) is higher in value than its corresponding shaded box (outcome of a choice not to drink). Assuming that Figure 3.5 is a true picture of these choices and their outcomes, if the higher valued outcome of the pair is always chosen, alcoholism will be the invariable result. This is the primrose path.[4]

Essential to the Herrnstein-Prelec theory (as well as to an economically based theory of Becker and Murphy, (1990)) is the descent in value, not only of the addictive activity, but of all activities together until stability is finally reached at C, representing a steady state of continuous drinking lower in value than continuous sobriety. Stable states such as C are shown as thick dots in Figures 3.5 to 3.10.) In the case of drinking, this descent is easy to envision. A person who drinks and keeps drinking loses not only the enjoyment of drinking, but also the enjoyment of health, social activity, work, and virtually everything else.

Although a single unit of drinking is worth less to an alcoholic than to a social drinker, it is still worth more, perhaps much more, than not drinking. This mutual deterioration of drinking and not drinking is represented in Figure 3.5 by the downward stepping of the open t-length boxes in tandem with the hatched t-length boxes. As the higher-valued t-length units of drinking are repeatedly chosen over the lower-valued t-length units of not drinking, the values of both alternatives sink together coming to rest finally at C. At every point along the path from B to C the higher-valued unit is chosen. Nevertheless, the final stable state C, is lower in value than the initial state A. Path ABC is the primrose path.

An alcoholic cannot retreat directly along the primrose path. The only way back from C to A is through point D, a decrease in unit value. In colloquial terms, the alcoholic is unhappy but would be still more miserable (for a while) if he stopped drinking. The route from C to D to A might be called "the straight and narrow path." At every point along this path there exists a more valuable t-length alternative. How to take the straight and narrow path and stay on it is *the* crucial question for a science of self-control.

MELIORATION.   It would make sense at this point to apply to complex ambivalence the discount functions introduced in the previous chapter. The difference between a person choosing narrowly, between t-length alternatives, and a person choosing widely, between T-length alternatives, may be quantified in terms of the constant k in Equation 2.2. Narrow choices imply high k's and severe discounting of distant events. Wide choices imply low k's and little discounting of distant events. Nevertheless, it will be convenient in this chapter and in all future discussions of complex ambivalence to continue to treat discounting as an all-or-none process. That is, alternatives are specified in terms of units. Melioration is defined as choice of the highest-valued t-length unit (Herrnstein and Vaughan, 1980). All events within the unit are given their full value; events beyond the unit are ignored. The meliorating organism simply chooses the unit of highest value. Units in turn may be fixed temporal intervals (t in the discussion above) or may be defined by stimuli as a "situation." For example, a party on a given evening may be defined as a unit in terms of its stimuli—the sights, sounds, smells of the room. Melioration is choice of the highest-valued unit (regardless of the effects of this choice beyond the unit—for example, the morning after the party). The person in Figure 3.5 choosing to drink (B) rather than not to drink (A), even though drinking decreases future value, is meliorating. Similarly, when you pay the minimum rather than the full amount on your credit card bill—even though by paying the minimum you will have to pay more in the long run—you are meliorating. You are choosing the highest-valued alternative over a limited period.

Your behavior could also be interpreted in terms of maximization: maximization of value, discounting the cost of future payments. Any behavior that can be explained in terms of meliorating (with judicious adjustment of t) can also be explained as maximization of discounted value[5] (with judicious adjustment of k in Equation 2.2). The reasons for using the concept of melioration in this chapter are, first, mathematical simplicity and, second, the fact that the concept of melioration leads naturally to that of behavioral restructuring.

RESTRUCTURING. A meliorating organism may achieve self-control by restructuring choice alternatives into larger units—by expanding t. In Figure 3.5 the duration of t (the effective choice horizon) has been set at one-tenth that of T; it takes ten t-length steps to get from B to C. In Figure 3.6 t

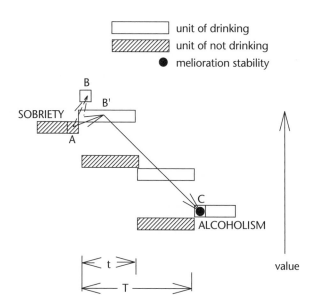

Figure 3.6. Moderate behavioral restructuring (increasing the duration of a behavioral unit) that decreases the value of drinking and makes sobriety easier to maintain.

has been expanded to one-half T; the values of the first five steps in Figure 3.5 are averaged and drawn as a single step five times as wide as in the previous figure. The average of the second five steps in Figure 3.5 are also averaged and drawn as a second step just above and to the left of point C. Because the smaller steps of Figure 3.5 are decreasing in value, the average value of the first five small steps is lower than that of the first small step. Thus, the value of the initial unit of drinking, B′ in Figure 3.6, is lower than that of the initial unit B in Figure 3.5. Still, the incentive to drink is positive in Figure 3.6 (arrow AB′ points upward) and melioration (choice of the highest-valued unit) would bring a person to stability at C in two large steps (rather than in ten small steps as before).

In Figure 3.7 t has been expanded yet again, now to a duration equal to T. With this further expansion the incentive to drink has become negative (arrow AB″ points slightly downward) and stability of a meliorating subject occurs at A—sobriety.

Self-control achieved by restructuring is compatible with common sense. A former alcoholic who decides anew each time a drink is offered whether or not to have that drink will likely drink more than one who is

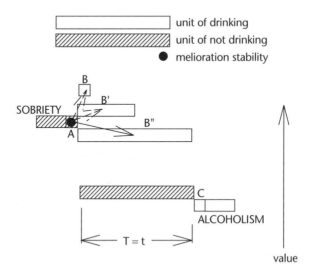

Figure 3.7. Major behavioral restructuring (vastly increasing the duration of a behavioral unit) that decreases the immediate value of drinking below that of sobriety.

able to decide at the beginning of the evening how much to drink in the course of the evening. And the latter is likely to drink more than one who decides at the beginning of the month how much to drink that month. All three are meliorating, are choosing the alternative with the highest value. As restructuring proceeds, as t increases in duration and approaches T, the effect of present behavior on future value (including hangovers, social rejection, financial ruin, bad health, and the like) gets incorporated into t; the unit of choice becomes more and more global, more and more meaningful.

In terms of the list of activities (ranging from swinging a hammer to being a good person) presented at the beginning of this chapter, few people would choose to swing a hammer for its own sake. Everyone would choose to be a good person rather than a bad one—if being good involved no sacrifice. (In the latter case, unfortunately, the alternatives are so abstract that few of us are able to choose between them as wholes.)

The problem of achieving self-control in cases of complex ambivalence thus reduces to the problem of restructuring choice alternatives so as to incorporate more context. I shall explore effective and ineffective solutions in later chapters, but first I need to explore the primrose path in more detail and uncover its causes.

CYCLING.   The difference between states A and C in Figure 3.5 is not only that A is above C in value but also that A is below point B while C is above point D. In going from A to B, value increases. Behavior that increases value is said to be positively reinforced. Choice of B over A is thus an instance of *positive reinforcement.* On the other hand, in going from C to D, value decreases. Behavior that decreases value is said to be punished; avoidance of a decrease in value is said to be negatively reinforced. Choice of C over D is thus an instance of *negative reinforcement* (Premack, 1965). Colloquially, for a nonaddict (at A) addictive activity (going to B) would be pleasurable, while, for an addict (at C) addictive activity (staying at C) merely avoids pain.[6]

Figure 3.8 repeats the conditions of Figure 3.5 ($t = 0.1T$), but for simplicity straight lines replace the boxes. The dashed line in Figure 3.8 represents average utility at various mixtures of addictive and nonaddictive activity proportional to the horizontal separation of A and C in the figure.

In the long run, for example, the average value of a t-length unit for a person who drank during 50 percent of the units would be at the midpoint

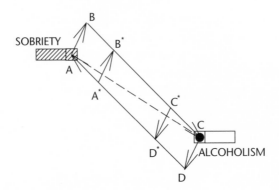

Figure 3.8. The dashed line represents the average value obtained by various rates of an addictive activity ranging from 0 percent of the time at point A to 100 percent at point C. The area above the dashed line is positive reinforcement; the area below the dashed line is negative reinforcement.

of the dashed line; that of a person who drank during 25 percent of the units would be one fourth of the way from A to C on the dashed line; that of a person who drank during 75 percent of the units would be three fourths of the way from A to C on the dashed line, and so forth. The region above the dashed line represents local improvement in value over the average. The region below the dashed line represents local diminution in value below the average. The dashed line thus separates regions of positive and negative reinforcement. Triangle ABC is an area of positive reinforcement; triangle CDA is an area of negative reinforcement.

Suppose that a person has become an addict and is at state C in Figure 3.8. There are now two motives for quitting—for taking the straight and narrow path from C to D to A. One motive is to increase average (or overall) utility; the other is to exchange negative for positive reinforcement. The latter is a very powerful force in human behavior which, according to Skinner (1971), is tantamount to exchanging slavery for freedom. (The literature of addiction is in fact full of references to addiction as slavery.) Moreover, while average utility is an abstract, temporally extended state, positive reinforcement is a discrete event—albeit, from the viewpoint of the addict at C, a future event. This ambivalence, whether or not to exchange negative reinforcement in the present for positive reinforcement in the future, is a case of the simple ambivalence discussed in the previous chapter. The dominant motive for quitting may well be to effect this exchange. However, because it is not socially acceptable to quit current addictive behavior only so as to enjoy addictive behavior more in the future, this motive may go unverbalized and even unrealized by addicts themselves.

Nevertheless, as a case of simple ambivalence, ambivalence between current negative and future positive reinforcement is controllable by commitment. The behavior of the addict who commits herself to a detoxification center, dries out, and upon release resumes addictive behavior, is not necessarily inconsistent (not necessarily economically irrational, that is). She has obtained exactly what she was after: an exchange of negative reinforcement for positive reinforcement.

As the course of addiction progresses from A to C, the proportion of positive reinforcement (the space between AC and BC in Figure 3.8) steadily diminishes, thereby increasing the addict's motive to turn back. At point C*, for example, the path C*D*A may be embarked on. As this path is pursued, the proportion of positive reinforcement that would be obtained by defecting from it and engaging in addictive behavior steadily increases. At point A*, for example, positive reinforcement (consequent upon a switch to B*) is predominant. There would be very little gain in the ratio of positive to negative reinforcement by continuing on the straight and narrow path all the way up to A. Thus a person might cycle around the path A*B*C*D*, between relatively moderate and relatively high levels of addictive consumption, as positive and negative reinforcement exerted their immediate and long-term effects. Such shuttling (between abstinence and relapse) is notoriously common among addicts (Marlatt and Gordon, 1980).

EFFECTS OF PRESENT CHOICE ON FUTURE VALUE.   The lines AD and BC represent the effect of present choice on future value. In the drinking example, it is assumed that, starting from state A, the more a person chooses to drink, the less valuable both drinking and nondrinking become. The other side of the coin is that, starting from C, the more a person chooses not to drink, the more valuable both nondrinking and drinking become. The course of these processes is illustrated in Figure 3.8 by the parallel lines AD and BC. But these lines need not be parallel.[7]

Figures 3.9 and 3.10 illustrate cases where the addictive activity has a stronger effect (Figure 3.9) or a weaker effect (Figure 3.10) on its own future value than it does on the future value of alternative activities. In Fig-

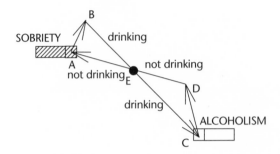

Figure 3.9. Conditions of melioration stability at a rate of addictive activity activity (alcoholic drinking) less than 100 percent.

ure 3.9, again with alcoholic drinking as an example, having a drink decreases both the value of future drinks and the value of other activities (social relations and such). For each unit of drinking the decrease in the future value of drinking is greater than the decrease in the future value of other activities (line BC is steeper than line AD). Under the conditions of Figure 3.9 a meliorator would begin to drink, proceeding down the primrose path to the intersection of the two lines—point E, representing a state in which drinking is chosen about half of the time. But to the right of E, not drinking is locally more valuable than drinking. Stability would be reached at state E. In Figure 3.9 point E is midway between A and C and represents drinking at 50 percent of the *t*-length opportunities to drink. But lines AD and BC may cross anywhere. If their intersection, point E, were close to A, stability would be reached at a state of moderate drinking.

Figure 3.10 illustrates the case opposite to that of Figure 3.9. Here the addictive activity has a weaker effect on its own future value than it does on the value of other activities. In Figure 3.10 each unit of drinking decreases the future value of drinking less than it decreases the future value of other activities (line BC is less steep than line AD). Again the lines cross somewhere between A and C, at point E. But point E no longer represents a stable state. It is now like the top of a hill with behavior like a ball that will only come to rest at one side (state A) or another (state C). To the left of E, not drinking is more valuable than drinking. A meliorator starting to the left of E will proceed to A (sobriety) and stay there. To the right of E, drinking is more valuable than not drinking. A meliorator starting to the right of E will proceed to state C (alcoholism) and stay there.

Behavior under the conditions of Figure 3.10 is bistable—stable at both

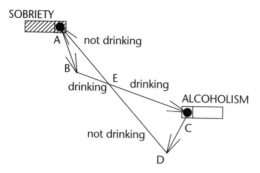

Figure 3.10. Conditions of melioration bistability at rates of an addictive (alcoholic drinking) of 0 percent or 100 percent.

A and C. The case may lead to the following scenario. A person is currently sober. Even though the value of drinking for this person is now intrinsically lower than that of not drinking, *extrinsic* forces, such as social demands, may encourage drinking. If those extrinsic forces are removed and behavior is kept well to the left of E, the person will return to sobriety. If those forces are not removed but are continuously applied (as perhaps in a college fraternity), behavior may proceed across point E. If it does, then the primrose path to C will be followed even after the forces are removed. Drinking will have become more intrinsically valuable than its alternatives.

The conditions of Figure 3.10 as well as those of Figure 3.9 correspond to many real-life addiction situations and are critical parts of the theory to be presented in the next chapter.

4

The Lonely Addict

The purpose of this chapter is to discuss a theory, "relative addiction," that accounts for the primrose path described in the previous chapter.[1] Relative addiction theory belongs under the heading of teleological behaviorism in the sense that it relies on processes of behavioral allocation such as melioration (Herrnstein and Vaughan, 1980) and economic maximization (Rachlin et al., 1981) rather than physiological or cognitive internal mechanisms.

Relative addiction theory says that social support, the benefit obtained from social activity, is crucial for both prevention and cure of addiction. Groups such as Alcoholics Anonymous and Gamblers Anonymous that stress social support generally believe it to be ancillary to the operation of some more fundamental process (physiological, cognitive, behavioral, or spiritual). Relative addiction theory, on the other hand, places social support or its lack at the center of the addiction process. It says that addicts are addicts *because* they lack social support—*because* they are lonely. According to relative addiction theory, lack of social support leads down the path to addiction just as directly as does the first drink, the first cigarette, the first line of cocaine. Before examining how lack of social support may cause addiction, we need to stipulate the operative behavioral dynamics.

Local and Overall Utility

In calculating utility, economic theory assumes first that a consumer's time horizon is infinite. When a choice is made, all known consequences, no matter how far in the future they may be, are assumed to be taken into account. But then, consequences are less powerful, the farther in the future they are; reinforcers and punishers are discounted by delay. As discussed in Chapter 2, animals, including humans, are said to be "impulsive" when they steeply discount future consequences and "self-controlled" when they weigh future consequences heavily. The science of microeconomics attempts to describe individual behavior, including the behavior of addicts, by specifying utility and discount functions and calculating their maxima (Becker, 1976, 1996). Behavioral economics is concerned with empirical determination of these functions (Rachlin et al., 1981).

As indicated in Chapter 3, this process may be simplified with melioration. Melioration abandons the assumption that all future consequences are discounted by some mathematical function of their delay. Instead, it categorizes delayed events in only two ways: as "local" events (within t, to use the terminology of Chapter 3) or as "nonlocal" events (beyond t). For each choice alternative there exists a local horizon, a point in the relatively near future, that defines a local period of time. Local utility is the sum of the benefits minus costs divided by the duration of the local period. Local events are given full weight in calculating utility (they are not discounted). Nonlocal events, those beyond the local horizon, are given no weight at all (they are completely discounted). If while sitting in a restaurant, for example, your local horizon extended only for the duration of the meal, you would fully count the benefits and costs of the menu alternatives over the meal's duration, but you would ignore possible weight gains or losses and health effects, which would occur almost wholly after the restaurant visit.

Each choice alternative has its own local utility. Choice of the alternative with the highest local utility, melioration (Herrnstein and Vaughan, 1980), is a form of maximization: maximization of local utility. Whether an animal is considered to be impulsive or self-controlled, then, depends on whether the local horizon, the line separating local from nonlocal events, is drawn in the near or distant future (whether t is of brief or long duration). A person who drinks without regard to tomorrow's hangover would be maximizing utility within the local boundary of tonight. A person who drinks (presumably more moderately) with regard to tomorrow's possible hangover would be maximizing utility within a local boundary beyond tomorrow morning. Heyman (1996a) has argued that the boundary line separating local from nonlocal events (the duration of t) may vary over a wide range (depending on the salience and relevance of environmental stimuli), thereby explaining how humans and nonhumans may be impulsive in one situation and self-controlled in another. A person may act quite differently, for example, in the presence versus the absence of a parent, a boss, or a spouse.

This chapter, like the previous one, adopts the language of melioration, distinguishing between *local utility* and *overall, or global, utility* (local plus nonlocal utility). Let me emphasize again that this usage is undertaken for the sake of explanatory convenience and mathematical simplicity, not because melioration is correct and economic maximization is incorrect. As indicated previously, melioration and maximization are not competing theories but are alternative modes of explanation—two languages (Rachlin, Green, and Tormey, 1988; Rachlin and Laibson, 1997). Any choice behavior that can be explained by melioration (choice of the highest undiscounted local utility) can also be explained by maximization (choice of the highest discounted overall utility).

In the standard operant concurrent-chain choice situation, an animal chooses not between individual reinforcers but between stimulus-defined "situations" (de Villiers, 1977). Within a situation the animal may be exposed to a reinforcement contingency for a time. With simple concurrent schedules the choice alternatives might be two food deliveries of differing magnitudes, as illustrated in Figure 2.4a. On the other hand, with concurrent-chain schedules, the choice alternatives (the "situations") might be five-minute exposures to one or another *rate* of food delivery, each signaled by a different colored light. The difference between simple choice procedures (simple concurrent schedules) and concurrent-chain schedules is like the difference between choosing between two cooks and choosing between two meals. With concurrent-chain schedules, as with hiring a cook, you have to bear with the consequences of your choice for at least a while.

With concurrent-chain schedules, local utility is defined as a function of all reinforcement parameters (rate, amount, delay) and response parameters (number, force, duration) during exposure to the stimulus-defined situation. In other words, local utility is a "net" rather than a "gross" amount; it is value minus cost. Although in the operant laboratory the response parameters are usually negligible relative to the reinforcement parameters, in the real-life situations to which laboratory results are applied, response parameters are *not* negligible. In life, rewards have their nonnegligible costs. Local utility may therefore be varied by increasing or decreasing either reinforcer value or reinforcer cost. If the price of cigarettes goes up, the local utility of smoking goes down. Moreover, amount per unit price may increase or decrease—as when candy bars cost the same but increase or (more often) decrease in size, or when cereal manufacturers put less or more air and more or less cereal into the same-sized, same-priced box.

NEGATIVE EFFECTS OF PRESENT CONSUMPTION ON FUTURE LOCAL UTILITY. Present consumption of a given commodity may affect the future local utility of that commodity or of other commodities. For example, if you eat a steak dinner now, you will probably spoil your appetite for a steak dinner an hour from now but increase your appetite for a sweet dessert. If you eat too much or eat too fast, you may have heartburn or indigestion later on. If you eat too much, you may gain a little excess weight farther along the road. The deleterious effect of present consumption on future activity is especially strong for activities normally considered to be addictive (Green and Kagel, 1996). Drinking alcohol, beyond a certain point, deteriorates health, social relationships, job performance, and almost all other activities, including the pleasure obtained from drinking itself. These reductions in future value decrease future local utility.

Present consumption may affect future utility in another, more direct way. As strong or unusual substances are consumed, the body mobilizes "opponent processes" that resist their effects (Siegel, 1976; Solomon, 1980). Opponent processes in turn reduce the net utility of a fixed amount of the commodity, requiring more to achieve the same effect—just as, with less cereal per box, you have to buy more boxes to satisfy the same appetite. Even the casual drinker or smoker experiences some reduced effect with continued use. For the alcoholic, the three-pack-a-day smoker, the heroin addict, this "tolerance" effect is magnified. Addicts regularly consume amounts of opiates that would kill nonaddicts.[2] The opponent processes underlying tolerance may become associated only with certain stimuli. A heroin addict, for example, tends to build up resistance to the primary narcotic effect of the heroin in situations where the drug is habitually taken. If heroin is taken only in one situation (in one way, in one room, at one time of day, with one other person or set of people present), and then the same dose is taken in a new situation, the effect of that very same dose will be much stronger than before—strong enough in some cases to be fatal (Siegel, 1988a; 1988b).

To borrow an economist's terminology (Becker, 1996), "tolerance" is the negative effect of a person's "stock" of an addictive substance (X) on utility. Stock represents the body's and the environment's "memories" of consumption. Stock increases with consumption and decreases over time. In Figure 4.1a, the leftmost point (B) represents the local utility of consuming X after X has been completely depleted from stock (after a prolonged period of nonconsumption of X). The rightmost point (C) represents the local utility of consuming X if stock of X is at maximum (after a prolonged period of consuming X). This figure illustrates the case where future local utility decreases as stock increases (tolerance). As an alcoholic drinks more and more, for example, stock of drinking increases and utility of future drinking decreases. But as time passes without drinking (as the alcoholic dries out), stock of drinking decreases and utility of future drinking increases.

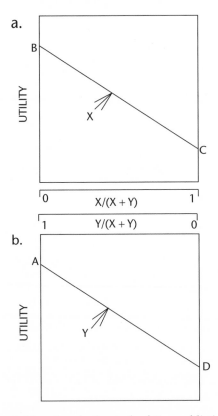

Figure 4.1. (a) Price habituation. As the stock of X, an addictive activity, increases (going from left to right), the utility of a unit of X decreases. (b) Price sensitization. As the stock of Y, a social activity, increases (going from right to left), the utility of a unit of Y increases.

Line BC of Figure 4.1a (corresponding to line BC in Figures 3.5 to 3.10) illustrates this effect. For simplicity, we still assume the effect to be linear. On the horizontal axis of Figure 4.1a, X stands for consumption of an addictive commodity over an extended time, a period well beyond the boundary of local utility, and Y stands for all other activity over that same extended period. As more and more of the addictive commodity is consumed, stock of X increases and stock of Y decreases; as more and time is spent on other activities, stock of Y increases and stock of X decreases. In other words, the consumer is supposed to move slowly to the right in Figure 4.1a as the addictive commodity is consumed, and slowly to the left as the addictive commodity is not consumed. Movement to the right decreases local utility of X; movement to the left increases local utility of X. This negative effect of present consumption on future local utility is called *price habituation* (Rachlin, 1997a).

POSITIVE EFFECTS OF PRESENT CONSUMPTION ON FUTURE LOCAL UTILITY. Some activities have an effect on future utility opposite to that of the addictive activities discussed above; the more the activity is performed, the greater its future local utility. In general, these activities involve learning of skills. Utility of skiing, tennis, golf, and other recreational sports tends to increase as more and more time is spent acquiring the skills necessary to enjoy and master them. Playing chess, reading classical literature, listening to serious music, are other examples. The more time you spend in these pursuits, the cheaper they become (the more cereal and the less air in the box).[3]

Just as an increase in the frequency of such activities tends to increase local utility, so a decrease in frequency tends to decrease local utility. The adolescent who spends large proportions of time reading poetry or playing the violin, who then out of necessity takes a time-consuming job or engages in time-consuming studies, will find an hour of reading poetry or violin playing not as enjoyable (more expensive) than it used to be when, later in life, time becomes available to take up these pursuits again.

A crucial assumption of relative addiction theory is that obtaining social support by means of social activity is this kind of skill. Although in our society, in most cases, parents and community provide free social support to children, childhood is also a learning period for highly complex social skills (Brazelton, Koslowski, and Main, 1974). If these skills are not acquired in childhood, they may never be acquired. For adults, as a general rule, the more socially active we are, the more social support we get; the less socially active we are, the less social support we get. In other words, the more socially active we are, the more utility we get from social activity—either through enhancement of the the intrinsic value of social activity itself or through reduction of the time, effort, or money it costs to increase social support by a given amount.

Correspondingly, the less socially active we are, the *less* social support we get—either through a decrease in enjoyment of social activity itself or an increase in its cost. Line AD of Figure 4.1b illustrates this effect. On the horizontal axis, Y stands for social activity and X stands for all other activities. Note that as $X/(X + Y)$ goes from zero to one, $Y/(X + Y)$ goes from one to zero. As a person spends more and more time in social activity (going from right to left in the diagram), stock of social activity increases. As a person spends less and less time in social activity (moving from left to right), stock depletes. The positive effect of present consumption on future local utility illustrated in Figure 4.1b is called *price sensitization* (Rachlin, 1997a).

A Return to the Primrose Path

In the discussion of the primrose path in Chapter 3, the choice alternatives were the addictive activity (illustrated by drinking) versus everything else. But "everything else" has no properties as such. In this chapter we refer to addictions in general terms but specify a particular alternative to addictive activity—social activity. Relative addiction theory depends on the existence of a reciprocal relationship between X (an addictive activity) and Y (social activity) such as that implied in Figure 4.1. In Figure 4.1a, Y is the context of X; in Figure 4.1b, X is the context of Y. Imagine there exist only two possible actions—addictive (X) and social (Y). As X increases, Y decreases; as Y increases, X decreases. If addictive activity and social activity constituted the universe of all available activities, the reciprocal relationship implied by Figure 4.1 would follow. But of course many activities other than those that are social and addictive are almost always available.

Another condition that would result in a reciprocal relationship between activities is economic substitutability (Rachlin and Burkhard, 1978). Consider, for example, the economic substitutes Coca Cola and Pepsi Cola. There is a market for cola drinks which, let us assume, remains fairly constant. Let us also assume that the taste difference between the two brands is negligible. Then relative consumption will depend on price, advertising effectiveness, shelf location, and so forth. Assuming constancy of the cola market and the absence of other competing brands, if people drank more Coke, they would drink less Pepsi and vice versa. Coke and Pepsi would be substitutable for each other but not for other commodities. These two commodities would in a sense be competing in their own arena, walled off from others.

A central assumption of relative addiction theory is that addictive activities and social activities are paired in this way—they are at least moderately substitutable for each other but not for any other activity. According to relative addiction theory, when the extrinsic price of social activity increases (say, by the death of a spouse or close friend), addictive activity may substitute to some extent for diminished social activity. That is, when people socialize less, they are more likely to become addicts and vice versa.

When two commodities are substitutable for each other but not for anything else, economists call this state of affairs *separability* (Becker, 1976). If this assumption were true in the case of socializing and addiction, the two classes of activity would vary inversely, as Figure 4.1 implies. Indeed, recent evidence (to be discussed in more detail later in this chapter) points to an inverse relationship between social and addictive activity. Decreases in social support are often accompanied by increases in addiction, and programs to reduce addiction work better when social support is present and worse when it is absent (Fisher, 1996, on cigarettes; Schuster et al., 1995, on cocaine; Vuchinich and Tucker, 1996a, on alcohol).

The crucial difference between Coke versus Pepsi and addictive versus social activity is that cola consumption, if it affects future local utilities of Coke and Pepsi, affects them in the same way. But consumption of addictive substances affects future local utility oppositely from the way social activity affects future local utility: addictive activity reduces its own future local utility; social activity increases its own future local utility.

Figure 4.2 combines Figures 4.1a and 4.1b. In Figure 4.2a the local utility of social activity (Y) is higher than that of addictive activity (X). The dashed line running from A (100 percent Y) to C (100 percent X) represents overall utility, the average of local utilities obtained over an extended period. The horizontal axis indicates a subject's overall distribution of time at X and Y. At the left end of the dashed line, at A, where socializing (Y) is always chosen over addictive activity (X), overall utility equals the local utility of social activity. (If a person always bought oranges and never

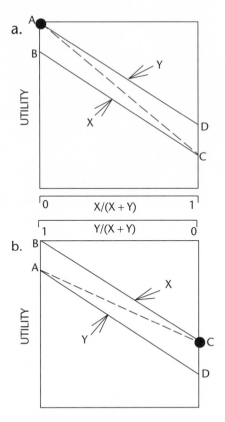

Figure 4.2. (a)The local utility of social activity (*Y*)is higher than that of addictive activity (*X*), with stability at point A. (b) The local utility of addictive activity (*X*) is higher than that of social activity (*Y*), with stability at point C.

bought any other fruit, the average price of a piece of fruit would be the price of an orange.) At the right of the dashed line, where addictive activity (*X*) is always chosen over socializing (*Y*), overall utility equals the local utility of addictive activity. In the center, *X* is chosen half of the time and *Y* the other half. Therefore, at the center, overall utility is halfway between the local utilities of *X* and *Y*. As a subject chooses one or the other alternative more frequently, overall utility is weighted proportionally.[4] There is no conflict in the conditions illustrated in Figure 4.2a. The point of highest local utility (A) is the same as the point of highest overall utility. A meliorating subject would choose the alternative with highest local utility (social activity, *Y*) and keep choosing it, coming to rest at point A (the heavy dot).

In Figure 4.2b (a variant of Figure 3.8) the local utility of addictive activity (X) is higher than that of social activity (Y). The conditions illustrated in Figure 4.2b create a conflict between maximization of local and overall utility. A meliorating person would always choose the activity with highest local utility (addictive activity, X) and keep choosing it. But repeated choices of X have two effects: (a) they directly reduce future local utility of X, and, (b) they imply rejection of the other alternative Y, thereby indirectly reducing future local utility of Y as well. A person who repeatedly chose the highest local utility (addictive activity, X) would come to rest at point C, the very lowest overall utility. If a social disaster occurred in the person's life that suddenly increased the extrinsic price of social support all along the line, economic conditions could go through a transition from those in Figure 4.2a to those in Figure 4.2b. The person's behavior would go from A in Figure 4.2a to B in Figure 4.2b and then gradually to C in Figure 4.2b—from no addictive activity to some addictive activity to complete addiction. In other words, the person could be following Herrnstein and Prelec's (1992) primrose path.

STABLE AND BISTABLE CONDITIONS.   Figure 4.2 illustrates conditions where lines AD and BC are parallel—where price habituation occurs at the same rate as price sensitization. But, as previously discussed, the two processes need not correspond in this way. Let us now reconsider the stable and bistable conditions illustrated at the end of the previous chapter (Figures 3.9 and 3.10). These figures are repeated, in the present chapter's terminology, in Figure 4.3. Figure 4.3a illustrates the condition where line BC (price-habituation) is steeper than line AD (price-sensitization). This is called *relative price habituation.* That is, addictive activity may be preferred to social activity up to the point where a person has "had too much," after which addictive activity becomes more and more aversive relative to social activity.

With relative price habituation, increases in addictive activity still decrease the local utility of both addictive and social activity, but the local utility of addictive activity decreases at a faster rate than that of social activity. Eventually, the local utility of social activity may be higher than that of addictive activity; lines AD and BC may cross, as in Figure 4.3a, providing a point of stability at the intersection. This state of affairs may well be the case for most people with respect to most addictive activities.

For some people, however, increases in some addictive activities may

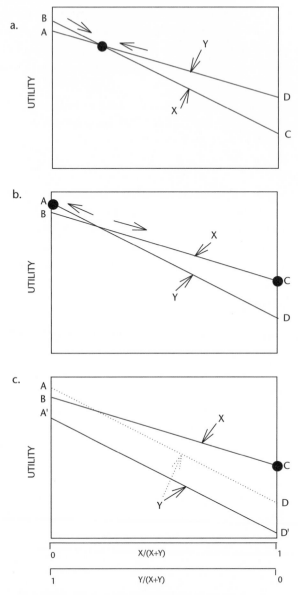

Figure 4.3. (a) Stability at a moderate level of *X*. (b) Bistability. (c) An increase in price of *Y* creates unistability at point C.

have a larger (indirect) effect on the future utility of social activity than the direct effect on the future utility of the addictive activity itself. For example, by spending more time drinking and less time with family, an alcoholic's social support may fade away faster than the pleasure obtained from drinking (which is also fading, but more slowly). That is, line AD (price sensitization) may be steeper than line BC (price habituation). This is called *relative price sensitization* and is shown in Figure 4.3b.

When the lines cross, a bistable condition results at the two extreme points. If the initial relative rate $X/(X + Y)$ is to the left of the intersection point, behavior will come to rest at point A, no addictive activity and all social activity ($X = 0; Y = 1$). If the initial relative rate is to the right of the intersection point, behavior will come to rest at point C, all addictive activity and no social activity ($X = 1; Y = 0$). Thus, the conditions of relative price sensitization do not doom a person to addiction. Yet, as Figure 4.3c illustrates, if the extrinsic price of social activity should suddenly increase (dropping local utility from AD to A'D'), a primrose path would be created with only one stable point—at C, complete addiction.

The following scenario would then characterize the progress of addiction according to relative addiction theory. A person begins at point A of Figure 4.3b as a socially active non addict. Occasional addictive activity such as social drinking (drinking for the purpose of enhancing social support) is quite safe because narrow excursions from point A would still be to the left of the intersection point, where the local utility of social activity is higher than that of addictive activity. As soon as the extrinsic pressure to engage in addictive activity (such as the contingency of social support on social drinking) ceases, behavior would drift back to point A. Should such extrinsic pressure persist (say, in an environment where social pressure to drink is continuous and intense), social contingencies could push the person up to and across the intersection point of Figure 4.3b, where melioration (choice of the highest local utility) would then bring behavior all the way to point C.

This is one path by which addiction may progress and it may well be the main path for young people. A young man pledges for a college fraternity, for example. A positive requirement for acceptance is heavy drinking, so he learns to drink and does drink. But other sources of social support (from his family, for instance) and other contingencies (the dependency of good grades on sobriety) may keep him from going too far. If other sources of social support do not exist, if other contingencies are less powerful, and if the pressure to drink from his fraternity brothers is consistently maintained, he may be pushed "over the edge" (past the point of intersection of lines AD and BC of Figure 4.3b). He may become an embarrassment to the fraternity or even an object of contempt for his inability to hold his liquor. At that point the utility he derives from drinking, although diminished, still exceeds that of the even more diminished social support (derived from his social activity within the fraternity).

Another path to addiction, illustrated in Figure 4.3c, would involve an increase in the price (hence, a decrease in the local utility) of social activity. This could come about through the death of a spouse or close friend or through being transferred to a job in another city (scenarios more likely as one grows older). Now, in Figure 4.3c, there is only one stable state—point C, complete addiction. Even if the conditions of Figure 4.3b were restored (remarriage, making new friends, and so forth) point C would remain a stable state. There contingencies may well act against addictive activity; in most neighborhoods addiction is socially condemned.[5] But the difference in the local utilities of addictive and social activities may be too extreme by then (point C may be too far above point D) for addiction to reverse.

PSEUDO SOCIAL SUPPORT.   It is often observed that addicts engage in addictive activity only in the company of certain other people (usually fellow addicts) and never in their absence. It may seem as if this social activity produces a degree of social support that complements rather than substitutes for addictive activity. However, as previously noted and as will be discussed further in Chapter 6, specific environmental stimuli easily become discriminative signals for addictive activity (as well as for internal opponent processes), just as for many of us TV watching may become a signal for eating. A particular group of people, like a particular room or a particular mode of drug taking, may come to serve as such a signal. When this is added to the fact that the substance being consumed may be more easily available in certain social situations, the observed "social activity" of addicts becomes explicable. Still, this social activity is not a source of social support in the sense that a family or community is. The opium addict does not go to the opium den for the social support (if any) to be found there.

Controlling Addiction

Note again that, except at the two extremes, overall utility (represented by the dashed lines in Figure 4.2) is an abstract, temporally extended state.

Utility at any given moment is, by definition, local. A point on the dashed line represents the proportion of addictive and social activities (the upper and lower solid lines) within some global boundary significantly wider than the boundary that defines local rates. In a typical concurrent-chain operant conditioning experiment with pigeons, for example, the local utilities would be given by rates of reinforcement in each of the specific situational alternatives ("terminal links"), while the overall rate of reinforcement would be the combined reinforcement rate over the entire experimental session. In Herrnstein and Prelec's (1992) extension of this model to human addiction, local utilities would be given by immediate costs and values of, for instance, a night of drinking and a night at home with one's family; global utility would be given by the average cost and value over a month or a year of such nights.

The main difference between choice by pigeons in concurrent-chain experiments and choice by humans in everyday life, aside from the vast discrepancy of temporal scale, is that for the pigeon future concurrent-chain situational alternatives are typically independent of present choices, whereas in human life present addictive or social activity may have strong negative or positive effects on future local utility, hence on current overall utility.

Nevertheless, some concurrent-chain experiments have explicitly varied future local reinforcement rate as a function of present choice. Perhaps the most instructive of these pits a fixed-ratio schedule against a progressive ratio schedule (Wanchisen, Tatham, and Hineline, 1992). These contingencies are illustrated in Figure 4.4. The cost of the fixed-ratio alternative remains constant. That is, a brief access to food is contingent on a fixed number of responses, the "cost." (In Figure 4.4 this fixed cost is twenty responses.) The progressive-ratio alternative starts out with a cost much lower than that of the fixed ratio (five responses in Figure 4.4). But current choices of either alternative explicitly affect the future cost in the progressive-ratio alternative. Each choice of the progressive ratio increases the next progressive-ratio cost (by five responses), while each choice of the fixed ratio sets the next progressive-ratio cost back to its initial response requirement.

Simply interpreted, melioration (choice of the alternative with the lowest cost, hence the highest local utility) predicts that the progressive-ratio alternative will be chosen until its cost grows to exceed that of the fixed-ratio alternative (where the lines cross in Figure 4.4). Then the fixed-ratio alternative will be chosen once, setting the progressive-ratio cost back to

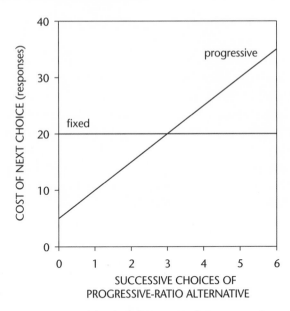

Figure 4.4. Contingencies of the Wanchisen group's 1992 experiment. Each successive choice of the progressive-ratio alternative increases the cost of the next choice of that alternative. Choice of the fixed-ratio alternative resets the cost of the progressive-ratio alternative to its minimum value.

its initial low value, whereupon the progressive-ratio alternative will again be chosen. This behavior fails to maximize overall utility, however, because it fails to take into account the effect of current choice on future local utility. Current choice of the fixed-ratio alternative not only yields some net local utility but also has a positive effect on future local utility, by reducing future cost of the progressive ratio alternative. For maximization of overall utility, the fixed-ratio alternative should be chosen—not when its cost is exceeded by that of the progressive ratio (after three successive fixed-ratio choices in Figure 4.4), but well before that point.

Imagine that Coca Colas cost two dollars ("fixed"), whereas Pepsis initially cost fifty cents but increase in price by fifty cents every time you buy one ("progressive"). Moreover, every time you buy a Coke the price of the next Pepsi resets to fifty cents. A meliorating consumer would buy three Pepsis, the last of which would cost a dollar and a half, and then switch to Coke (which costs two dollars, the same as the next Pepsi would be), and repeat the cycle. The average cost would be $1.25 per can [(.50 + 1.00 + 1.50 + 2.00)/4]. Making the switch one can earlier, however, yields a lower average cost of $1.17 per can [(.50 + 1.00 + 2.00)/3]. This sequence maximizes utility. Note that the switch to Coke occurs at a point where the immediate cost of the very next Pepsi ($1.50) would have been lower than the immediate cost of the Coke ($2.00). And note that switching two cans earlier, alternating between the two colas, would increase the average cost to $1.25 per can [(.50 + 2.00)/2]. In the example of Figure 4.4, the corresponding pattern (two choices of the progressive ratio and then a switch to the fixed ratio) maximizes utility (minimizes total cost).

In tests of concurrent fixed-ratio versus progressive-ratio schedules, animals (rats, pigeons, people) apparently do not meliorate. That is, they switch from the progressive to the fixed alternative well before the point of equality, much closer to the point where overall utility is maximized (and overall cost is minimized). According to Herrnstein (1991), such apparent deviations from melioration are due to restructuring. That is, the local horizon, the boundary line dividing local from overall utility, is drawn farther and farther in the future. In the case of progressive-ratio schedules, the local reinforcement rate is determined not on the basis of a single exposure to the fixed or progressive alternative, but on the basis of a sequence of exposures. In the Coke versus Pepsi illustration, a person could restructure alternatives from individual cans to individual strings of cans of Pepsi followed by a Coke. *Local* utilities would then be given by the figures in the brackets above rather than by individual cans. Melioration would consist of choice of the lowest-costing string. *Overall* utility would then have to be defined in still wider terms—perhaps the effects on future health of cola consumption versus other foods.

From this perspective, overall and local utilities of behavior are relative positions on a continuum with abstract, temporally extended patterns of acts on one end and specific brief, individual responses on the other. Just as any pattern, no matter how wide, can be conceived as part of some still wider pattern, so any act, no matter how narrow, can be conceived as composed of still narrower acts. Restructuring would consist of incorporation of more and more context into local utility. In terms of Figure 4.2b, restructuring would bridge over the solid lines and present choices as various positions on the dashed line. If choices were framed in this way, it would be easy to choose the alternative of highest utility.

The question for self-control is how to engender restructuring. This is the subject of the next chapter, which claims that restructuring occurs when behavior is organized into temporal patterns.

Evidence for Relative Addiction

One way to test whether social activity is substitutable for addictive activity is to compare consumption of the addictive substance by socially active subjects and by socially deprived subjects. If the two activities were substitutable, socially deprived subjects would consume more of the addictive substance than socially active subjects do (because the latter need no substitute for social support). It is of course impossible to perform precisely controlled experiments on this question with human subjects, but it *is* possible to do so with nonhumans. Indeed, several experiments have found that socially isolated rats consume significantly more addictive substances than socially active rats do (Roske et al., 1994, on alcohol; Wolffgramm, 1990, on ethanol; Wolffgramm and Heyne, 1995, on ethanol and an opiate).

Heyman and Tanz (1995), using pigeon subjects, studied a conflict much like that illustrated in Figure 4.2b. One alternative response tended to increase local utility and decrease overall utility while the other did the reverse. Signals could be provided that indicated when overall utility was increasing and when it was decreasing. These signals essentially particularized and localized overall utility, which otherwise was abstract and temporally extended. When the signals were absent, the pigeons tended to choose the alternative that maximized local utility (thereby minimizing overall utility). When the signals were present, however, the pigeons were able to choose the alternative that maximized overall utility.

Heyman (1996a) draws an analogy between these results and corresponding ease or difficulty in controlling addictive behavior in everyday life. For example, many American soldiers became addicted to heroin in Vietnam. Yet when they came home, despite withdrawal symptoms and drug availability, the vast majority stopped taking the drug. According to Heyman, in Vietnam there were no signals to indicate the decreases in global utility contingent on addictive behavior, whereas at home signals everywhere related addictive behavior to ill health, joblessness, and social rejection. These signals enabled the veterans to restructure their behavior into wider patterns. When this happens, local utility is defined more widely, the boundary between local and overall utility is farther in the future, and more context is incorporated into local utility. Melioration then approaches maximization of global utility.

Without denying the relevance of such signals, relative addiction theory would focus on the conditions of social support in Vietnam and later at home. Although intense social relationships are undoubtedly formed in combat conditions (not merely the pseudo relationships discussed earlier), by their very nature they must be brief and are frequently terminated by transfer or casualty. The risk of loss would discount the value of social relationships initiated under combat conditions. Heroin, on the other hand, would be a relatively reliable friend. The cheapness of heroin and other drugs relative to social support in Vietnam is exactly the condition that relative addiction theory predicts would produce addiction. A further determinant of addiction, according to relative addiction theory, is the relative steepness of the slopes of the price-habituation and price-sensitization lines. The greater the degree of relative price sensitization (accompanied by a relatively low price for addictive activity), the more likely addiction is. The rapidity with which social relationships are formed and lost in combat might well cause the price-sensitization line to be very steep, whereas, back home, social relations would at least initially be cheap and, once formed, would be less risky.

Relative addiction theory would therefore predict that veterans' difficulty of social adjustment to civilian life should be strongly negatively correlated with their ease of recovery from addiction. This in fact the case. In a study of Vietnam drug users, Robins (1974) reports that, of the (minority of) soldiers addicted to narcotics in Vietnam who continued their use of narcotics after discharge, 42 percent (of those who were married) became divorced during the 8–12 months between discharge and the time of the study. The corresponding figure for those who discontinued narcotic use after discharge was 7 percent. As Robins says (p. 74), "Drug users in the post-Vietnam period, and particularly narcotics users, carried a heavy burden of poor social adjustment." It is not evident from this study whether the poor social adjustment was the cause of the continued narcotics use or vice versa. According to the relative addiction model, social maladjustment and addiction are so intertwined that the causal direction is difficult or impossible to discern.

Recent evidence from studies with human subjects by Fisher (1996) indicates that cigarette smoking and social interaction behave as commodities X and Y are supposed by relative addiction theory to behave. On the basis of several studies of smoking and social support, Fisher summarizes evidence for their mutual substitutability: people with more social support smoke less than those with less social support; smoking cessation programs work better when they are accompanied by increased social support; the sudden withdrawal of social support (by widowhood or divorce) tends to be accompanied by an increase in smoking.

Fisher says (p. 227):

(a) Similar operations such as stressful events, personal losses, and performance challenges are likely to instigate choices for either social support or smoking.

(b) Psychological effects such as depressed mood, anxiety, or need for arousal appear to follow the operations noted in (a) and to be associated with increased interest in both smoking and social support.

(c) The common effects of social support and smoking appear to include anxiety reduction, mood elevation and performance enhancement.

Although smoking and social interaction may be substitutable for each other, they are distinctly different in the relation between consumption and demand. Nicotine generates its own antagonists in the body (McMorrow and Foxx, 1983); therefore, up to a point, greater and greater doses of the drug are required for the same mood-elevating effect. This is price habituation. Of course, at first a degree of sensitization develops as the neophyte learns to smoke, but once this threshold is crossed, smoking may accelerate to an extreme (USDHHS, 1988).

The relation between the demand for social support and its consumption would seem to be more complex. For most children, social interaction is freely available (that is, cheap), but eventually considerable skill must be acquired to maintain it (Ainsworth and Bowlby, 1991; Brazelton, Koslowski, and Main, 1974). In new social circumstances the skill must be altered or reacquired; without practice, it grows rusty (just as baseball players need spring training after a winter of inactivity). By the time adulthood is reached, some people are clearly better than others at securing and maintaining social support. It is thus fair to say that social interaction is in general price sensitized—the more it is performed, the cheaper it gets; the less it is performed, the more expensive it gets.

If social interaction and cigarette smoking are substitutable, what is the common need or drive they satisfy? Fisher (1996) speculates that anxiety-reduction, mood elevation and performance enhancement are the common factors. These psychological factors may achieve their effects through different mechanisms, or they may be common effects of a single mechanism such as a hormone or stimulation in a certain area of the brain. Hypothalamic electric brain stimulation (a brief train of very low intensity electric pulses from a wire implanted directly in the hypothalamic area of the brain) can reinforce a rat's lever presses. Green and Rachlin (1991) found that hypothalamic electrical brain stimulation was economically substitutable to some extent for both eating and drinking, two commodities not at all substitutable for each other. It should not be surprising, therefore, that two such apparently diverse activities as smoking and social interaction are mutually substitutable.

Elaboration of the underlying physical mechanism of addiction is beyond the scope of a teleological theory such as relative addiction theory. Nevertheless, if the present theory is correct, the addictive nature of smoking lies not in some special physiological properties unique to smoking but in the fact that smoking is price habituated and also substitutable for a price-sensitized activity.

As previously indicated, social interaction is substitutable for other addictive activities such as consumption of alcohol and other drugs. Indirect evidence for such substitutability is the high price elasticity of these activities (DeGrandpre and Bickel, 1996; Heyman, 1996b; Vuchinich and Tucker, 1996a). High price elasticity means that when the price goes up, consumption goes sharply down and vice versa. Low price elasticity means that consumption stays about the same as price varies. Luxuries such as expensive automobiles and yachts usually have high price elasticity. Necessities such as bread and milk usually have low price elasticity. It may seem that substances consumed by addicts should have low price elasticity— they should be necessities for addicts. Nevertheless, in study after study a surprising fact emerges: addicts' consumption of addictive commodities is quite sensitive to price.[6] When the price goes up addicts consume less of the addictive substance; when the price goes down, they consume more.[7]

More direct evidence comes from a study by Vuchinich and Tucker (1996b) of relapses of alcoholics who had participated in a treatment program. Relapse was significantly more frequent among those with low social support. A comprehensive review of alcohol treatment techniques (Miller et al., 1995) found training in social skills to be much more effective than any of the more frequently used long-term techniques (involving drugs, aversion therapy, twelve-step methods, and the like).

Schuster and coworkers (1995) examined outcome data from a voucher-based treatment of heroin abusers in methadone treatment who also had a history of heavy cocaine abuse. The addicts earned progressively more points (exchangeable for goods) as they continued to abstain. Initial periods of abstinence were in a sense investments in the higher rewards to be earned later. Relapse resulted in loss of the investment. The treatment program successfully reduced cocaine use among most of the addicts. However, a fraction of the participants had been diagnosed as having an antisocial personality disorder (APD), and the program was notably unsuccessful with those subjects. This fraction was small in the sample but disproportionately large relative to the fraction of people with APD in the general population. Thus it appears that APD is initially linked with drug use and, when present, retards treatment. This is what would be expected if drugs could substitute for social support.

Whether or not the present theory is correct, high price elasticity for addictive activities means that *something* must be substitutable for them. Social interaction seems a likely candidate.

In real social systems the price of social interaction (in terms of time, effort, and money) varies very widely. For children whose parents care for them, the price is essentially zero; for children whose parents do not care for them, the price must be prohibitive. For adults, the gain or loss of family and friends can cause sharp variations in price. We should, therefore, expect addiction in general to vary widely and (compensating for price) be inversely proportional to the price of social interaction within any social group.

A major feature of relative addiction is its dependence on initial conditions. For each pair of commodities there exists a point of stable or unstable equilibrium. With relative price sensitization, the bistable conditions illustrated in Figure 4.3b apply. An interesting situation arises when the negatively addictive activity becomes extrinsically instrumental for obtaining the positive commodity—for example, when smoking or drinking or crack taking becomes a condition of social interaction. The phrase "social drinking" implies the pervasiveness of such a contingency. The social drinker drinks in part to reduce the cost of social support. In such circumstances, the initial ratio X/Y (drinking/socializing) is not zero and might hover just below equilibrium (slightly to the left of the intersection point in Figure 4.3b). There a small change in price (a reduction in the price of drinking or an increase in that of socializing) could tip the balance (by elevating BC relative to AD as in Figure 4.3c), moving consumption to a single stable point C. By the time the conditions of Figure 4.3b were restored, consumption could have come to rest at C. At the other extreme, contingencies would work the other way. Addiction is usually socially condemned. Now, at C, the immediate negative effect of quitting (moving from C to D) would far outweigh the negative effect of the condemnation.

Perhaps this is the reason for a phenomenon studied in cigarette consumption called the *ratchet effect* (Young, 1983); as the money price of cigarettes decreases, consumption rises sharply; but when the money price later increases, consumption of cigarettes does not fall nearly as sharply. Apparently for cigarettes (and perhaps for other addictive commodities), the elasticity of demand differs for upward and downward variation of the money price. According to the relative addiction model, a ratchet effect would occur in an individual if a decrease in the money price of cigarettes served to start her on the path to addiction (to push her over the X/Y point of equilibrium). Once past the equilibrium point, she would progress to addiction ($X/Y \to \infty$). At that point it would take a massive price decrease to push her back over the equilibrium point. Relative addiction theory predicts, then, that the ratchet effect should be stronger, the longer the interval between the initial price decrease and the subsequent price rise (because the longer the interval, the further toward addiction the addict will have progressed). This thesis has yet to be tested.

Relative addiction theory suggests that Fisher is on the right track in looking for substitutability in such apparently disparate activities as cigarette smoking and social interaction. Discovery of other such price-sensitized substitutes for harmful addictions might lead to more effective treatment methods. Fisher's evidence implies that those who advocate making drugs more expensive and those who advocate social programs for addicts are both, in a sense, correct. Both increasing the price of drugs and decreasing the price of social support should tend to decrease drug taking. But to bring an addict all the way back to and over the point of unstable equilibrium, the relative price change would have to be very large. Perhaps the two avenues should be pursued, although it may well be more difficult for society to increase the price of drugs to very high levels (say, by making criminal penalties severe and certain) than to reduce the price of social support to near-zero levels.[8]

Appendix: The Conditions of Addiction

We are looking for a function relating relative consumption at time t, $(X/Y)_t$, to relative consumption at time $t - 1$, $(X/Y)_{t-1}$. Then, as t steps along, we will examine when the function stabilizes and when it progresses to extremes. The time marker t is here taken to represent an interval during which consumption activities (X and Y) occur in various proportions (Rachlin and Burkhard, 1978). The utility U of the package, $X_t\, Y_t$, may be expressed as

$$U = aX_t^n + bY_t^n, \tag{4.1}$$

where a and b are scale factors and n (< 1) is a constant representing substitutability between X and Y. Equation 4.1, called a CES function, is much used to describe economic data. In psychology, the equation has described consumption patterns of rats choosing between imperfect substitutes (food, water, flavored liquids, electrical brain stimulation), and it implies matching of relative response to relative reinforcement (Rachlin, 1978). Thus, by extension, it accounts for all of the choice data with humans and nonhumans described by Herrnstein's matching law (Herrnstein, 1997).

As n approaches one, the activities approach perfect substitutability—the utility of the package approaches the simple sum of the quantities (multiplied by scale factors) consumed. For example, if X were Coca Cola and Y were Pepsi Cola, the utility of a mixed package of bottles of Coke and Pepsi would, for most consumers, be close to the total number of bottles in the package (a and b allowing for different-sized bottles). Values of n greater than one are conceivable but would imply that the marginal utility of an activity could increase as its amount increased. This would violate the law of diminishing marginal utility. We therefore assume that n does not exceed one.

As n approaches zero the activities become less substitutable (like Coke and 7-Up); and as n becomes more and more negative, the activities become complements (like Coke and pretzels). The usual illustrations of strong complementarity are left shoes and right shoes or bicycle wheels and bicycle frames. The concepts of substitutability and complementarity connect with the psychological concept of motivation in the sense that the more of an activity you do, the less you need or want its substitutes and the more you need or want its complements.

Let us assume further that at any period some fixed amount (W_t) of resources (time, effort, money, or some combination thereof) is available to distribute between X_t and Y_t:

$$p_t X_t + q_t Y_t = W_t, \tag{4.2}$$

where p and q are true prices of X and Y. Rachlin (1978) showed that utility (Equation 4.1, under the constraints of Equation 4.2) is maximized when

$$\left(\frac{X}{Y}\right)_t = \left(\frac{pb}{qa}\right)_t^{\frac{1}{n-1}}. \tag{4.3}$$

As the activities become more and more substitutable ($n \rightarrow 1$), X/Y approaches zero or infinity depending on relative price; assuming that $a = b$, if the true price p of a unit of X is higher than the true price q of a unit of Y, then all consumption will go to Y and vice versa (as is usually the case with Coke and Pepsi—people buy whichever is cheaper). If the activities are perfectly complementary (like wearing left and right shoes), then n becomes negatively infinite and $X = Y$ (as is usually the case with left and right shoes—people wear them in pairs).

Now let us consider how Equation 4.3 would change over time with consumption of X and Y. We are concerned here with relative, not absolute consumption. Absolute consumption is regulated by the substitutability of X and Y together for other activities. Since by assumption the demand for the quality common to X and Y (s) is inelastic (s is assumed to be available only from X or Y), the absolute rate of consumption of X and Y together will be fairly constant. A simple expression of alteration of relative price with relative consumption is

$$\left(\frac{p}{q}\right)_t = \left(\frac{X}{Y}\right)_{t-1}^m \left(\frac{p}{q}\right)_{t-1}, \quad -1 < m < 1 \tag{4.4}$$

The exponent m is a measure of the shift in s between X and Y from trial to trial. At $m = -1$, X loses all s and Y gains all s. At $m = 1$, X gains all s and Y loses all s.

When $m = 0$, relative price is independent of consumption. When $m > 0$, relative price varies directly with prior relative consumption; this is *relative price habituation*. When $m < 0$, relative price varies inversely with prior relative consumption; this is *relative price sensitization*.

Substituting Equation 3 in Equation 4:

$$\left(\frac{X}{Y}\right)_t = \left(\frac{X}{Y}\right)_{t-1}^{\frac{m}{n-1}+1} \tag{4.5}$$

Let us say the exponent $(m/(n-1)+1) = r$ and ask what happens as r varies. When r varies between zero and one, X/Y approaches unity more or less rapidly from its initial value. At $r = 0$, X/Y jumps immediately to unity. At $r = 1$, X/Y stays at its initial value. Thus, $0 < r < 1$ is a stable range for X/Y. However, if $r > 1$, and X is initially greater than Y, X/Y grows to infinity. If $r > 1$ and Y is initially greater than X, X/Y approaches zero. Thus, $r > 1$ is an unstable range for X/Y. Negative values of r mirror the effects of positive values, except that stability is approached by oscillations of decreasing amplitude and extremes are approached by oscillations of increasing amplitude. We assume here that r is always positive (oscillations occurring within rather than between successive intervals).

Now let us consider the exponent m of Equation 4.4. Recall that for consumption of normal commodities, $n < 1$. Thus, $n - 1$ must be negative. For instability,

$$r = \frac{m}{n-1} + 1 > 1, \quad \frac{m}{n-1} > 0.$$

Since $n - 1$ is negative and the fraction $m/(n-1)$ is positive, m must be negative. Negative values of m (relative price sensitization) therefore result in instability of time allocation to X and Y. On the other hand, positive values of m (relative price habituation) produce values of r less than unity. Therefore relative price-habituation results in stable consumption allocations.

Note that even with negative values of m, harmful addiction does not automatically follow. If the initial value of X is less than that of Y and m is negative, all consumption shifts to Y. By assumption, Y is price sensitized. High levels of many price sensitized activities, such as listening to classical music, reading Trollope novels, and socializing, are not normally harmful. Still, even these activities may become harmful if done to excess and some such activities (television watching or web surfing) are considered addictions at high levels.

On the other hand, if m is negative and the initial value of X is greater than that of Y, all consumption shifts to X. By assumption, X is price habituated. High levels of at least some price-habituated activities, such as drinking alcohol, sniffing cocaine, and smoking cigarettes, are indeed normally harmful.

CHAPTER

5

Soft Commitment

When in his *Principles of Psychology*, William James compares habit to an "enormous flywheel of society, its most precious conservative agent," the metaphor is apt because a flywheel is a kind of soft commitment device. It is always possible to put on the brakes, of course, but the faster the flywheel spins the greater the effort required to stop it. Once you set a flywheel spinning, you are in a sense committed to keep it going. You are not *strictly* committed; you can stop the flywheel—but at a cost. Hence the commitment is soft not strict. But to say commitment is soft, is not to say that the cost of defection from it is necessarily low.

Very brief behavioral patterns, for example, are notoriously difficult to interrupt—so difficult that we hardly think of them as patterns at all, we think of them as brief individual acts. Consider a sneeze. Although a sneeze seems always to emerge as a unit, it may be analyzed into components (the first perceptible tickle, the first tentative sniff, the sharp intake of breath, the clutch in the back of the nose, the pressure of the air, the formation of the tongue and jaw, the gust of exhaled breath, the modulation of the sound to "achoo," "wachaa," or any of their thousands of individual variations, and the sigh of relief afterward). Each component in turn may be analyzed almost indefinitely. Each has its own pattern and each its own ease or difficulty of modification and inhibition. Yet, at least for most of its components, inhibition is so difficult, hence so infrequent, that we see a sneeze as a single act. Other brief acts—coughing, urination, certain components of the sex act—are equally difficult to interrupt. Once they are begun, their momentum (an actual physical momentum in some cases) keeps them going. They may be interrupted, but only at a cost.

Less clearly, but just as certainly, longer-term patterns are costly to interrupt. Consider again the act of listening to a three-minute song. We do not like to be interrupted in that act, and the closer we are to the end of the song the less we like it. On a more molar level, as we get absorbed in a television program, a play, or a concert, interruption becomes more costly. Because long-duration activities attain their value by virtue of their organization (their pattern, their gestalt), interrupting them degrades the value of the whole—not just the value of the part during and after the point of interruption.

It is worth pointing out that even interruption by a momentary pleasure may be costly. As my friends and family will attest, I greatly enjoy engaging in vociferous argument on some philosophical or psychological subject. I also love to be hugged or kissed (by the right person). But when the latter interrupts the former, the hug or kiss might as well be a brief electric shock. In fact, the shock might well be less intrusive, since (below a certain level of intensity) its interruptive effect is shorter. And the cost imposed by the interruption is greater, the closer it is to the end of the argument.

When we initiate a pattern of behavior whose interruption is costly, we are committing ourselves to its completion. This is soft commitment. It is "soft" because there is always a way out—we can interrupt the pattern. It is "commitment" because the interruption is costly. Soft commitment is like punishment commitment (discussed in Chapter 2) in the sense that it may be revoked at a cost. But in the case of punishment commitment the cost is contingent upon, and imposed after, the impulsive act (after the smaller-sooner reward is obtained) while in the case of soft commitment the cost is contingent upon interruption of the pattern and thus imposed before or simultaneously with the impulsive act.

To return to the example of Figure 3.2, the sum of the values of listening to each three-minute division of a one-hour symphony is less (much less, we are assuming) than the value of listening to the whole symphony. Yet (we are also assuming) there is some positive value in those components. In many cases, however, the components of a pattern have virtually no value relative to the pattern as a whole. As an example, consider my parking problem in my home city of New York. The cost of a permanent space in a garage is $300 per month, or $3,600 per year. That I cannot afford. Instead I park on the street. It is often very difficult to find a parking space on the street. Sometimes, to find a space, I have to drive around for an hour or more. Instead of endlessly driving around and around, I have over the years established the following rule: drive twice over a fixed route (which takes ten to fifteen minutes) and then, if I don't find a space, put the car into a garage overnight. The cost of a garage for a single night is $20. If I stick to my rule I will have to garage the car overnight about ten times a year, for a total cost of $200 per year. That I *can* afford. The problem is that I find it very difficult to stick to my rule. After driving twice over my route I cannot help but weigh the following two options: (1) drive around the block just one more time or (2) pay the $20 for the garage. Seen that way, it is always worth driving around the block one more time. Thus, occasionally, I break my rule and drive around the block one more time. (And, as so many times in life, this self-destructive act is occasionally rewarded; I find a space.) Let us analyze this process.

In economics there is a concept known as *sunk costs.* These are essentially past investments that you have made in a project. When considering whether to make future investments, you should, according to economics, ignore sunk costs. What counts for a given present investment are the costs and returns on *that* investment. For example, it takes about five years between the conception and completion of a large commercial building. Suppose that during the fourth year, when the frame of the building is already up, the costs of completion suddenly escalate and the real estate market collapses. Should the building be abandoned? Well, yes, if the problem is simply as stated. But there may be other factors to consider. If the uncompleted building will stand out like a sore thumb, and if the builder plans on continuing to do business in that city, then perhaps it is worth completing the building. Otherwise potential investors in future buildings might worry about the loss of their investments and instead put their money with another builder who "foolishly" finishes every project once he begins it, regardless of current conditions. In other words, what seem to be sunk costs in a narrow context may not be so sunk when the context is expanded.

Similarly, when driving around the block looking for a parking space, I need to consider events beyond the next few minutes. I especially need to consider the times during the coming year when I will be in the same situation again. My rule (twice around the route then into the garage) is meaningful only in the context of many instances of looking for a parking space. It is meaningless in the context of this one instance. In this narrow context my two times around the route are sunk costs and should be ignored in deciding whether to circle one more time. Nevertheless, in the context of a year's worth of parking my rule makes perfect sense. The two times around the block are not sunk costs at all, but part of a general pattern of behavior that is ongoing.

I know in advance, however, that at the moment of decision, when my rule says to garage the car, that rule will seem absurd, just as getting up early in the morning seems absurd to Archie Goodwin (see Chapter 2). I also know that if, despite their apparent absurdity, I stubbornly follow the various rules I have made for myself, I will be much happier in the long run. That is, I have a habit—a soft habit, to be sure—of following such personal rules. And this habit acts as a flywheel in my life, as a "conservative agent" in James's words. (This is not to say that it is desirable to obsessively make rules and obsessively follow them all the time.)

Soft Commitment with Simple Ambivalence

The crossing discount functions of Chapter 2 illustrate how commitment works in cases of simple ambivalence (see Figures 2.5a and 2.9). At some point in time (t_A) a larger-later reward is preferred to a smaller-sooner reward; later (at t_B) these preferences will reverse. Before they do, however, an act is performed which either eliminates the possibility of obtaining the smaller-sooner reward (strict commitment) or attaches such a heavy penalty to it (punishment commitment) that the larger reward is actually obtained.

Another method of avoiding choice of the smaller-sooner reward at the point where preferences will have reversed, the point where the smaller reward is actually preferred (t_B), is to begin (at t_A) a behavioral pattern leading to choice of the larger reward that will carry the initial choice over the point of preference reversal. This is soft commitment.

Soft commitment has been studied in the laboratory with pigeons exposed to a standard simple-ambivalence procedure (Siegel and Rachlin, 1995). The reward alternatives were the following: First, 2.5 seconds access to mixed grain available almost immediately (after a 0.5-second delay) followed by a 5-second blackout, henceforth called the smaller-sooner reward (or SS). Second, 4 seconds access to mixed grain preceded by a 4-second delay, henceforth called the larger-later reward (or LL). Note that both alternatives take 8 seconds to elapse, but SS provides a small reward early in the 8-second period while LL provides a large reward late in the 8-second period.

From Chapter 2 we know that when presented with the straightforward choice between LL, obtained by a single peck on a red button, and SS, obtained by a single peck on a green button (illustrated in Figure 5.1a), pigeons strongly prefer SS. Indeed, in this experiment, after hundreds of choices, the pigeons chose SS more than 95 percent of the time. After confirming this well-established preference, Siegel and I exposed the pigeons to a different sort of choice, illustrated in Figure 5.1b. Instead of a single peck on either button, the pigeons were required to make 31 pecks on either button. The button pecked on peck 31 determined which reward was obtained; if peck 31 was on the green button, SS was obtained; if peck 31 was on the red button, LL was obtained (for half of the pigeons the colors were reversed). This apparently minor change in procedure had a very strong effect on the rewards obtained. Now the pigeons obtained SS only 36 percent of the time, and obtained the larger reward (LL) the other 64 percent.

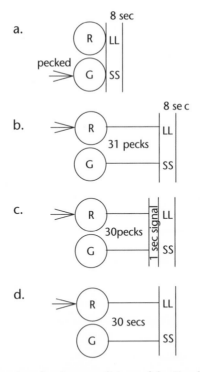

Figure 5.1. Contingencies of various conditions of the Siegel and Rachlin (1995) experiment on soft commitment. The arrows indicate a typical pigeon's choices (button pecked) between alternatives.

The reason for this preference reversal is twofold. First, it took about 30 seconds on average for a pigeon to make the 31 pecks. From the parameters of the hyperbolic discount functions determined in other experiments, it is evident that 30 seconds added to the delay of both LL and SS is well beyond the point where the functions cross–where LL begins to be preferred. Thus, when the pigeons started to peck, when they made the first of the 31 pecks, they actually preferred LL. Second, although it was possible to switch between the red and green buttons at any point during the 31 pecks, once a pigeon began to peck on a button, it kept pecking on that same button. If the first of the 31 pecks was on the red button, the last of the 31 pecks was likely to be on the red button too. Given that a pigeon pecked the red button (leading to LL) on the first peck, the probability that it would switch and peck the green (leading to SS) on the second peck was less than .01. Given that a pigeon pecked the red button on the first 6 pecks, the probability that it would switch and peck green on peck 7 was zero and remained virtually zero until the end.

The schedule of reinforcement used in this experiment is technically a "fixed-ratio" schedule, which typically results in very rigid behavior patterns (Skinner, 1938). After a reinforcement or a blackout, there is usually a pause (proportional in duration to the response requirement) and then very rapid responding until the requirement is met. That was the pattern observed in our pigeon experiment. The pause is the flexible part of the pattern in the sense that its duration is sensitive to the parameters of the reward. Once responding starts, it proceeds at the same rigidly constant (and very high) rate regardless of the reward parameters. Note that however long they paused, the pigeons were no closer to obtaining the reward than when they started; 31 pecks still had to be made. Thus, the rigid pattern always began 31 pecks from the SS and LL rewards. It was their natural tendency to engage in this fixed-ratio pattern that allowed the pigeons to obtain the larger reward. The pattern itself acted like a flywheel, committing the pigeons to their initial choice. The pigeons could have switched but they did not, and they did not because their behavioral pattern was rigid.[1]

Two further procedures, illustrated in Figures 5.1c and 5.1d, relaxed the rigidity of the pattern in different ways. In the procedure of Figure 5.1c, a brief (1-second) signal was inserted between pecks 30 and 31 to essentially tell the pigeon that the next peck would produce either SS or LL. After peck 30 both buttons turned dark and a white light at the top of the cage (called a house light) was turned on. One second later, the white light was turned off and the buttons were again lit red and green. The next peck produced SS or LL. We were asking, with this procedure, whether such a brief interruption would break up the pattern and cause the pigeons to defect from the path leading to LL. Would the brief signal cause the pigeons to treat the 30 pecks made prior to the signal as essentially sunk costs, to be ignored when making peck 31? If so, peck 31 would surely be made on the button that produced SS, and SS would be obtained.

We found that despite the brief interruption the pattern held. Although with the brief signal the pigeons would begin to peck a little less frequently than they did before on the button leading to LL, once they did begin to peck on that button, they persisted through peck 30, across the 1-second interruption, to peck 31, finally obtaining LL. Ultimately, with the interruption, LL was obtained about half the time (as compared to 4 percent of the time with straightforward choice between SS and LL and 64 percent of the time with the uninterrupted fixed-ratio 31).

A second method of weakening the pattern was to change the schedule of reinforcement from a fixed-ratio to a fixed-interval schedule. A fixed-ratio schedule delivers a reward after a certain number of responses. As noted, this schedule generates a pattern of pausing followed by very rapid responding. A fixed-interval schedule reinforces the first response after a certain time has elapsed. In the present case the time was 30 seconds. The green and red buttons were lit during the 30 seconds but, regardless of how many pecks were made on the two buttons during this time, neither SS nor LL was obtained. Instead, the first peck after the 30 seconds had elapsed produced either SS or LL, depending on whether the green or red button was pecked.

A fixed-interval schedule generates a brief pause in responding (proportional in duration to the interval) and then a gradual acceleration to a high rate as the interval elapses.[2] This acceleration is not smooth; rather, it consists of shorter and shorter pauses with longer and longer bursts of rapid responding. Thus, with fixed-interval schedules, there are many self-generated interruptions and, in our experiment, many opportunities to switch between the red and green buttons. Indeed, this was what we found. Although at the beginning of the 30-second interval pigeons strongly tended to peck on the button leading to LL, they would often switch to the SS button as the interval progressed. As a result, they obtained LL only about 25 percent of the time. Still, this fixed-interval pattern was much more efficient (in terms of obtaining more food) than the simple choice between SS and LL.

In summary, although the pigeons clearly preferred SS to LL in a simple choice between them, they preferred LL to SS when both were preceded by an interval of about 30 seconds. The more rigid and the less frequently interrupted its behavioral pattern during that interval, the more likely a pigeon was to stay with its initial choice of the larger reward, and to obtain it. Commitment in the various conditions of the experiment was imposed not by physical restraint on choice but by the pigeons' own behavior. In the fixed-ratio procedure, for example, pigeons preferred the sequence 31 pecks + LL, to the sequence 31 pecks + SS. When these entire sequences became objects of choice the preferred sequence was obtained.

As stated in previous chapters, the serious self-control problems of everyday human life are not usually cases of simple ambivalence. Those cases can be handled with devices such as alarm clocks and punishment commitment. The serious self-control problems of everyday human life arise as complex ambivalence, where the larger reward is abstract, amorphous, and spread out in time, whereas the smaller reward is distinct and always preferred to a component of the larger. The response patterns exhibited by the pigeons in the above experiment on simple ambivalence were short and the interruptions were still shorter. Moreover, the patterns were naturally produced under the reinforcement schedules imposed. These conditions do not usually prevail in cases of complex ambivalence in human life, to which we turn next.

The Paradox of Complex Ambivalence

Complex ambivalence occurs when a component of a pattern (such as listening to any three-minute section of an hour-long symphony) is less valued than its alternative (listening to a three-minute song) but the whole pattern together (listening to the whole symphony) is worth more than the series of alternative choices (listening to twenty three-minute songs). Given this definition, it is possible to view simple ambivalence not as a different process from complex ambivalence, but as a reduction of complex ambivalence to its basic elements. Consider the pattern 31 pecks on a button, followed by LL (in the fixed-ratio condition of the experiment just discussed). The reward alternative, LL (despite being itself a compound of blackouts and access to mixed grain), may be treated as a unitary terminal component of the larger pattern. The 31 button pecks leading to LL (despite being a compound of 31 pecks each in turn divisible into many submovements) may be treated as the initial component of the larger pattern.

The initial components of a pattern are not necessarily sunk costs, to be ignored in future decisions, but rather are investments in the pattern's completion. The components of a pattern stand to each other as economic complements. Compare the pattern 31 pecks on a red button followed by LL, with the pattern 31 pecks on a green button followed by SS. Pigeons are indifferent between pecking a red or a green button, and they strongly prefer SS to LL. Adding up the isolated values of the components, pigeons should prefer 31 pecks + SS to 31 pecks + LL. Actually, they prefer the reverse. This preference reversal occurs because the combination (the gestalt) of 31 pecks and LL (in that order) is worth more than the sum of its isolated parts. This is another way of saying that 31 pecks and LL are economic complements.[3] (Analogously, a left shoe alone or its economic complement, a right shoe alone, is virtually worthless. Utility is attained only when the shoes are paired.)

This sort of preference reversal (between patterns and components of patterns) becomes even more crucial in cases of complex ambivalence in human life. For an alcoholic, an hour of drinking may always be worth more than an hour of socializing, but a week of drinking (a pattern whose components are successive hours of drinking) may be worth less than a week of socializing (a pattern whose components are successive hours of socializing).

Recall the quote from Chapter 3: "However good or bad you feel, heroin makes you feel better." It is difficult to understand how some activity that *always* makes you feel better can reduce your happiness in the long run. Therefore let us once again review Herrnstein and Prelec's primrose path theory of complex ambivalence, this time calculating utilities for various choice patterns. The reader may thereby form a more precise conception of the fundamental self-control conflict in complex ambivalence.

Figure 5.2 repeats yet again the simplified primrose path of Figure 3.8, but places the parallelogram on a grid so that points may be numerically identified. Let us assume that choice opportunities (trials) occur at fixed intervals. Let us further assume that the utility to be gained by a choice of X or Y strictly depends on the proportion of X and Y choices over the last ten trials.[4] A moving window of ten trials steps along from trial to trial, within which current choice affects future local utility. (A choice has no effect on utility farther in the future than ten trials.) The horizontal axis

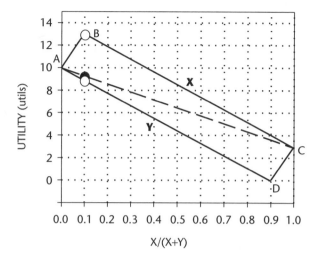

Figure 5.2. The primrose path on Cartesian coordinates.

shows the proportion of choices within the ten-trial window between X, a negatively addictive activity, and Y, a positively addictive activity.[5] The vertical axis of Figure 5.2 is utility in arbitrary units which will be called utils. The vertical axis measures local utilities (u_x and u_y) of a unit of X or Y, given that the last ten choices between X and Y have been in the proportion shown on the horizontal axis; every time a choice is made, that choice plus the previous nine choices go into calculating $X/(X + Y)$.

First consider point A, representing 0 percent choice of X and 100 percent choice of Y. This means that, over the previous ten choices between X and Y, Y has been chosen every single time. As an illustration, suppose that Jane is a former heroin addict. If X is taking heroin and Y is a social activity such as calling a friend or visiting a relative, then we are assuming that Jane has been socializing and has not taken heroin over the previous ten opportunities to do so, and (probably contrary to fact) all the deleterious effects of any heroin she may have taken prior to that point have exited from her body and her social relationships. She is therefore feeling good.

She is now about to make another choice. According to the diagram, at point A, and only at point A, the utility of switching to activity X (u_x) is 13 utils (represented in Figure 5.2 by the open circle labeled B). That is, Jane is feeling good, but taking heroin now would make her feel better. If Jane instead goes to visit her mother—if she chooses Y, and $X/(X+Y)$ remains at zero—the options remain as they were (at point A) and she again may choose between local utilities of 10 and 13 utils. The paradox is that to remain in her happy state she must always choose the lesser-valued immediate alternative. Let her once choose the higher-valued alternative and (given the assumptions embodied in Figure 5.2) her overall happiness (the average utility of her choices) will be reduced.

Let us now calculate average utility assuming that Y has been chosen in the recent past (Jane has been socializing and not taking heroin), X is chosen one single time (Jane slips just once), and Y is again repeatedly chosen (she goes back to socializing). The single X-choice may be seen as a disturbance in a stream of Y-choices. What is the effect of the disturbance? As long as Y is chosen, $X/(X+Y)$ remains constant at zero, where utility is 10 utils.

Suppose, on one trial, X is chosen instead of Y. The immediate utility jumps up from 10 to 13 utils (Jane gets high), but now $X/(X+Y) = 0.1$ rather than zero. If Jane begins to repeatedly choose Y again, $X/(X+Y)$ will remain at 0.1 for nine more trials. The value of choosing Y at $X/(X+Y) = 0.1$ is now about 8.9 utils rather than 10 as before (as shown by the lower open circle on line AD at $X/(X+Y) = 0.1$—and, because $X/(X+Y)$ is calculated over ten trials (the effects of the heroin last for ten trials), the value of choosing Y remains at 8.9 utils for nine more trials.

In summary, by choosing X rather than Y, Jane immediately gains 13 rather than 10 utils; but when she switches back to Y, she gains 8.9 rather than 10 utils on each of the next nine trials. That is if after one slip Jane goes back to socializing, she will feel just a little worse than she did before. The average utility over the ten trials is $[13 + (8.9 \times 9)]/10 = 9.3$ utils per trial, shown by the filled-in circle on the dashed line AC. Choosing X twice would only make matters worse. The first X choice would be worth 13 utils as before, but at $X/(X+Y) = 0.2$ the second X choice would be worth only 11.9 utils. If at this point Y were again repeatedly chosen, $X/(X+Y)$ would remain at 0.2 for eight more trials worth 7.8 utils per trial. Then, as the first X choice slipped out the window, $X/(X+Y)$ would decrease to 0.1 and the next Y choice would be worth 8.9 utils. Finally, point A would be recaptured and 10 utils again earned for each Y choice. The entire disturbance caused by two X choices would have lasted for eleven trials and the average utility over those trials would be $[13 + 11.9 + (7.8 \times 8) + 8.9]/11 = 8.75$ utils per trial. Compare this with an average of 9.3 utils with one X choice

and 10 utils with no *X* choices. The dashed line in Figure 5.2 represents average utility over ten trials as *X*/(*X*+*Y*) varies; the more *X* is chosen, the
lower the average utility.

The state of affairs illustrated in Figure 5.2 certainly does not represent
all addictive processes. The giraffe-like diagram of Figure 5.3 may be more
typical. It illustrates the case where a moderate amount of the addictive activity is actually beneficial in the long run. The harmfulness of the addictive process does not materialize below a certain point. Many addictive
substances may have a beneficial effect below some threshold amount: alcohol is perhaps the prime example. At low levels (moderate social drinking) it is relatively harmless and may even prolong life. The problem is that
the point at which the long-term benefits of moderate consumption convert into long-term harmfulness is very fuzzy. In contrast, the line between
no consumption and any consumption at all is quite distinct.

Under the conditions diagrammed in Figure 5.3, one or two successive *X*
choices improve average utility. Somewhere between two and five successive *X* choices, however, average utility begins to turn down and, with
longer and longer strings of *X* choices, approaches point C (3 utils), just as
it does in Figure 5.2.

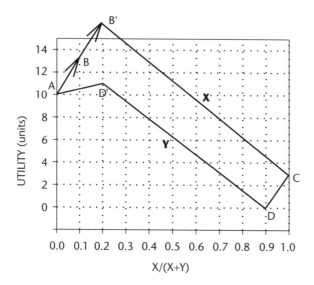

Figure 5.3. The primrose path in the case where a moderate amount of addictive
activity is beneficial in the long run.

Again, we are considering strings of X choices of various lengths as disturbances in a background of Y choices. That is, we are looking for the beneficial or harmful effects of shorter or longer periods of consumption of a substance such as alcohol on a background of alternative behavior such as social activity. We are assuming a background level of 10 utils per Y-choice.[6]

Figure 5.4 shows the average utilities of disturbances of increasing duration as a function of the number of X choices in the disturbance under the giraffe-like conditions of Figure 5.3. With few X choices, average utility increases above 10 utils. As the string of X choices increases, however, the average approaches 3 utils. Figure 5.4 shows that moderate consumption, under the conditions illustrated in Figure 5.3, may increase overall utility. But for a myopic consumer, this brief increase is irrelevant. Such a consumer will always choose the higher local utility which, in Figure 5.3 as in Figure 5.2, is always X. In both cases repeated choices of X drive average utility (over the duration of the disturbance) down to its minimum.

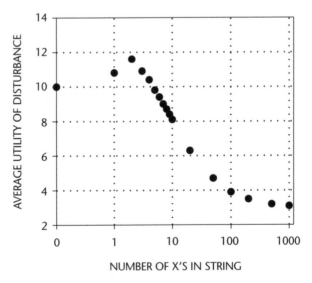

NUMBER OF X'S IN STRING

Figure 5.4. An organism under conditions of Figure 5.3 has been consistently choosing Y in the past, earning an average of 10 utils per press. Then a string of X's are chosen of a length given on the horizontal axis. Then Y is again consistently chosen. Each point represents the average utility of all the choices until stability at 10 units is again attained.

SOFT COMMITMENT IN COMPLEX AMBIVALENCE. The analysis of Figure 5.4 shows how extended sequences of addictive choices may reduce the utility of behavior that in moderation would be harmless or beneficial. The inverse also holds true: sequences of nonaddictive choices may raise utility. People trying to control themselves are of course mainly interested in the latter process.

The effect of a string of nonaddictive choices (Y choices) on a background of addiction (X choices) is the mirror image of that of a string of addictive choices (X choices) on a background of nonaddiction (Y choices). Consider the effect of five successive Y choices on a background of X choices under the conditions of Figure 5.2 (the same would apply for Figure 5.3). Jane has completely succumbed to her heroin habit. (She is now at point C.) She injects herself with heroin at every opportunity and never socializes (except to obtain and consume heroin). If she continues to use heroin (to choose X), she will continue to feel miserable (to gain only 3 utils per choice). If she stops using heroin (chooses Y), she will feel even worse (dropping to 0 utils). If she remains clean (continues to choose Y), however, she will slowly begin to feel better (rising from 0 utils to 1.2 utils to 2.3 utils to 3.4 utils to 4.5 utils in five successive Y choices). The effects of this period of abstinence (this five Y-choice "disturbance" in a continuous string of X choices) will last for a while (fourteen choices from the first Y-choice) and on the average she will feel better during the period (averaging 5.6 utils over the fourteen choices) than she did before (3 utils).

To attain the benefit of an average, or global, improvement, however, Jane has to undergo a local decline. And at every point along the way, she has to forgo the immediate "feeling better" that an injection of heroin would grant. The essence of self-control, in this case, would be for Jane to choose not between one injection of heroin and one social engagement (3 utils versus 0 utils) but between the long-term effects of several successive injections of heroin and several successive social engagements. To rid herself of her habit, Jane has to establish patterns in her behavior and choose between those patterns. The following experiment, with human subjects (Stony Brook undergraduates), attempts to show how a person may come to choose between patterns rather than between individual acts.

PATTERNING WITH COMPLEX AMBIVALENCE. A game devised by Herrnstein, Prelec, and Vaughan (1986) directly opposes particular acts to patterns of acts in a manner corresponding to Figure 5.2. In this human choice procedure, undergraduate subjects are each faced with repeated choices between pressing one of two concurrently available buttons (Y and X). In the simplest version of the game, points exchangeable for money (corresponding to the utils of Figure 5.2) are given to the subjects according to the following rules:

1. Each choice of Y adds N points;
2. Each choice of X adds $(N + 3)$ points;
3. N at each choice is equal to the number of Y's in the previous ten choices.[7]

Subjects usually are not told the rules, just instructed to get as many points as possible over the course of the experimental session (fifty to a hundred trials).

Any particular choice of X is clearly better than Y, since three more points are thereby added to the subject's score. However, in general it is better to choose Y since (by rule 3) each choice of Y adds one unit to N over the next ten trials; the three-point gain of an X-choice eventually is more than offset by the ten-point loss involved in having an X-choice remembered in N for the next ten trials. As in the primrose path addiction model illustrated in Figure 5.2 and analyzed in this chapter, an X-choice "poisons" N for ten trials. In this version a subject would maximize earnings by always choosing Y (except on the very last three trials), averaging 10 points per trial. The worst possible performance would be to always choose X, averaging 3 points per trial. In the long run the more Y-choices, the more points earned.

Most (undergraduate) subjects playing the game choose X most of the time, thereby failing to maximize earnings. Very few subjects spontaneously learn the rules sufficiently to verbalize them. When subjects are given fairly broad hints about the rules, they tend, immediately after the hint, to increase Y-choices but then gradually drift back to their original submaximal performance.

The following experiment (Kudadjie-Gyamfi and Rachlin, 1996) is an attempt to test the effect of patterning on self-control (maximization) with human subjects. The version of the game used, differing somewhat from the one described above, gave a single point (convertible to cash at the rate of 10 cents per point) for Y-choices and X-choices alike, but varied *delays* of point-gain by choice of different alternatives. The total cumulative delay time was fixed (at 325 seconds). Subjects chose by pressing buttons marked

A (functioning as *Y*) and *B* (functioning as *X*). A computer screen displayed delay time left and total points earned. After pressing either button, the subject waited for a certain delay period while the delay timer on the computer screen counted down. At the end of the delay the timer stopped counting and one point was added to the subject's displayed score. When the delay timer reached zero, the experiment ended. The subjects would maximize total reward by minimizing average delay. The rules (not revealed to the subjects) were the following:

1. Each choice of *Y* yields 1 point delayed by $(N + 3)$ seconds;
2. Each choice of *X* yields 1 point delayed by *N* seconds;
3. *N* at each choice is equal to the number of *X*'s in the previous ten choices.

Again, the *particular* consequences of choosing *X* were better than those of choosing *Y* (less delay), whereas the *general* consequence of choosing *X* was to increase *N*, thereby increasing average delay. Of the sixty subjects in this experiment, none could verbalize the rules after the experiment although almost all subjects understood that it was sensible to at least occasionally choose *Y*. Most subjects distributed their choices between *Y* and *X*.

The four groups of subjects differed only with respect to the patterning of trials. All subjects played under the set of rules stated above. The trial patterns of the four groups were as follows:

Control group 1: . . . *COCOCO* . . .
Control group 2: . . . 10*sCO* 10*sCO* 10*sCO* . . .
Control group 3: . . . 30*sCO* 30*sCO* 30*sCO* . . .
Experimental group: . . . 30*sCOCOCO* 30*sCOCOCO* 30*sCOCOCO* . . .

where *C* = choice, *O* = outcome, and 10*s* and 30*s* represent intertrial intervals. (The delay timer did not count down during those intervals.) The experimental group was the only one with patterned trials—triples of rapid trials separated by 30*s* intervals. The patterning, it was hypothesized, would group trials into threes and emphasize the consequences of groups of trials instead of specific trials. Relative to the experimental group, control group 1 had the same local rate of trials, control group 2 had the same overall rate of trials, and control group 3 had the same intertrial interval. Because total delay time was held constant, number of trials (hence, number of points) depended on *Y*-choices: the greater the percentage of *Y*-choices, the shorter the average delay and the greater the number of trials. The lowest average number of trials for any group was forty-two, for control group 1; the greatest was fifty-eight, for the experimental group. Figure 5.5 shows the percentage of Y-choices within the first forty trials for all groups. The experimental group chose Y significantly more times than any of the control groups, while control group 1 chose Y significantly fewer times.

Analysis of choices within the grouped triples of the experimental group indicates that the probability of a Y-choice in the first of the three grouped trials was .48. However, if a Y-choice was made on the first, the probability of a Y-choice on the second of the three contiguous trials was .54. And, if the first two were Y-choices, the probability of a Y-choice on the third trial was .80. Thus, the tendency we found with pigeons to persist in a choice leading to a larger long-term reward, once that choice had been initially made, appears with humans. This is so even though with this procedure (as opposed to the pigeon experiments) patterns of choices were interrupted by outcomes after each choice.

It may be argued that although the problem posed in this experiment is formally analogous to everyday self-control problems, it is fundamentally different because it is a cognitive problem whereas self-control in everyday life is fundamentally a motivational problem. We often seem to "know what is good for us" but nonetheless do otherwise. The distinction typi-

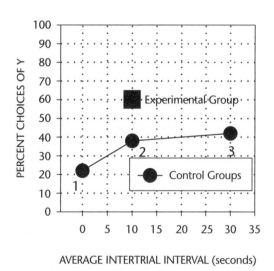

AVERAGE INTERTRIAL INTERVAL (seconds)

Figure 5.5. Results of the Kudadjie-Gyamfi and Rachlin (1996) experiment.

cally made between cognition and motivation is a distinction between higher and lower internal mechanisms. To grant that distinction (as it is usually understood) would be to abandon the teleological-behavioral analysis with which we began. All the same, it is true that if the subjects of this experiment were explicitly taught the rules and rigorously tested for their understanding, none would have ever chosen X. The delays in the experiment were for points exchangeable for money. Eventual consumption could not occur in any case until after the experiment was over. To defect and choose fewer total points would be tantamount to failure to understand the rules. However, we know from the experiments with various degrees of hints (Herrnstein et al., 1993) that subjects who merely repeated the rules verbally would not necessarily choose Y exclusively (as they would if they really "knew" the rules).

True knowledge cannot be mere repetition of a rule verbally—like an actor on a stage. To know a rule must mean at least to behave in a manner consistent with the rule (and perhaps, *in addition,* to verbalize the rule). People who behave consistently with a general rule are, to that extent, controlling themselves. Verbal agreement or disagreement would seem to be irrelevant for self-control (however relevant it may be for knowledge). In any case, the operations that fostered self-control in the pigeon experiment correspond to those that fostered better performance in the human experiment. (We shall return to the issue of cognition versus motivation in Chapter 6.)

Reduction of Variability as Soft Commitment

Why does soft commitment increase self-control? When we commit ourselves to a behavioral pattern, we are reducing our future options, hence the potential variability of our future behavior. As soon as we embark on a particular behavioral pattern, we have abandoned all other potential patterns. The difference between the prisoner and the free person is that the free person may potentially do what the prisoner can do, *plus* other things.

A pigeon presented with the choice between a smaller-sooner reward and a larger-later reward may consistently and monotonously prefer the former. If at an earlier time, however, the pigeon had committed itself to the larger-later reward, it would have reduced the potential, if not the actual, variability of its behavior. In other words, it would have reduced its freedom. Commitment *means* reduction of freedom, and freedom *means* potential behavioral variability.[8] Thus commitment *means* reduction of potential behavioral variability.

In a series of experiments with pigeons, Catania and colleagues (see for example, Cerutti and Catania, 1997) found that if a reward is obtainable by a narrow path (by pecking a single button) and the very same reward is obtainable by a wider path (by pecking either of two buttons or by pecking a larger button) the wider path is preferred even though the actual variability of behavior, once the wider path is chosen, may be no greater than it would have been on the narrower path. That is, pigeons, like people, prefer more to less freedom of choice even though they may not actually take advantage of it. The reduction in value of a reward by reduction in variability of its consumption or the increase in value of a reward by increase in variability of its consumption may be highly significant in everyday human life. People will quit high-paying jobs to go into business for themselves in order to "be their own boss," even though they may end up working harder and earning less money.

The fact that variability reduction depresses the value of reward may be used as a form of self-control if the potential variability of consumption of the smaller-sooner reward is voluntarily reduced. That is, decrease in variability of a smaller-sooner reward will make that reward less valuable and increase the probability of choosing a larger-later or more abstract reward.

Consider the following experiment, part of a series now under way at Stony Brook. By advertisement in the student newspaper we recruited cigarette smokers who were *not* trying to quit. The subjects were paid for participating, but payment was in no way dependent on their smoking or not smoking. All subjects were instructed to count the number of cigarettes they smoked ("self-monitoring") and to report the total to us each evening by leaving a message on a phone recorder. After three weeks, half of the subjects continued with self-monitoring and half were asked to try to reduce not their smoking as such, but the variability of their smoking. They were asked to do this by smoking as much as they wanted on a given day of each week but then trying their best to smoke the same number of cigarettes each day (no more and no less) for the rest of the week. They were told that there was no penalty of any kind for exceeding or failing to reach their goal and that we were much more interested in accuracy of reporting than in how much they smoked. After three weeks of variability reduction the subjects were returned to simple self-monitoring for another three weeks.

The experiment has not been completed but the results so far are clear. By attempting to decrease the *variability* in their smoking, our subjects are also decreasing the *amount* of their smoking. Trying to reduce variability essentially forces the subjects to focus on their behavioral patterns over a week rather than over the few minutes that it takes to smoke a cigarette.

We are also finding some decrease in smoking by those subjects who simply continue to monitor their smoking. This is a standard finding, to be discussed further in the next chapter. But, within the group of subjects who did no more than monitor their smoking, some subjects also spontaneously decreased its variability. These subjects smoked less than the other self-monitoring subjects.[9]

In summary, the group of subjects who reduced the variability of their smoking also reduced the amount. Reduction in the variability of an addictive behavior is a form of soft commitment. By restricting freedom of choice, variability reduction adds "weight" to any instance of the behavior; it focuses attention on the behavior's long-term consequences.

Consider the person who keeps a supply of Dove ice-cream bars in the freezer and is in the habit of eating one or two of them every night, or the person who is in the habit of having two or three glasses of scotch every night before going to sleep. Now suppose that person adopts the following rule: however many Dove bars (or scotches) I have tonight, I will have an equal number each night for the rest of the week. Without the rule's adoption, each Dove bar (or scotch) consumed tonight would entail only its own consequences and could be, in theory, the last one ever consumed. With the rule's adoption, each Dove bar or scotch is in effect seven of them strung out in time. No longer is it possible to say, "Just this once." The pleasures of consumption are no longer restricted to the moment; they are extended in time and therefore more easily compared with future disadvantages. In other words, the decision to eat the Dove bar, to drink the scotch, to smoke the cigarette, has been given weight.

Soft Commitment and Happiness

Figure 5.4 is a way of representing Aristotle's "golden mean" in terms of utility. Aristotle did not know about the "general mean theorem" which says that, depending on how it is calculated (depending on the value of a constant in a general mean equation), the mean of a group of numbers may be anywhere between the lowest and the highest of all the numbers

(Aczl, 1948). Clearly the golden mean, the most highly valued point be-tween extremes, may be, depending on circumstances, anywhere between those extremes or even at one extreme. Moreover, as Aristotle emphasized, one extreme may be much worse than the other.

Figure 5.4 is a profile, of a sort, assumed to apply to alcohol consump-tion by some hypothetical individual. Other commodities and individuals would be characterized by other profiles. If we assume for the moment that Figure 5.4 fairly represents the effects of drinking alcohol, a mean (of drinking on about 20 percent of opportunities to drink) between total ab-stinence and total indulgence is higher in average utility than either ex-treme, but total abstinence (the left end of Figure 5.4) is much higher in utility than total indulgence (the right end).

Other activities may have golden means in different places. There may be no rate of cigarette smoking of higher average value than no smoking at all. (Rates below those harmful to health—one cigarette per year, for exam-ple—may be irritating rather than pleasant.) Thus, the golden mean for smoking may be at the extreme of no smoking at all. For necessities such as eating, on the other hand, moderation is clearly better than extremes in ei-ther direction. For eating, unlike the picture presented in Figure 5.4, total abstinence would be the worse of the two extremes. When total abstinence is harmful, its pursuit may be seen as a certain kind of addiction, what we called in Chapter 3 a revolt against indulgence. Anorexia (self-starvation) is a kind of (almost total) abstinence that results in death. Extreme absti-nence from leisure, or workaholism, results in health problems, depression, and general unhappiness.

When total indulgence is harmful in the long run, as in the case of alco-holism, we tend to call that behavior an *impulsive addiction.* When total abstinence is harmful in the long run, as in the case of anorexia, we tend to call that behavior a *compulsive addiction.* Compulsive addictions cannot generally be attributed to myopia or to steep temporal discounting. They are rather the taking to extremes of otherwise highly valued patterns. As Ainslie (1992) notes, people search for "bright lines," clear demarcations between beneficial and harmful behavior. The brightest of bright lines is the one that divides no consumption at all from any consumption. When the commodity in question is not a necessity (as alcohol is not) total absti-nence does no harm. But when the commodity is a vital necessity, such as food, or a necessity for a balanced life, such as leisure, points near the extreme of total abstinence may be of lower utility (that is, more harmful) than points near the extreme of total indulgence. Anorexics and workaholics have in a sense taken an easy way out of total indulgence, devised an overly simple solution to a complex problem, a cutting of the Gordian knot.

At the extreme of total indulgence lie most addictions that are usually labeled "impulsive." In Figures 5.2 and 5.3 these addictions are given the lowest possible average value (arbitrarily, 3 utils).[10] Such addictions may be attributed in most cases to myopia or steep temporal discounting.[11]

A person can gain entrance to an exciting social milieu in some instances only at the price of some degree of indulgence. This is of course true of moderate social drinking but it may also be true of heavy drinking (as in fraternities) or drug taking. The "compulsion" or "craving" to drink or take drugs may be just as strong in the context of the social group where such behavior is socially reinforced as that induced directly by the intoxicating effects of the drink or drug. These intoxicating effects may in fact serve mainly as discriminative stimuli for social behavior; they may not themselves be primary reinforcers. (The next chapter will discuss in detail the important role of discriminative stimuli in self-control.)

Certain long-term, or global, reinforcers (social acceptance by a certain group) may thus act on the same behavior as very short-term, or local, reinforcers (having a drink or taking a drug now) and in opposition to other long-term reinforcers (social acceptance by family). The actual reinforcers of an individual addictive act may be difficult to identify, not only for outsiders, but for addicts themselves. The person in the best position to identify those reinforcers would be a friend or family member in close contact with the addict from day to day. Ironically, if the theory of Chapter 4 is correct, such close contact is exactly what an addict lacks and is expensive for the addict to obtain.

Italo Calvino (1988), in his essay "Lightness" in *Six Memos for the Next Millennium,* quotes the poet Paul Valéry (p. 16): "One should be light like a bird, and not like a feather." Valéry advocates a directed lightness, a lightness of thought rather than a lightness of whim. In life, Calvino and Valéry imply, we need to be spontaneous, but only in the context of some framework that allows us to attain higher levels of spontaneity; a feather is a slave to the wind, while a bird *uses* the wind. A happy life will strike the right balance between lightness and heaviness. Soft commitment is that sort of balance.

6

Rules and Probability

The theme of this chapter is behavioral context. First I discuss the immediate context of an act or pattern of acts. This context consists of the stimuli signaling a given relationship between an act and its consequences—discriminative stimuli. Next I examine the wider context of an act or pattern of acts (the context of the context, so to speak). The concept of contextual control is then elaborated and extended to human language, and I show how verbal rules come to serve as behavioral guides.

I discuss probability in this chapter for two reasons. First, it is a paradigm of an abstract concept that is at the same time quantitatively specifiable. By analyzing the meaning of a verbal probability statement such as "The probability of the coin landing heads up is one-half," I address the more general question of the relation of language to behavior. Second, to make a reward less probable is to discount that reward; probability is a mode of discounting analogous to temporal discounting, hence to self-control.

Local discriminative stimuli serve to bridge between past and present acts because of a "history of reinforcement"—the wider temporal context of those stimuli and those acts (a person's experience with verbal rules or traffic lights and cars, for example). Ultimately, an individual's entire history of reinforcement may be seen as the widest context (within the individual's lifetime) of the present act.[1]

Discriminative Stimuli

Unlikely as it seems, our deepest desires are situational. That is, we do not carry our cravings around with us wherever we go. Rather, our cravings come and go depending on where we are. The desire to eat a snack, so irresistible while watching TV, often vanishes while playing ping pong or working or cleaning the bathroom. Of course it is difficult to eat while playing ping pong. Still, why should the *desire* to eat vanish with the *opportunity* to eat? The reason for this selectivity of desire is that situations differ in the behavior that is reinforced or punished within them. "When in Rome do as the Romans do" means that the Romans are familiar with the contingencies of reinforcement that apply in Rome, whereas you (assuming you are not a Roman) are not. A situation or a stimulus that signals the operation of a certain contingency of reinforcement is called, technically, a discriminative stimulus.

A discriminative stimulus is a guide to behavior. The simplest type is a discrete signal like a red or green traffic light. The green light tells you to go and the red light tells you to stop. What exactly does that mean? It means that going when the light is green will be reinforced (by getting where you are going) and that going when the light is red may be punished (by a traffic ticket, by an accident, by social disapproval).

A pigeon can be trained to peck a green button and be rewarded by a food delivery after every tenth peck as long as the button is green. Then the button's color can be changed to red and pecks not reinforced ("extinction"). If green and red buttons are alternated (like traffic lights) the pigeon will soon learn to peck rapidly on the button whenever it is green and not to peck when the button is red. The pigeon's behavior is controlled by the colored buttons in the same sense that traffic is controlled by the traffic lights. A person watching the pigeon peck the green button and not peck the red button without having seen the initial training might think that the green button directly causes the pecks while the red button lacks this property. Similarly, a visitor from Mars watching traffic might think that green lights somehow caused cars to move while red lights caused them to stop. But there is no direct (that is, efficient) causal relationship between a discriminative stimulus and the behavior it controls. Rather, a discriminative stimulus *guides* behavior; it signals a particular relation between behavior and reinforcement (a particular set of behavior-environment contingencies).

Discriminative stimuli may be simple or complex and the behavior they control may be simple or complex. One situation (watching TV) differs from another (playing ping pong) primarily by virtue of differences in the very complex networks of behavior-environment contingencies they signal. Within each situation, subsets of discriminative stimuli—consisting of the observed actions of others, linguistic rules, maps, verbally or pictorially expressed probabilities, and so forth—will have different meanings (will signal different contingencies) and therefore guide behavior in different directions. This is another way of saying that the context of a discriminative stimulus may determine its meaning.

Many psychology experiments have illustrated the importance of context in situations where the reinforcement contingencies are complex. (See, for example, Catania, Matthews, and Shimhoff, 1982; Hayes et al., 1986.) The following hypothetical experiment combines and summarizes the results of these studies.

Suppose three human experimental subjects are each given a difficult problem to solve. For the first subject, this one is the latest in a series of problems differing in detail but all of which may be solved by using the same rule (not told to the subject). The problems may be algebra word problems, for example, all requiring that a single equation be set up. Initially, let us assume, these problems were solved slowly but by now the first subject has caught on to the rule and is solving them quite rapidly. This first subject, we are assuming, has "learned to learn" how to solve this kind of problem.

The second subject is not given any prior problems but is instead informed of the rule by which the problem may be solved and instructed in its use. The second subject, let us further assume, solves the current problem just as quickly as the first subject does.

The third subject is neither given experience with these kinds of problems nor told the rule. All else being equal, the third subject will take longer to solve the problem than the other two subjects but, let us suppose, eventually solves it.

Now all three subjects are given a new problem; although similar on the surface to the previous ones, it cannot be solved using the earlier rule. The invariable result of these studies is that the third subject solves the new problem significantly sooner than the first two subjects. The first two subjects are essentially equivalent in what they learned about these problems; the experience of the first subject is equivalent to the verbal instruction given to the second. In fact, both the first and second subjects are relying on previous experience: the first, directly; the second, through the experience to which the rule refers.[2] But the rule that has been so useful up to now has its downside: it retards adaptability to new situations.

An experiment at Stony Brook by Kudadjie-Gyamfi (1998) illustrates this type of study. Recall from Chapter 5 the procedure used by Kudadjie-Gyamfi and Rachlin (1996), in which human subjects made choices by pressing button X or Y. A subject in that experiment would maximize overall earnings by always choosing Y, the lower of the two local rewards. Remember that presenting trials in temporal patterns (rhythms) tended to increase Y choices (Figure 5.5).

Using this procedure, with trials unpatterned, Kudadjie-Gyamfi gave subjects a hint by telling them that choosing Y tended to improve rewards for future choices. The subjects subsequently improved their performance and chose Y about as much as did subjects with patterned trials. Then, without informing the subjects, Kudadjie-Gyamfi changed the contingencies so that N increased or decreased randomly from trial to trial. Because their behavior no longer controlled N, the subjects' current choices no longer influenced future local utility; earnings would now be maximized by always choosing X. Yet the subjects who had been given the hint continued to choose Y at the same rate as before—following the old rule rather than the new contingencies.

The lesson of these studies is that rules are useful but may be situation specific. A discriminative stimulus that signals a certain relationship between behavior and reinforcement in one situation (in the presence of a given broader discriminative stimulus) may signal a different, even an opposite, relationship between behavior and reinforcement in another situation (as in the differing reinforcement contingencies for driving in Great Britain and the United States).

I turn next to a series of experiments on complex behavioral patterning with nonhumans. They demonstrate that animals without language may come to pattern their behavior in highly complex ways—that is, to follow arbitrary (nonnatural) rules.

COMPOUND DISCRIMINATIVE STIMULI.   An experiment by Nevin and Liebold (1966) with a single pigeon illustrates the remarkable situation specificity of discriminative stimuli. The experimenters combined two already complex procedures called matching to sample and nonmatching to sample. In the matching to sample procedure, there are three buttons in a horizontal row on the wall of the experimental chamber. The center button is first lit either red or green (randomly from trial to trial). The pigeon pecks the center button. Then the side buttons are lit; one is red, the other is green (colors randomly assigned to sides from trial to trial). If the pigeon pecks the side button that is the same color as the center button (matches to sample), it receives a small food reward and the next trial starts. If the pigeon pecks the side button opposite in color to the center button, a short blackout occurs, no food is received, and the next trial starts. In other words, the red center button is a discriminative stimulus for pecking the red side button, and the green center button is a discriminative stimulus for pecking the green side button. After several sessions made up of hundreds of trials, pigeons usually learn to match to sample. The nonmatching to sample procedure is the opposite: the red center button is a discriminative stimulus for pecking the *green* side button and the green center button is a discriminative stimulus for pecking the *red* side button. With a bit more difficulty, pigeons also learn to nonmatch to sample.

Nevin and Liebold added another layer of discrimination to this already complex process. A yellow light was mounted on the ceiling of the experimental chamber. When the light was on, the contingencies in effect were those of matching to sample; when the light was off, the contingencies in effect were those of nonmatching to sample. That is, the yellow light served as a contextual discriminative stimulus that reversed the meaning of other discriminative stimuli. After extensive training, the pigeon was able to behave appropriately with the yellow light on and off.

In the Nevin and Liebold experiment, the center button remained lit while the pigeon chose between the side buttons. Other experimenters have trained pigeons, rats, and other animals to match to sample or nonmatch to sample in the absence of the lit center button (see Balsam, 1988, for a review). That is, the center button is lit, is pecked, and then is unlit for a few seconds. Next, the side buttons are lit and the pigeon chooses between them. This procedure is often used to study memory in nonhuman animals. Within a minute of delay between sample and comparison stimuli, pigeons' choices become random. The ability of humans to label stimuli with words and to rehearse those words during the delay enables us to remember over vastly longer periods of time. When that ability is taken away (by interference or some other means) we do not remember isolated events much better than a pigeon does.

In a series of experiments by Olton and his colleagues (summarized in Olton, 1979), rats were placed in a maze containing a central chamber and a number of arms (usually eight) radiating outward. At the other ends of the arms were goal boxes that might or might not contain food. (The rats could not see or smell the food from the central chamber.) In one experiment, all of the goal boxes contained food. The rats in this experiment quickly learned to visit each arm just once, eat the food in the goal box, and not visit that arm again. That is, the rats became very efficient about getting the food and not revisiting the empty arms even though there were no *local* discriminative stimuli signaling food (sights or smells of food). The discriminative stimuli by which the rats' behavior was guided were the *global* spatial cues present (the maze was open so the rats could see the room with its fixed walls, windows, doors, and furniture) in the context of the rats' own past behavior relative to those cues.

Still another series of experiments by Terrace and colleagues shows that pigeons can learn to peck a series of different-colored buttons (say, red, green, blue, and yellow) in a specific order regardless of the location of the buttons. On one trial, the buttons from left to right would be red, yellow, blue, and green; on the next trial, yellow, blue, red, and green, and so on. Whatever the order in space, the pigeons always had to obey the following rule: peck the red button first, the green button second, the blue button third, and the yellow button last. There were no feedback stimuli to tell the pigeons how they were doing while pecking. Only correct completed sequences were reinforced. As in the Olton experiments, the discriminative stimulus was the current environment in the context of the pigeons' own previous behavior. Significantly for self-control, pigeons learned longer button sequences when the stimuli were temporally or spatially organized into "chunks" of two or three individual items.

In further experiments, Terrace showed that the same principles applied to monkeys pressing buttons. But monkeys could learn longer sequences and learn them faster than pigeons could. More significantly, monkeys were much better than pigeons at skipping over missing items in a sequence. That is, when monkeys were trained on a five-item sequence, say, and only items 1, 2, 4, and 5 were presented, they would still press the buttons in correct order; pigeons, trained correspondingly, were as likely to peck button 5 as button 4 after button 2 (Terrace, 1993). This shows that monkeys could structure a highly complex task into patterns and treat those patterns as units in themselves, whereas for pigeons (in these complex tasks) the units were always single pecks.[3]

Finally, an experiment by Wasserman, DeVolder, and Coppage (1992) tested the ability of pigeons to learn that two classes of discriminative stimuli are *functionally equivalent*. The ability to learn functional equivalence is an essential element of the ability to use language. For example, the two different-sounding names Mark Twain and Samuel Clemens stand for the same person—they mean the same thing. If you first learn that the two names both stand for the same person, and then you learn that Mark Twain wrote *Tom Sawyer,* you automatically know that Samuel Clemens wrote *Tom Sawyer.* You don't have to learn this fact.

Can pigeons make the same sort of inference? Wasserman and colleagues showed that they can. The discriminative stimuli they used were a large group of different pictures (slides projected on a screen in the chamber) in four categories: cats, flowers, cars, and chairs.[4] The experimental chamber had four different-colored buttons that the pigeons could peck (B1, B2, B3, B4). Only two of the buttons were lit at any one time. In the first phase of the experiment, B1 and B2 were lit. Slides from two categories (say, cats and flowers) were established as discriminative stimuli for pecking B1 (that is, when a cat or flower slide was shown, pecks on B1 were reinforced and pecks on B2 were not), while slides from the other two categories (cars and chairs) were established as discriminative stimuli for pecking B2. The pigeons learned to discriminate between cats or flowers on the one hand, and cars or chairs on the other. (When a car or chair slide was shown, pecks on B2 were reinforced and pecks on B1 were not.) In this first phase, cats were functionally equivalent to (functioned the same way as) flowers; cars were functionally equivalent to chairs.

In the second phase of the experiment, only buttons B3 and B4 were lit. One category from the first pair (say, cats) was established as a discriminative stimulus for pecking B3 and one category from the second pair (say, cars) was established as a discriminative stimulus for pecking B4. The pigeons soon learned to make this new discrimination.

In the experiment's final phase, buttons B3 and B4 were again lit and the pigeons were presented with examples from the other categories of each pair (flowers and chairs). The question was, would the pigeons peck B3 in the presence of the flowers and B4 in the presence of the chairs? Indeed, the pigeons were able to make this logical leap. They learned that in the context of this experiment flowers were functionally equivalent to cats, while chairs were functionally equivalent to cars.

Why go through all these complicated experiments with pigeons and rats? Not to show how smart they are. The purpose is rather to show how complex behavioral patterning may become, even without language. With language, learned patterns of behavior may be much more complicated and extend over much longer periods. The ability to construct grammatical sentences, to remember them, and to use them as behavioral guides is unique to humans. Although language functions in many ways for us, its main function, like that of any complex discriminative stimulus, is to guide behavior. The guided behavior in turn may be linguistic behavior or nonlinguistic behavior—of others or of the speaker. In all cases the *meaning* of a sentence is to be found in the contingencies of reinforcement to which it refers. If there are no contingencies of reinforcement, no prior experience of the listener, to which the sentence applies, then the sentence has no meaning, or rather it may be classified as nonsense (which may, in another context, have a metaphoric, ironic, or satiric meaning). Even apparently pure descriptions are largely behavioral guides. As it stands, "The grass is green" may have no behavioral referent. Nevertheless, no one (except a person suffering from schizophrenia) walks around saying "The grass is green" for no reason. In its context, "The grass is green" may mean It's not brown so you don't have to water it, or it may be part of instruction in English, or an example of a simple declarative sentence designed to change the behavior, including the verbal behavior, of the listener—as the sentence is used here.

In a psychology experiment, verbal instructions to a human subject take the place of hundreds of hours of exposure to a set of reinforcement contingencies for a nonhuman subject. Verbal instructions, and rules in general, serve as mediators between past experience and current behavior. Experimental psychologists assume that the explicit verbal instructions they give to subjects signal the primary reinforcement contingencies that govern the subjects' behavior in the experimental context. This assumption is often unjustified, however. Other reinforcers, such as the experimenter's approval—being deemed intelligent, moral, or not gullible—or simply getting quickly out of the experiment, may strongly influence behavior and in fact dominate the explicit instructions.

CRAVING.   The force behind a drug addict's irresistible craving for drugs is similar in nature and sometimes even in intensity to the cravings everyone experiences at times—to scratch an itch, for example. What is it about an itch that makes us want to scratch it? Certainly the itch does not directly cause the scratch. The relief is just as great when someone else scratches us as when we scratch ourselves. Moreover, an itch is not a pain. A pain is negative by definition; but an itch is not simply negative. What is it?

According to Ainslie (1992), an itch is a discriminative stimulus signaling that scratching has become a very strong but very brief reward. While the itch is there, scratching is a reinforcer. When the itch is absent, scratching is just scratching. The problem with scratching a mosquito bite, however, is the same as that with an addiction—a reduction of overall value and an exchange of positive for negative reinforcement. That is, a trip down the primrose path. What, for the first few scratches, had been a positive pleasure soon becomes merely the (very temporary) removal of the discriminative stimulus. The difference between an itch and an addiction is that with an itch the time course of the process is so brief (the primrose path is so steep) that the descent is clearly perceptible (like a cliff as opposed to a long shallow hill) and therefore may be avoided.

Although an itch is a discriminative stimulus for brief immediate positive reinforcement, it also becomes associated with the punishment that ensues after a minute or two of scratching. Creams and lotions are thus self-control devices; they help us to avoid a discriminative stimulus signaling a brief positive reward with overall negative consequences. Fortunately for us, the discriminative stimulus for scratching (built into our physiology) is specific and localized, and the negative consequences follow quickly on the heels of the positive consequences. Thus, however intense our craving to scratch an itch may be, this is one addiction we can usually handle. Unfortunately for the dieter, the alcoholic, and the crack addict, while some discriminative stimuli for these addictions (such as the smell of food or alcohol), are physiological and proximal, many other discriminative stimuli (such as the ambience of a bakery, bar, or crack house) may become associated with the positive consequences of these activities and relatively unassociated with their delayed and abstract negative consequences. There are no creams or lotions that will remove these stimuli.

Nevertheless, the nature and even the intensity of the craving we all have to scratch a mosquito bite is no different from the craving of the crack addict to take crack or of the alcoholic to drink alcohol. When we find ourselves, despite our resolutions and our better judgment, scratching an itch—sometimes without even realizing what we are doing—we can put ourselves in the shoes of the addict at the lower end of the primrose path.

USING DISCRIMINATIVE STIMULI.   The relation of itches to scratching is innate. The relation of TV watching to reinforcement from eating snacks (to cite my own problem) is learned—and may be unlearned. The rule *Never eat while watching television,* is difficult for me to establish over long periods. The food commercials and the depiction of eating in TV programs are powerful discriminative stimuli to get up and have a snack. As with scratching, I sometimes find myself unconsciously performing or about to perform the addictive activity (standing in front of the open freezer with a pint of ice cream in my hand) without even realizing how I got to that point. Instead, it is just barely possible for me to enforce the following rule: *If you must eat now you have to turn off the TV while you are eating and turn it back on only after you have finished.*

This second rule is not inconsistent with the first. It seems reasonable, but it is surprisingly difficult to follow. Trying to enforce it creates a tremendous feeling of ambivalence, because the TV watching has become a necessary part of my enjoyment of the food. That is, TV watching and food eating have become economic complements (like left shoes and right shoes) in my life. Their value together is much higher than that of either activity alone. And it is exactly this enhanced value that I am reluctant to give up. Nevertheless, the arbitrariness of this association seems so irrational to me that I can indeed force myself to turn off the TV during a commercial and wolf down some mocha-almond-fudge ice cream (a particular weakness). The interesting (and revealing) part of this process is that it only takes three or four such separations of TV and eating before the craving to eat loses its compulsive power and becomes weak enough so that turning off the set (even during a commercial) becomes simply not worth the effort. It is not that I have lost my taste for mocha-almond-fudge, but that the TV has lost its discriminative power over the act of eating it.

For a person who is chronically overweight, life is full of such discriminative stimuli. In New York City, for example, it is virtually impossible to walk down the street without being assailed by smells of food from restaurants, bakeries, and pushcart vendors. It seems that half of the people one encounters on the street are eating something. For them, taking a walk—an exercise activity usually highly effective in *substituting* for eating, becomes instead a discriminative stimulus for eating—an economic *complement* to eating; in other words, a booby trap.

Exercise, like social activity, may be a positive addiction that may become a substitute for any negative addiction (see Chapter 4). It is an especially effective substitute for overeating because it uses up calories. But eating while exercising defeats the very purpose of exercising. An overweight person who eats while exercising is like an alcoholic who drinks while socializing. The overweight New Yorker who finds herself on the street with a hot dog that has unconsciously made its way into her hands should ask the vendor for a bag, put the hot dog in it, take a bus back home, run up to her apartment, and eat the hot dog there. This of course is very difficult to do. Yet if it were done once or twice, the connection between eating and walking would be broken (there would be no more unconscious food buying) and there would be one less booby trap in her life.

Movie exhibitors profit much more from food sales than from admissions. Everything about a modern multiplex theater, from lighting and traffic patterns to cup holders on the armrests to the content of the movies themselves, is designed to make moviegoing a discriminative stimulus for eating—to make these two activities economic complements. Breaking this connection, perhaps by enforcing the rule *If I must have the popcorn and soda now I'll finish them outside in the lobby,* will establish a behavioral pattern that can last. If everyone did this, it would immediately become universally clear that the craving for popcorn comes not from inside us but from the outside; eating would just not be worth missing the movie for.

Anyone can go on a diet and lose weight. The trick, as we all know, is to keep the weight off, not to relapse. If during a diet the discriminative stimuli for eating are allowed to retain their power, then after the diet eating will quickly and automatically return to its previous levels. But if the discriminative stimuli that control eating are identified, and if their connections to eating are broken one by one, patterns will be established and maintained for long periods. And a weapon will have been added to the dieter's armamentarium that may be taken out and used whenever a relapse is detected.

The same reasoning applies to other addictions. The habit of smoking, for example, is notoriously signaled by various discriminative stimuli—after meals or sex, during various social occasions, upon getting up in the morning, while reading or working. Breaking one or two of these connections of course is not sufficient to reduce smoking. Whatever is not smoked in one situation may be compensated for in another. Still, attacking these situations one by one is easier than trying to attack them all at once. A smoker who reduces the number of discriminative stimuli controlling his smoking is in a sense corralling his cravings, thereby making them easier to deal with.

Breaking the connection between discriminative stimuli and addictive behavior is only half of the addict's job. The other much more difficult half is to *establish* connections between discriminative stimuli and nonaddictive behavior. We have seen the power of discriminative stimuli that signal *local* reinforcement contingencies; we turn now to the question of how discriminative stimuli may signal *global* reinforcement contingencies.

Discriminative Stimuli and Self-Control

In the last chapter I discussed a phenomenon of economics called the sunk costs fallacy. A project is begun that requires continuous investment over time. At some point before the project is complete, future investment is deemed to be unprofitable. The project should be abandoned at that point but, because they have already made the previous investment (the sunk costs), decisionmakers are reluctant to do so.

For instance, a chain clothing store may decide to enhance its image by opening a branch on Fifth Avenue in New York City, even though it might be unprofitable. (Visitors, seeing the firm's store amid other very expensive clothing stores, may value the merchandise in their home-town branch slightly more.) After a few years, losses from the Fifth Avenue branch are higher than anticipated. Should it now be closed? Is it a fallacy to keep the branch open merely because the firm has already invested so much in it?

The problem is that while the benefits of keeping the branch open are vague and impossible to measure, the costs are vivid and clear. The firm's comptroller, the person assigned to watch the budget, is more likely to press for closing (especially if the firm's current overall profits are low), while the firm's president is more likely to press for keeping the branch open (especially if his or her name is over the door). These officers embody, respectively, the firm's short-term and long-term interests (Northcraft and Wolf, 1984). If we treat the firm as analogous to an individual, the sunk cost problem is a problem of self-control. As in any self-control problem, there is no inherently right or wrong answer. Because the benefits of sticking to a prior decision are difficult to measure, and because the costs are easy to measure the costs may seem real and the benefits illusory. The sunk cost "fallacy" is thus a necessary counterweight to our tendency to overweight benefits that are immediate, specific, clearly definable, or precisely measurable, and to underweight benefits that are distant in time, abstract, not clearly definable, or not precisely measurable.[5]

To put this point another way: Stick to your earlier decision about future rewards even though it may now seem wrong. As we have seen in earlier chapters, this rule is not always detrimental. There is often a valid reason to ignore present judgments; the present is necessarily closer in time to future reward than the past was. And judgments of value close in time to reward are notoriously unreliable; as reward grows nearer we often change our minds and later come to regret having done so.

Recall the behavior of the pigeons in the experiment of Siegel and Rachlin (1995). These pigeons chose a smaller-sooner reward (SS) over a larger-later reward (LL) when both were obtainable by a single peck, but they chose and obtained LL when 31 pecks were required—even though they could have switched after peck 30. This is an example of the sunk cost fallacy. At the point just before peck 31, the 30 initial pecks were essentially sunk costs—an initial investment in LL that should have been ignored when deciding between SS and LL on the next peck. Yet they were not ignored. When the 30 initial pecks were made on the LL button, the chances were virtually 100 percent that LL would be chosen on peck 31, whereas without that investment the pigeons would have chosen and obtained the smaller reward. Thus, being influenced by sunk costs served the pigeons well in the experiment, as this tendency undoubtedly does in nature.

The pattern of behavior exhibited by the pigeons was extremely simple: pause for a second or two and then peck rapidly. The discriminative stimulus controlling that pattern was the green button in the context of the experimental chamber. The patterns of everyday human behavior are of course much more complex. To a large extent, however, everyday human life is improved by the tendency to preserve a pattern of behavior once it has begun—to stick with earlier decisions, with resolutions, with promises we have made to other people and to ourselves, to finish the job we started—in other words, to be influenced by sunk costs. As the next chapter will show, our personal and social reputations for consistency in patterning are so significant that, one way or another, they form the very basis of our self-concepts.[6]

Many of the verbal rules, axioms, and advice we extract from our experience, including formal education, are essentially aids in maintaining a planned pattern of behavior despite immediate temptations to deviate from that pattern. Water needs no map to go downhill. But when the path to our destination is not the one we would naturally take at the moment, a map or a verbal plan comes in handy. The difficulty of achieving consistent behavioral patterning lies in the abstract nature of its benefits and the abstract nature of the behavior itself. It is more difficult to play a melody, for example, than to repeat a single note over and over again. The melody has to be planned in advance, whereas the single note needs no plan. That is the value of discriminative stimuli in self-control.

GLOBAL CONTINGENCIES.   An experiment with pigeons by Heyman and Tanz (1995) illustrates the power of discriminative stimuli to signal global contingencies. The choice faced by the pigeons in this experiment was much like the choice faced by the human subjects in the Kudadjie-Gyamfi and Rachlin (1996) experiment. The pigeons chose between pecking two different-colored buttons. If the pigeons distributed their pecks on the buttons so as to maximize the *local* reinforcement rate, they would in fact minimize the *overall* reinforcement rate. Faced with these contingencies, the pigeons did maximize local at the expense of overall reinforcement rate. Then, "to help the pigeons learn what was 'good' for them" (Heyman, 1996a, p. 571), a light in the experimental chamber turned from blue to white to signal increases in the overall reinforcement rate. With this signal the pigeons altered their behavior and began to maximize overall reinforcement rate, ignoring local reinforcement rate. The signal therefore did help the pigeons to learn what was good for them.

I mentioned in Chapter 4 that many soldiers who became addicted to heroin in Vietnam had little difficulty in breaking their addiction once they came home. The principles discussed in this chapter provide a reason why this was so. The superordinate stimuli present in Vietnam (like the yellow light in the Nevin and Liebold experiment) were discriminative stimuli for one set of reinforcement contingencies (high value of drug taking relative to social support), while the drastically different superordinate stimuli present at home were discriminative stimuli for another set (high value of social support relative to drug taking). Nonetheless, while the value of taking heroin is realized as soon as the drug is injected, the value of social support takes a while to develop and is not easily perceived. To phrase it differently, the value of heroin is local while that of social support is global or abstract.

People who develop an addiction, not in a drastically different environment like Vietnam but here at home where they will live for the rest of their lives, should nevertheless provide some strong stimulus to distinguish the new situation from the old—a haven, as it were, from their addiction. Then, they have to expand that haven so that it encompasses the whole of their lives. Institutions such as hospitals and clinics may initially serve in this capacity but it is very difficult to expand their control outside their walls. Institutions may act in an addict's life in just the opposite way from how Vietnam acted. They may become distinct discriminative stimuli for abstinence while the addict's home environment remains a discriminative stimulus for addictive behavior. Therapeutic environments closer to home, like Alcoholics Anonymous, may not reduce addiction as efficiently as a clinic but they have the advantage of more easily expanding their behavioral control from local to global contingencies in the addict's life.

DELAY OF GRATIFICATION.   Recall from Chapter 2 the delay of gratification procedure (Mischel, Shoda, and Rodriguez, 1989): The experimenter puts a less-preferred reward (a pretzel for example) in front of a child. She tells him that she will leave the room and will return with a more-preferred reward (a marshmallow, for example). The child may signal the experimenter to come back into the room (by ringing a bell) before the experimenter does so on her own. If the child makes the signal, he gets the small reward (the pretzel) and forfeits the large one (the marshmallow). If the child refrains from signaling until the experimenter comes back, he gets the large reward. The experimenters observe how long each child waits (delays gratification) before signaling.

Delay of gratification depends on age of the subjects and other variables that might be expected to affect the steepness of discount functions. As argued in Chapter 2, the expected delay to the larger reward increases with elapsed waiting time.[7] Steeper discounting will bring the current value of the large reward below that of the smaller immediate reward and the child will signal for the experimenter to return.

Delay of gratification is highly sensitive to instructions and to waiting conditions. When the rewards are exposed or when children are told to think about consuming them (about how "crunchy and tasty" the pretzel is), they ring the bell sooner. When the rewards are hidden, or when children are given a task to do during the waiting period, or when they are told to imagine the small reward as a nonconsumable object (a toy log, for example) they wait much longer before ringing the bell.

The words that the experimenter says to the child establish a context; that is, they are discriminative stimuli for actions appropriate to various situations. The larger reward (the marshmallow) has a large social component. The child wants to please the adult, to behave well, and it has been made clear that waiting is behaving well. The alternatives in the delay of gratification procedure are not just small versus large rewards but also particular rewards (eating the pretzel) versus more abstract rewards (pleasing an adult or being a good child).[8]

Providing discriminative stimuli for consumption (like the sight of the pretzel or the words "crunchy and tasty") increases the likelihood that consummatory behavior will be highly valued. Providing discriminative stimuli for an activity that conflicts with consumption (playing with a pretzel is incompatible with eating it) increases the likelihood that behavior incompatible with consumption will be highly valued; hence the child waits longer.

MONITORING.   Perhaps the most serious obstacle to self-control is faulty perception of one's own behavior. It is much more difficult for an alcoholic to perceive how much he is drinking than it is for his friends and family members to perceive how much he is drinking. The same is true of smoking—even though cigarettes are easily countable and come in packs that also are easily countable. A heavy smoker may know that she consumes three packs a day because she has to buy three packs, but that realization is in a sense forced upon her. *While* she is smoking, she has only a dim idea of where she is in the count. Consequently, maintaining a running total of how many cigarettes have been smoked so far each day, and keeping that total in an easily accessible place like a handbag or shirt pocket (providing a source of feedback) is often enough to reduce smoking.

Recall the ongoing study of smoking patterns at Stony Brook. Smokers are asked to reduce the variability of the number of cigarettes they smoke each day by keeping the number constant over five-day periods. That is, they smoke freely on day 1, keeping track of the number of cigarettes they smoke that day (by putting the butts in a plastic bag or removing a tab from a card). On days 2 through 5, they try to smoke the exact same number each day. We have seen that focusing the smoker's attention on patterns over five-day periods reduces smoking significantly below that of smokers who only monitor their smoking. Interestingly, however, the smokers who are just keeping count of the number of cigarettes smoked each day (the control group) are also significantly reducing their smoking.

Why does monitoring work as a self-control method? Just smoking a cigarette that *happens* to be the twenty-fifth cigarette smoked that day is quite different from smoking a cigarette that is known to be the twenty-fifth cigarette smoked that day. In the former case, the act of smoking the cigarette stands alone as the most valuable alternative available within the next five minutes; in the latter case, smoking this cigarette is part of a larger pattern that is much less highly valued.

The experiment shows that providing a discriminative stimulus for number of cigarettes smoked over five days is more effective in reducing smoking than providing a discriminative stimulus for number of cigarettes smoked over a single day. But even providing a daily discriminative stimulus is more effective in reducing smoking than not providing any—other than the smoker's own unaided, cloudy perception.

An example of the power of monitoring to aid in self-control is an experiment by Castro and Rachlin (1980) with people trying to lose weight. The original purpose of the experiment was to test whether it is possible for people to effectively reward or punish themselves. It was known that if dieters rewarded themselves by taking, from a dish next to a scale at a weekly weigh-in, an amount of money proportional to the weight they had lost that week, they would lose more weight than dieters who simply weighed themselves (Mahoney, 1974). Our experiment replicated this finding, but we had another group of dieters who "punished" themselves by *putting into* the dish an amount of money proportional to the weight they had *lost.* Instead of gaining weight, which they would have done if this procedure was an effective punishment for weight loss, these dieters actually lost more weight than those who "rewarded" themselves. Thus, it was not self-reward that caused dieters to lose weight when they took money from the dish, but the feedback provided by the money. This feedback was more salient when money was put into the dish than when money was taken out (monetary losses have been frequently found to be much more effective than equal monetary gains) and so was more effective as a discriminative stimulus for weight loss.[9]

The problem with self-monitoring as a means of self-control is that it is almost as difficult to get yourself to monitor your own behavior as to control that behavior in the first place. Self-monitoring is often the hardest part of a self-control program. Several subjects in the smoking study at Stony Brook dropped out (losing as much as $100 in participation fees) because they found self-monitoring so onerous.

I have a book, a pamphlet really, called "Dial Away Your Fat," originally published in 1937 and still in print. It contains a not-very-useful table listing calories in certain foods and a cardboard dial on the front which can be used to count calories. When my weight rises above a certain point, I take the book from the drawer, put it in my shirt pocket, and use it to count calories. It works like a charm. The only problem is that I can hardly bring myself to put it in my pocket and I often "forget" to do so. Monitoring is effective but monitoring is difficult. It is harder for me to count calories than to reduce calories once they are being counted.

A second problem with self-monitoring is the same as that with any discriminative stimulus for self-control. When the stimulus is taken away, the self-control disappears as well. When I take the calorie book out of my pocket, my weight starts to creep up. Thus self-monitoring cannot be a permanent solution to a serious self-control problem like drug addiction or alcoholism. What is needed in those cases, as previous chapters indicate, is the development of long-term patterns of a positive addiction such as social activity. These patterns depend in turn on the establishment of clear discriminative stimuli distinguishing them from long-term patterns of negative addiction. This is, to be sure, a difficult and lengthy process— but it is one that will last. Self-monitoring may be the first and perhaps the most difficult step in the development of the process.

Probability

The function of a verbal rule is to reach back into the past—into the hearer's reinforcement history—and apply that history to the present situation so as to guide current behavior. A verbal statement of a probability is a quantitative verbal rule. Like any verbal statement it is a guide to behavior, but a probability statement is a graduated guide. The difference between "If you cross the street against the light you may get hit by a car" and "If you cross the street against the light the probability of your being hit by a car is .25" is a difference in precision. Both statements are discriminative stimuli and both rely on a certain reinforcement history (experience with cars, streets, punishment by parents, effects of the environment in general, as well as other instances of compound discriminative stimuli). The probability statement relies on an additional kind of history—a history of experience with random events such as outcomes of spinners, playing cards, dice, and so forth.

The weather report "75 percent chance of rain" is a discriminative stimulus that refers to a set of complex contingencies that have occurred in the past—relationships between previous conditions (like those prevailing today) and outcomes (rain or no rain). The weather report serves as an accurate guide to behavior only to the extent that it adequately represents those prior contingencies. In the psychology laboratory a verbal probability, a picture of a spinner or pair of dice, a hand of cards, or any gambling device presented to a human subject, is a discriminative stimulus dependent on that subject's prior experience with such devices. In experiments with nonhumans no such prior experience may be assumed. To present a probability to a pigeon, for example, there is no substitute for many experimental sessions of exposure to that probability.[10]

CALCULATING PROBABILITIES.   The mathematics of probability is the mathematics of fractions. The first question to ask about fractions is, fractions of what? In terms of pure mathematics, the answer is, fractions of the number one, or fractions of a unit. When we apply the mathematics of fractions to other spheres, it becomes necessary to say what a unit is.

Let us consider a few conceivable units, illustrated in Figure 6.1. The rule that must be followed is that the fraction cannot go above one or below zero. If it does, terms have to be redefined; it will be impossible to apply the mathematics of fractions to the other spheres where, after all, our interest lies. There is no collection of individuals greater than all, no proposition more certain than a true one, no object that occupies more space than everywhere, and no event that occurs more often than always. Correspondingly, there is no collection of individuals fewer than none, no proposition less certain than a false one, no object that occupies less space than nowhere, and no event more rare than one that never happens.

A case can be made to consider any of the nonmathematical dimensions of Figure 6.1 as a fundamental probability and to derive the rest of the probabilities from it. For instance, one person may argue that space and time may be broken into individual elements on the all-none dimension. Logical propositions must be propositions about something; otherwise they cannot be true or false. Thus logic, as well as space and time, can be reduced to individual elements ranging from none to all. Another person might argue that the words on this page, if they mean anything, can be reduced to logical propositions. That person might say that probabilities apply not to individual objects themselves, nor to objects in space and time but to propositions—sentences—such as those of a weather report or

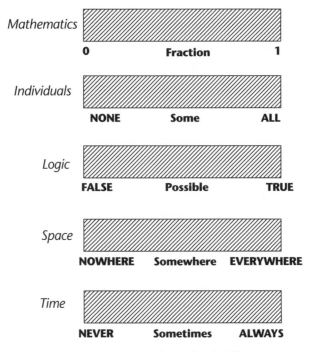

Figure 6.1. Conceptions of probability.

those we may say to ourselves. A probability exists in our language, not in things; a chair cannot be probable, any more than it can be true or false. Thus, all probabilities reduce to logical propositions.

A third and fourth person, arguing together, could say that space and time define our concept of a *thing*. Nothing exists outside both of these dimensions. For these two people, language is only a kind of action—writing or speaking—existing in space and time. Individuals, logic, everything must be expressible in space and time; hence probability is also so expressible. If these two people should continue the argument, together, you can easily imagine one turning on the other and the subsequent debate over whether space or time is more fundamental.

Here I will be ecumenical and apply the mathematics of fractions whenever convenient and consistent with the definition of probability as a graduated guide to behavior. A person's behavior may be guided by individual fractions (the fraction of students at a given college who go on to graduate or professional school) ranging from none to all, by propositional statements ("If you cheat on your income tax, you'll get caught") ranging from false to true, and by spatiotemporal events (traffic jams on a given road) ranging from nowhere and never to everywhere and always.

There is no such thing as a one-shot probability. To speak of the probability that the world will end tomorrow is to assume that in a very large number of worlds like ours some fraction of them will end on a given day. This fraction might be based directly on astronomical observations of such events as worlds ending in other solar systems or might be calculated as the coincidence of other events that we can observe. Many apparent one-shot probabilities are based on such coincidences. The likelihood of a nuclear war, for example, may be approximated by multiplying the probabilities of a series of mistakes and miscommunications, each of which may have occurred with some frequency in the past. The fact that a nuclear war (excluding World War II) has never happened does not mean that its probability is zero.

PROBABILITIES AND SIMPLE AMBIVALENCE.   Imagine that you are standing on one side of a door and on the other side is a man with a spinner and a dollar bill. The spinner is divided into n sections, one black and the rest $(n - 1)$ white. When you knock on the door, the man immediately spins the spinner's arrow. The arrow takes c seconds to come to rest. If it lands on the black section, the man passes the dollar bill to you through a slot in the door. If it lands on a white section, the man waits t seconds and then spins again. He keeps spinning, waiting t seconds between spins, until finally the arrow lands on black. He passes the dollar bill through the slot and stops. How long would you expect to wait between knocking and receiving the dollar? The expected waiting time (d) depends on the probability of the arrow's landing on black $(p = 1/n)$, the trial duration (c), and the intertrial interval (t) according to the following formula:

$$d = \frac{c+t}{p} - t. \tag{6.1}$$

Let us assume that the trial duration c is essentially zero (the spinner takes a negligible time to come to rest). Then,

$$d = t(1/p - 1) = t\theta \tag{6.2}$$

where θ is the "odds against" the spinner's landing on black. Equation 6.2 says that the expected waiting time to a probabilistic event is proportional to the odds against its happening. If, as in the above example, the probability of the spinner's landing on black were .1, the odds against the spinner's landing on black would be $(1/.1 - 1)$, or 9 to 1. If the man waited 1 minute between spins ($t = 1$), your average or "expected" waiting time between the knock and the dollar would be 9 minutes. If the spinner consisted of all black sections, then $p = 1, \theta = 0$, and your expected waiting time would be zero. That is, you would surely get the dollar after the first spin (which we are assuming takes a negligible time). If the spinner consisted of all white sections, then $p = 0, \theta = \infty$, and you would never get the dollar. In general, the lower the probability or the longer the intertrial interval, the longer the delay.

If Equation 6.2 expresses a meaningful relationship between probability and delay then the waiting time d derived from a probability should discount a reward in the same way as a delay discounts reward. Recall Mazur's hyperbolic delay discount function (Equation 2.2):

$$v = \frac{V}{1 + kD} \tag{2.2}$$

Equation 2.2 expresses the value of a delayed reward (v) as a function of its value if it were immediate (V) and its delay (D). If hyperbolic discounting also applies to probabilistic rewards we should be able to substitute delay d, as calculated by Equation 6.2, for delay D in Mazur's hyperbolic delay discount function:

$$v = \frac{V}{1 + kD} = \frac{V}{1 + kt\theta} \tag{6.3}$$

To test Equation 6.3, Raineri and I asked human subjects to make a series of hypothetical choices between probabilistic (but immediate) reinforcers on the one hand and delayed (but certain) reinforcers on the other (Raineri and Rachlin, 1993). Our subjects were asked to choose between $1,000 with a given probability (for example, $p = .5$) to be received immediately and $1,000 for sure with a delay of zero. Of course all subjects chose the latter. Then we increased the delay of the certain $1,000 in steps until finally the probabilistic $1,000 was chosen. For example, a subject might have preferred the immediate $1,000 with $p = .5$ to $1,000 delayed by two years, but preferred $1,000 delayed by one year to $1,000 with $p = .5$. If so, we assumed a point of indifference at 1.5 years. This is a titration procedure. The experimental subject was essentially used as a scale to balance the probabilistic and delayed rewards.

After obtaining a point of indifference at one probability, we changed the probability and began again until we had obtained indifference points over the whole range of probabilities. Each subject was tested at all probabilities and each probability was tested twice, once with the titrated delays starting from zero and increasing (as described above), and once with the delays starting at a very high value (how high depended on the probability) and decreasing. Setting the delayed reward (Equation 2.2) equal to the probabilistic reward (Equation 6.3),

$$\frac{V}{1+kD}=\frac{V}{1+kt\theta}, \quad D=t\theta, \quad D=t(1/p-1) \tag{6.4}$$

Figure 6.2 shows our results, with probability on the horizontal axis and the equivalent delay on the vertical axis. (The constant t was a single free parameter.) The solid line is the prediction of Equation 6.4. Clearly, our subjects were able to balance probabilistic and delayed rewards as Equation 6.4 predicts.

If probability discounting corresponds to delay discounting there should be probabilistic processes corresponding to the delay discounting

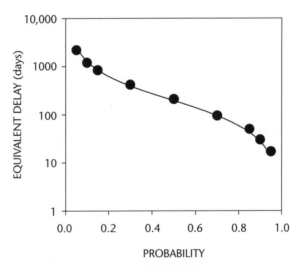

Figure 6.2. Results of the Raineri and Rachlin (1993) experiment.

processes discussed in Chapter 2. Indeed this is the case. Just as organisms tend to favor smaller immediate rewards over larger delayed rewards, they tend to favor smaller certain rewards over larger probabilistic ones. For example, most people prefer $100 for sure to $210 with a probability of .5. The expected value of a reward is its probability multiplied by its amount. Expected value is the average amount of reward per trial over a long series of trials. The expected value of the sure $100 is $100, while that of the probabilistic $210 is $105. Nevertheless, people prefer the sure reward.

We do not usually identify this fiscal conservatism with impulsiveness, yet the processes correspond. In real-life situations, probabilistic rewards may be obtained sooner or later by persistence. The worker who leaves a steady job to start a business that has the potential to pay three times as much as the job may have to fail several times before succeeding. Depending on the riskiness of the business, success (the large reward) may be more or less delayed. Thus, to give up the steady job is an act of self-control as we have defined it here. It is to give up a smaller present good for a larger uncertain (hence delayed) one.

Just as a programmed uncertainty, like repeated spinner trials, implies a delay, so does a programmed delay imply uncertainty. As indicated in Chapter 2, our modern culture tends to make delayed rewards more certain than they were in more primitive societies. A bird in the hand is worth two in the bush, but just half of two in a supermarket case. But even in our culture, delayed rewards are never perfectly certain. A bank may fail, and is more likely to fail the longer we keep our money there. And humans are mortal. We may die before collecting a large and apparently certain reward for which we have given up some momentary pleasure.[11]

As shown in Chapter 2, hyperbolic delay discounting predicts a preference reversal between an initially preferred smaller-sooner reward and an initially dispreferred larger-later reward. As a common delay, added to both rewards, gets larger and larger, the larger-later reward comes to be preferred. (Conversely, if a larger-later reward is initially preferred to a smaller-sooner reward, subtracting a common delay from both rewards may reverse that preference.) A corresponding phenomenon occurs with probabilities and is known as Allais' paradox (Allais, 1953). If an initially preferred smaller-surer reward and an initially dispreferred larger less-sure reward are both made equally less sure (by reducing the probability of both by an equal fraction), preferences may reverse.

Consider the worker who has decided to hold onto a low-paying certain job rather than go into a business that will potentially pay three times as much as the job but has only a 50 percent chance of succeeding. The economy goes into recession and both probabilities decrease by half; the formerly secure job now has a 50 percent chance of being eliminated (by downsizing) and the business has only a 25 percent chance of succeeding. The worker is now more likely to quit the job and try the business.

With both probability and delay discounting, common additional discounting blurs the distinction between the probabilities or delays of the alternatives under consideration and makes the differences in amount of the rewards (the V's in the discount equations) relatively more salient.

In the case of delay discounting, it is this preference reversal phenomenon that allows commitment to the larger alternative. Figure 6.3a (similar

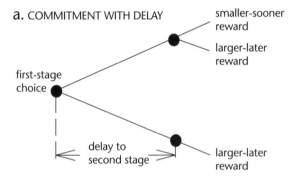

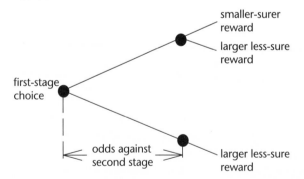

Figure 6.3. (a) Strict commitment with delay. (b) Analogous structure of commitment with probability.

to Figure 2.9a) shows how commitment works with delays. When a large and a small reward are both in the distant future (the large reward slightly more distant) the large reward is preferred. As time passes and the distance to both rewards diminishes, and if no commitment process is instituted (if the upper path is chosen at the first stage in Figure 6.3a), the smaller reward will eventually be available immediately and will be chosen. However, if a commitment is made at the first stage to the alternative preferred at that time (if the lower path is chosen), the larger reward will be obtained.

Rachlin, Castrogiovanni, and Cross (1987) constructed a probabilistic commitment paradigm, illustrated in Figure 6.3b, equivalent to the delay commitment paradigm. Using a spinner with numbered sectors (like a roulette wheel), we varied probability by changing the number of sectors signifying a win or a loss. Each trial began with a first-stage choice between a given probability of proceeding to a second-choice stage (the upper path in Figure 6.3b) or an equal probability of proceeding to a single alternative (the lower path).

When choosing at the second stage between a larger less-sure (monetary) reward and a smaller-surer reward, the subjects (Stony Brook undergraduates) tended to choose the smaller-surer reward. And when the probability at the first stage of going on to the next stage was high (15/18), subjects chose the upper path (and at that point chose and obtained the smaller-surer reward). When the probability at the first stage was low (3/18), subjects chose the lower path leading to commitment to the larger less-sure reward. Thus, as with delay, commitment to a larger reward depended on the degree of the common additional discounting of both rewards.[12] Recall that, by analogy to delay discounting, when the expected value of the risky option is higher than that of the more secure option, choosing the *more secure* option is *impulsive*.

PROBABILITIES AND COMPLEX AMBIVALENCE. Complex ambivalence is a conflict between abstract rewards (like generally being sober) and specific rewards (like having a drink now). Probabilities also may be abstract or specific and a conflict may arise in the behavior they guide. Suppose you were on a beach and saw a man coming out of the water in flippers, mask, and wetsuit. You and your friends, bored at the beach, bet on what his profession is. You might bet that he is a navy frogman on the grounds that navy frogmen are more likely to be dressed in that way than members of any other profession. But you would have better odds of winning if you bet that he is a lawyer, simply because there are so many more lawyers than frogmen.

The fractions of lawyers and frogmen in the population are called base rates. Being population statistics, base rates are more abstract in the sense that they are farther away from the case at hand than specific probabilities such as the fraction of lawyers or frogmen who wear wet suits. That is, if you drew a circle representing the population, you could then draw a second circle representing the number of lawyers in the population wholly within the first circle, and a third circle representing the number of lawyers who ever wore a wet suit wholly within the second one. As the circles get smaller, the information they convey grows more specific (eventually tightening around one particular person).

Just as people tend to ignore abstract alternatives in clear-cut self-control situations, they tend to ignore base rates when making decisions (Tversky and Kahneman, 1982). If, as has been argued above, base rates and specific probabilities are discriminative stimuli, that is, guides to behavior, then when base rates and specific probabilities conflict, ignoring base rates is a kind of impulsiveness.

Ignoring base rates becomes more serious (than making bets on the beach) in the case of medical decisions. Making up statistics for the sake of illustration, let us suppose that at any given time 5,000 Americans have pneumonia while 5,000,000 have a common cold. Assume that all 5,000 with pneumonia have the symptoms of headache, congestion, cough, and high fever. Suppose also that only 1 percent of the people who have a cold (that is, 50,000 people) have this particular cluster of symptoms. Because the immediate probabilities are so extreme (100 percent for pneumonia and only 1 percent for a cold), when we have these symptoms we tend to believe that we have pneumonia. Yet the odds are still 10 to 1 (50,000 to 5,000) that it is only a cold. (Of course, even if these made-up statistics were true, I am not implying that you shouldn't go to the doctor and find out for sure.)

If base-rate neglect is a kind of impulsiveness, what can be done about it? We know that, with delay, clear discriminative stimuli for abstract contingencies tend to decrease impulsiveness and increase self-control (Heyman, 1996a; Heyman and Tanz, 1995). It has also been found, in probability experiments with both human and nonhuman subjects, that clear discriminative stimuli increase the influence of base rates on choice.

As Fantino (1998, p. 357) says, "The base-rate problem may be seen as one of multiple [discriminative] stimulus control, in this instance control by the base rates and control by the case cue [the particular probability]."

Cognition and Motivation in Self-Control

So ignoring base rates may become a self-control problem. Is also a cognitive problem. As with the primrose path experimental procedure described in the previous chapter (Kudadjie-Gyamfi and Rachlin, 1996), cognition and motivation are not readily separable. According to Plato, there is no fundamental difference between knowledge (cognition) and self-control (motivation). (See Rachlin, 1994, for a detailed discussion of Plato's psychology.) Plato's fundamental concern was to distinguish between the particular and the abstract. He identified the abstract/particular dimension with the dimensions of good/bad, reality/illusion, long duration/short duration, and knowledge/ignorance. According to Plato, a wise person is by definition a good person. If a person is not good, that person is not wise. You cannot truly know what is good for you and yet do what is bad for you. Or, as Plato put it, "we cannot want what is bad for us" (*Gorgias*, 486e) except out of ignorance. Thus knowledge cannot be hidden; it has to be exhibited in good behavior. If it is not so exhibited it is not true knowledge.

Good behavior in turn is behavior directed to abstract ends (abstract rewards, in our terms). Behavior directed to particular ends can achieve abstract ends only by accident. The squirrel that "saves" nuts, like all nonhuman animals, is exhibiting self-control only by accident—because in this case the behavior that serves immediate ends (the pleasure of burying nuts) also serves abstract ends (preservation of its life over the winter). The squirrel may thus be good without being smart. For human beings, in cases where pleasure conflicts with goodness (in cases of simple or complex ambivalence), knowledge and goodness (cognition and motivation) do coincide. They cannot be relegated, as much modern psychology tries to do, to different parts of the brain. The next chapter will extend this argument from individual good (self-control) to social good (cooperation).

The reason for discussing this philosophical issue at such length is that probability seems to be a strictly cognitive variable, whereas delay seems to be a strictly motivational variable. But we cannot go on to discuss such issues as gambling (in the appendix to this chapter) and social cooperation (in the next chapter) without seeing these two variables as mutually interchangeable. The Kudadjie-Gyamfi and Rachlin (1996) primrose-path experiment was discussed in the last chapter in terms of programmed delays (when subjects chose the shorter immediate delay they increased delay overall). The experiment may also be seen in terms of probability discounting. At the end of the experiment, none of the subjects could verbalize the delay contingencies. Various amounts of reinforcement may have been associated probabilistically with pressing either button. Moreover, the subjects in any self-control experiment and in real-life self-control situations may be seen as gambling on their own future behavior. The smoker who refuses a single cigarette is essentially betting that he will continue to refuse cigarettes. Otherwise his single act of self-control will have been meaningless—he might as well have taken the cigarette. Thus, refusing the cigarette is a choice of a larger less-probable reward (good health) over a smaller more-probable reward (the pleasure of smoking the cigarette) just as much as it is a choice between a larger delayed reward over a smaller immediate reward. Every act of self-control may be viewed in terms of delays or probabilities. And, as the next chapter will show, so can every act of social cooperation—even those that appear to be altruistic.

Appendix: The Attraction of Gambling

If risk taking is self-control and risk avoidance is a lack of self-control, how can gambling, which certainly is taking a risk, also be a lack of self-control? Let me begin to try to resolve this apparent contradiction with a true story.

My fellow guests at a recent seder at the home of my son-in-law's parents were mostly retired people in their sixties or seventies. When I mentioned at this gathering that I was doing research on the psychology of gambling, I expected a smattering of interest but not the outpouring that actually occurred. It turned out that every single one of these motherly and fatherly old folks (my age, actually) was a regular, if not a compulsive, casino gambler. One man described without shame how he would go into a trance at the poker machine and gamble rapidly without thinking; a woman told me how she would switch from one slot machine to another until she found a "hot" one.

I should have known. Atlantic City and Foxwoods are meccas for busloads of elderly people from various organizations in the area. You pay about $20 for the bus and get a certificate for the bus fare (plus or minus a few dollars) redeemable in quarters on the casino floor.

Why do they do it, I asked, when over the long run they have no chance of winning? The more experienced they are, the more they should recognize that fact. Yes, they do recognize it. But why go? The answer around the seder table was universal—for the excitement. One gray-haired woman described, with a glint in her eye worthy of a crack addict, how gambling was her life. If they took away her machines, she didn't know what she would do. But what was so exciting about losing money? Why not just ceremoniously burn the hundred or so dollars she often lost in Atlantic City? The question drew laughs around the table. It was the gambling itself, the possibility of winning or losing, that made the casino so exciting. Moreover, the excitement of gambling was well worth $100 to her. A movie and dinner out would cost as much, occupy less time (of which she had plenty), and not be half as much fun. *Why* the possibility of winning and losing was so exciting, she could not say.

For an explanation of the thrill of gambling one must turn to research findings. Laboratory research with people playing for very low stakes (what research funding agencies can afford and what human-subject protection committees will permit) and nonhuman animals playing for high stakes (very hungry pigeons and rats spending effort and winning food rewards) demonstrates unequivocally that random rewards (the kind provided by gambling) generate rapid, compulsive behavior.

A hungry rat can be trained to press a heavy lever (a rat-sized version of the lever of a one-armed bandit) to receive, on a random basis, a few pellets of food. Technically, gambling is a "*random*-ratio schedule of reinforcement." A schedule of reinforcement is in essence a rule that relates rewards received to behavior emitted. On the other hand, a piecework wage that pays a fixed amount for a specified number of items produced would be a "*fixed*-ratio schedule."

A rat choosing between two levers, one paying off on a fixed-ratio schedule (say, one pellet for every tenth lever press) and the other, an equivalent random-ratio schedule (1 in 10 probability of any given lever press paying off) far prefers the random-ratio schedule. The rat is gambling with calories of energy for a payoff in calories of food. The experimenter can adjust the odds that a given lever press will pay off so that on average the rat receives more calories, the same amount, or fewer calories than it uses in pressing the bar. But it does not matter. Over a wide range of odds the rat strongly prefers the random-ratio schedule to the equivalent fixed-ratio schedule, and with the random-ratio schedule will press the lever as quickly as it can, pausing only when it is exhausted.

A rat pressing the lever at the longest odds, where calories out exceed calories in, would eventually starve to death if not otherwise fed. Hungry pigeons pecking at buttons and well-fed undergraduates pressing buttons to obtain small cash rewards also respond very rapidly with random-ratio schedules and prefer them to equivalent fixed-ratio schedules.

Such behavior seems to contradict people's usual tendency to avoid risk. People generally prefer sure things to risky prospects. The women at the seder who risks an average of $100 per week at casino slot machines also prefers $100 for sure to $200 if a flipped coin comes up heads. She would prefer to take the sure $100 to the casino, convert it to quarters, and bet it there. This is true even though she knows that the casino offers much less favorable odds of winning than the strict even-money heads-or-tails bet.

The excitement of gambling seems to depend on repetitive actions (like pulling the arm of a one-armed bandit) and many small bets as opposed to one large bet. When I told the woman at the seder that once, passing through Las Vegas, I put $50 on a single number at roulette, lost, and left the casino, she said, "Where's the fun in that?" (She was right, it wasn't much fun.) The attraction of gambling depends on repeated outcomes—losses and wins—extending over hours, days, weeks, months of betting. What is it about repetitiveness itself that makes gambling attractive? Analysis of the way people organize the losses and wins that repetitive gambling entails, produces a likely answer. I call it the string theory of gambling.

When a person gambles over and over again, outcomes (wins and losses) form strings. Below is a string of wins (W's) and losses (L's) determined by hypothetically flipping a coin and repeatedly betting on heads. The number below each string is the number of dollars won or lost in an even-money one-dollar bet on each flip. With adjustments for different odds, the string could equally well apply to winning and losing poker hands, roulette bets, scratch-off lottery cards, sports bets, or lever pulls on a one-armed bandit.

W	L W	L L W	W	L L L W	L L L W	W	W	W	L L W	W
+1	0	−1	+1	−2	−2	+1	+1	+1	−1	+1

According to string theory, the gambler unconsciously organizes long outcome strings into substrings of losses followed by wins, as in the above illustration. That is, after each win the gambler, as it were, takes stock and begins anew. (Similarly, a rat will pause very briefly after receiving a pellet before beginning to press the lever again.) The spaces above after each win represent this division into substrings.

Let us now suppose that the gambler has just won and is facing the next string. He knows that he will sooner or later win again. The only question is, will it be sooner or later? If sooner, the substring will be short (there are six instances of the shortest possible substring—an immediate win—in the above illustration); if later, the substring will be long (there are two instances of relatively long strings—three losses followed by a win—in the above illustration).

The point to note is that short substrings are proportionally better than long substrings. In an even-money bet of $1, one-outcome substrings (immediate wins) are net wins of $1, two-outcome substrings (a loss and a win) are washes, three-outcome substrings (two losses and a win) are net $1 losses, and four-outcome substrings (three losses and a win) are net $2 losses. If the net value of a string is not calculated until the string ends, then the gain or loss of a short string will be realized sooner, whereas the gain or loss of a long string will be realized later—that is, the gain or loss of a long string is delayed. If a gain or loss is delayed, it is discounted. Because short strings (in the above case only the shortest string) are net wins and long strings are net losses, the gambler's losses are subjectively discounted; the gambler's gains are subjectively valued at their full strength. Although the sum of all the numbers in the above example is zero (no actual gain or loss), the sum of all the discounted values would be highly positive.[13]

A fair gamble is a gamble in which the probability of winning times the amount won equals the amount bet. If casinos, racetracks, or the state returned all money bet to gamblers in the form of winnings, these gambles would be fair. Since none of these institutions returns all money bet, the gambles are less than fair. If a gamble *were* fair, the shorter net win substrings would be frequent enough to exactly balance out all of the longer net loss substrings and in the long run the gambler would come out even. In an unfair gamble, the longer substrings outweigh the shorter ones and the gambler loses in the long run. Anyone who consciously or unconsciously organized outcomes into substrings, as string theory says, and then evaluated all substrings veridically would never bet on unfair gambles. But no one can evaluate all substrings veridically. Instead, the longer, negatively valued substrings are discounted.

To summarize, the force underlying the attraction of gambling is a tendency some of us have to organize strings of wins and losses into substrings of so many losses (ranging from zero to infinity) followed by a win. People who are attracted to gambling ignore repeated losses until they finally cap them off with a win. Gamblers treat a string of losses as an investment; the eventual win is the return on the investment. When there are few losses in a substring (the substring is short), the overall value of the investment is positive; when there are many losses in a substring (the substring is long), the overall value is negative.

In a casino, where all gambles have negative overall (expected) values for the bettor (otherwise the casinos would make no money), the net losses must overbalance the net wins. However, gamblers, like all organisms, "discount" (or diminish the subjective value of) future events. The longer the substring, the more distant in the future its end, the less important it is, subjectively. Since these long substrings are all net losses, the longer the string, the bigger the loss and the more it is discounted. Although in reality the losses overbalance the wins, *subjectively* the (sooner) wins overbalance the (later) losses and may do so even in casinos, where the overall values for the bettor are negative.

Why then are we all not compulsive gamblers? The answer is that not all of us organize strings of gambles into substrings consisting of losses followed by a win. For nongamblers the losses are too important to ignore. Nongamblers see each bet as an individual event, and when considering gambles as individual events, people tend to avoid risk. The woman at the seder, a woman who lived through the Depression and learned well the value of a dollar, is horrified at the thought of risking $50 on a single bet. But losing $100 a quarter at a time is exciting to her. Each 25-cent bet sneaks in under her threshold of danger and can be ignored until suddenly a $5, or $10, or $100 win ends the string.

The pernicious quality of casinos is that they offer a veritable menu of bets. You can pick from among combinations of amount bet and odds of winning where the loss will be below your threshold of danger and the win (accompanied in the casino by bells, whistles, the clatter of coins) above your threshold of excitement. Of course losses, no matter how small, add up and in a casino must eventually add up to more than the wins. (Our forebears must have been trying to protect us against our tendency to ignore small losses when they set a minimum of $2 per bet at racetracks in most states—in the days when $2 was a meaningful sum to most people.)[14]

The people at the seder, coming from a Depression background, are probably not in danger of spending their rent money in the casino. They take a certain amount of money with them, usually lose it, occasionally win, blow the winnings on an expensive dinner or a present for their grandchild, and come away happier. They are essentially paying the casino to transfer their steady income (from Social Security or a pension) to a variable income. Where's the harm?

The harm comes when the excitement of winning becomes the main source of satisfaction in a person's life. An older individual is especially vulnerable because the network of social support may have eroded over the years (obviously not true of the people at the seder) and the cost of social support may be high. Then, as the eventual losses add up and other sources of satisfaction (friends, family, work) are inevitably exhausted, winning becomes the gambler's *only* source of satisfaction and gambling his only concern. If the compulsive gambler at that point is feeling happy, then a win will make him feel happier; if the gambler is feeling unhappy then a win will still make him feel better. But to win he has to gamble, and gambling slowly but surely is going to make him feel worse and worse in an absolute sense. At that point he is hooked.

What can be done about compulsive gambling? First, the state should get out of the gambling business. The returns from lotteries to states, although tangible and immediate, cannot be worth the ultimate cost. A rat choosing between a fixed income of food per lever press (one pellet for each ten presses, say) and a variable income (a probability of 1 in 10 of earning a pellet per lever press) will choose the variable income every time. It is not surprising therefore that some people (young active persons, not only retirees) spend more time gambling than working. This scenario can only be harmful to the state. By taking the short-term money and ignoring the long-term harm, the state is itself in the position of an addict. It is as if the state were running opium dens or crack houses.

On a personal level, it may be possible for gamblers to change the way they organize their behavior. The object would be to create substrings based on a fixed number of *bets* rather than an eventual win (or fixed number of wins). The slots player should change machines after every ten bets, *not* after a win or a loss. Many casino gamblers keep two accounts, one for their stake (the amount they had, coming into the casino), the other for winnings. Then the player bets from the winnings (bets with "the casino's money").

It would be far better to do just the opposite. For example, suppose you came with $200, the amount you can afford to lose. Let's say you bet $5 in roulette and win back $45. You should put $5 back into your stake account and $40 into a winnings account. Throughout the day you should only bet with your stake account, never touching your winnings, When your stake is exhausted, you should quit. If at that point you have more than $200 in the winnings account, all well and good, you won. If you have less than $200 in the winnings account (as will be the case most of the time), you lost. Go home.

Of course, this method of accounting takes a lot of the fun out of gambling and probably will not work for a compulsive gambler. She cannot just go home. That is where all her troubles lie and that is where she should start the attack on her gambling—by increasing nongambling social activity, reducing the cost of social support, getting a life.

7

Self-Control and
Social Cooperation

The following passage from Anthony Trollope's 1875 novel, *The Way We Live Now,* presents an analogy between a character's selfishness and his impulsiveness (p. 17):

> Whether Sir Felix . . . had become what he was solely by bad training, or whether he had been born bad, who shall say? It is hardly possible that he should not have been better had he been taken away as an infant and subjected to moral training by moral teachers. And yet again it is hardly possible that any training or want of training should have produced a heart so utterly incapable of feeling for others as was his. He could not even feel his own misfortunes unless they touched the outward comforts of the moment. It seemed that he lacked sufficient imagination to realize future misery though the futurity to be considered was divided from the present but by a single month, a single week,—but by a single night.

Trollope here attributes Sir Felix's selfishness, his social narrowness, to his lack of self-control, the narrowness of his time horizon. The purpose of the present chapter is to examine more closely this analogy between the social and temporal spheres.

For the last ten years or so, whenever I present the results of my research on self-control at university colloquia or conferences, I have begun by saying that I want to give the audience a phenomenal experience of complex ambivalence by means of playing a game. Index cards are handed to 10 randomly selected people and the others are asked to imagine that they have received one of the cards. They are requested to choose among hypothetical monetary prizes by writing either *Y* or *X* on the card. The rules of the game (projected on a screen behind me while I talk) are as follows:

1. If you choose *Y* you get $100 times *N*.
2. If you choose *X* you get $100 times *N* plus a bonus of $300.
3. *N* equals the number of people (of the 10) who choose Y.

Let us analyze this game (which is called a multiperson prisoner's dilemma game).

Imagine you have one of the cards and that you know that the other 9 players have chosen *Y*. If you choose *Y* too, by rule 3 $N = 10$ and by rule 1 you each get $1,000. If, however, you choose *X*, by rule 3 $N = 9$ and by rule 2 you get $1,200 [($100 × 9) plus $300]. Thus, if everyone else chooses *Y*, you get $200 more if you choose *X* than if you too choose *Y*.

Now imagine you know that the other 9 players have chosen *X*. If you choose *X* too, then $N = 0$ and you each get just the $300 bonus. If, on the other hand, you choose *Y*, $N = 1$ and by rule 1 you get $100. Thus, if everyone else chooses *X*, you get $200 more if you too choose *X* than if you choose *Y*.

In fact, it does not matter what anyone else chooses. You will always get $200 more if you choose *X* than if you choose *Y*. By choosing *X* rather than *Y* you decrease *N* by 1 (rule 3), losing $100 but gaining the $300 bonus. The resultant is a $200 gain for choosing *X*. Logic thus says to choose *X*, and any lawyer would advise you to do so. The dilemma (the source of ambivalence) is that if everyone follows the advice of their lawyers and indeed chooses *X*, $N = 0$ and each gets $300; while if everyone ignores the advice of their lawyers and chooses *Y*, $N = 10$ and each gets $1,000. Therefore, *Y* choices ("cooperation") benefit the group as a whole, while *X* choices ("defection") benefit the individual at the expense of the group.

At this point I ask the 10 people holding cards to make their choices, imagining as best they can what they would choose if the money were real and letting no one else see what they have chosen. Then I collect the cards and hold them until I finish my lecture. I have done this demonstration or its equivalent dozens of times with audiences ranging from Japanese psychologists to Italian economists. The result is about an even split between cooperation and defection, indicating that the game does create ambiguity.

There are some variations, however. The record for the highest percentage of cooperation is held by a group of Italian economists, most of them Marxists. They may have been trying to send a message to the American capitalist psychologist lecturer! One audience was a mixture of American and Japanese psychologists. In this case I gave out 20 cards and asked them to place a "J" or an "A" on the card to indicate their nationality. My lecture followed one by a Japanese psychologist about the difference between Japanese "sushi" psychology (cooperative) and American, "hamburger" psychology (competitive). I therefore expected the Japanese to cooperate more and defect less than the Americans did. The result was exactly the opposite—the Japanese cooperated less and defected more. Interestingly, this result was predicted by the theory of the Japanese social psychologist Toshio Yamagishi, which says that in a social dilemma, where the choice made by the subjects is *private,* Americans will cooperate more than Japanese (Yamagishi and Yamagishi, 1994).[1]

Figure 7.1 represents the contingencies of the prisoner's dilemma game that I ask my audience to play. The diagram is unfamiliar to the audience but not to the reader of this book. It is an exact analogue to the primrose path discussed in Chapters 3, 4, and 5 except that the abscissa represents not *time* but *social space.* Point A represents the condition where everyone cooperates; point C represents the condition where everyone defects. The dashed line represents the (hypothetical) average earnings per person at each value of N. Clearly, the more people who cooperate, the greater the average earnings. But, as is shown by the two solid lines—ABC (the return to each player who defects) and ADC (the return to each player who cooperates)—an individual always earns more by defecting than by cooperat-

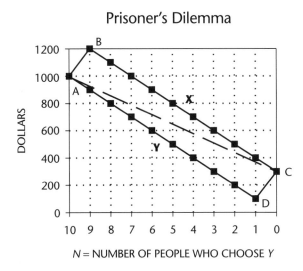

Figure 7.1. The contingencies of the group prisoner's dilemma experiment.

ing. Thus social cooperation is to social defection as individual self-control is to individual impulsiveness.

I have introduced this chapter with the above demonstration for the same reason that I introduce my lectures with it: to give the reader a feeling for complex ambivalence in a social setting. Later in the chapter I shall return to the relation of self-control and social cooperation in a context of complex ambivalence. For now let me take a step back and discuss several experiments that explore the self-control/social cooperation analogy in a more molecular context.

The Probability of Reciprocation

Because there seems to be a relationship between the structure of self-control and the structure of social cooperation, it is important to know whether experience in one sphere transfers to the other. Jay Brown of the psychology laboratory at the State University of New York at Stony Brook is working on this problem; I now describe some of his completed research (Brown and Rachlin, 1999).

The object of the experiments was to compare self-control with social cooperation by humans playing a game. The game was played either by a single player ("alone") to study self-control, or by a pair of players ("together") to study social cooperation. The subjects were all female undergraduates at Stony Brook.

The game board is diagrammed in Figure 7.2a. It consisted of a rectangular plastic tray divided into four compartments ("boxes"). Each box contained three items:

A red or green index card with a picture of a door ("red doors" or "green doors").
A red or green key.
1, 2, 3, or 4 nickels as shown in Figure 7.2. (In subsequent experiments 1, 2, 5, or 6 nickels were in the boxes.)

The upper boxes both contained red doors; the lower boxes both contained green doors. The left boxes both contained red keys; the right boxes both contained green keys. Note that each right box held one more nickel than the box to its left, and each upper box held two more nickels than the one below it. All the items in the boxes were visible to the players.

a.

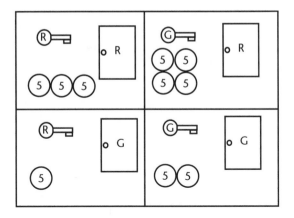

b.   CURRENT
                                       TRIAL

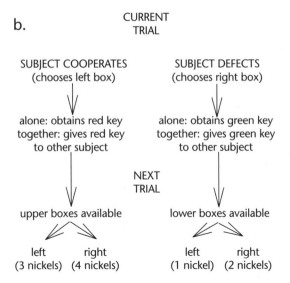

| SUBJECT COOPERATES | SUBJECT DEFECTS |
| (chooses left box) | (chooses right box) |

alone: obtains red key   alone: obtains green key
together: gives red key   together: gives green key
to other subject   to other subject

                         NEXT
                         TRIAL

upper boxes available   lower boxes available

left   right   left   right
(3 nickels) (4 nickels)   (1 nickel) (2 nickels)

Figure 7.2. (a) The game board used in Brown's experiments. (b) The contingencies in those experiments.

THE SELF-CONTROL GAME ("ALONE"). Each trial began with the apparatus as pictured in Figure 7.2. To start, a player was given a red key. The player could use that key to "open" one or the other red door (to choose either the upper left or upper right box). That key was then surrendered. If the upper left box was chosen, the player was permitted to take the 3 nickels and the red key from that box. If the upper right box was chosen, the player was permitted to take the 4 nickels and the green key from that box. Then the nickel(s) and key taken were replaced by the experimenter and the next trial began. If a red key had been received on the previous trial, the player could again choose between the two red doors as before; if a green key had been received on the previous trial, the player could use the key to "open" one of the green doors (to choose a key and nickels from either the lower left or lower right box). The sequence is shown in Figure 7.2b.

The alone game is a self-control procedure in the sense that the behavior leading to the higher current reward (choosing the right box with 2 or 4 nickels plus a green key) conflicted with the behavior that maximized overall reward (choosing the left box with 1 or 3 nickels plus a red key). Choosing the right box always earned the player one more nickel than choosing the left box did, but at the cost of obtaining a green key. With the green key the player paid for the 1-nickel gain (for choosing the right box) on the previous trial with an average 2-nickel loss (having to choose between the lower boxes) on the next trial.

The best overall strategy in the alone game is always to choose the left box, always receive a red key, and always earn 3 nickels. Always choosing the right box yields a fixed return of 2 nickels per trial. Alternating between the left and right boxes yields an average return of 2.5 nickels [(3 + 2)/2 or (4 + 1)/2] per trial. Only on the very last trial does it pay to choose the right box; but the subjects did not know when the experiment would end.

The alone version of the game duplicates the contingencies of a prisoner's dilemma game against an opponent playing tit for tat (Axelrod, 1997). Tit for tat says; cooperate on the first trial, and from then on cooperate if your opponent cooperated on the previous trial and defect if your opponent defected on the previous trial. Consider what it would be like to play a repeated prisoner's dilemma game against an opponent who plays tit for tat. If you were to cooperate on the present trial, you would be able to choose next time between the higher rewards (because the other player would have cooperated). If you were to defect on the present trial, you would be forced to choose next time between the lower two rewards (because the other player would have defected). These are the very contingencies set up by the keys and doors of the alone condition.

Because current choice of the lower available reward always leads to a higher next-trial reward, current choice in the alone game depends on the degree to which the (higher) next-trial reward is discounted. Since it cannot be obtained until the next trial, the higher future reward may be discounted by delay. But another possible source of discounting is probabilistic discounting. A player may currently discount higher future reward by the probability that she herself will fail to choose the lower reward on subsequent trials.

Suppose a player has repeatedly chosen the higher current-trial reward in the past, earning 2 nickels per trial. If she chooses the lower current-trial reward on this trial only, and the higher current-trial reward on all subsequent trials, she will earn 1 nickel on this trial, 4 nickels on the next trial (for an average of 2.5 nickels), then return to 2 nickels per trial. This might not be enough incentive to choose the 1 nickel on the current trial. Yet if she chooses the lower current reward on this trial and continues to do so, she will eventually earn 3 nickels per trial, a 50 percent increase. This may well be a sufficient incentive to choose the 1 nickel now. However, if by past experience a player believes it unlikely that she will choose the lower current-trial reward in the future, there is little incentive to do so in the present. As discussed in the last chapter, probabilistic discounting may apply as well in everyday-life self-control situations. If by past experience a dieter believes it highly improbable that high-calorie foods will be resisted tomorrow and on subsequent days, there is no reason to resist them today.

THE SOCIAL COOPERATION TASK ("TOGETHER").   The game as played by two players together was the same as when played alone, except that the two players, playing on a single game board, made choices on alternate trials. After using her key to open a box, each player took the nickels in the box for herself and then handed the key to the other player. Thus, after the first trial, whether a player was permitted to choose between the upper boxes (3 or 4 nickels) or between the lower boxes (1 or 2 nickels) depended on the other player's choice on the previous trial. This sequence is also shown in Figure 7.2b. The players were not allowed to discuss the game. Their only means of communication was through the choices they made. This task has the essential properties of a prisoner's dilemma game.[2]

Playing this game together, income would be maximized (at 3 nickels per trial) for each player if both players repeatedly chose the left box (co-operated). However, the individual player would always gain more on the present trial by choosing the right box (defecting). The penalty for defecting—having to choose between the lower boxes—is suffered not by the player who defects but by the other player, who inherits the green key.

There is an ambivalence in the together game as there is in the alone game. A player wants to choose the right box with the higher number of nickels (2 rather than 1 or 4 rather than 3). That is, she wants to defect. She also wants to have a red key (to be able to choose between 4 and 3 nickels rather than between 2 and 1). She will only have a red key if her partner chose the left box (if her partner cooperated) on the previous trial. Since her partner has the very same motives, one way for a player to get her partner to cooperate on the next trial might be to cooperate herself on the present trial. Thus, each player has a reason to defect and a reason to cooperate.

Cooperating is the very worst strategy in this game, unless the other player also cooperates. Therefore the only reason to cooperate (within the demands of the game) is to influence the other player to cooperate subsequently. The reward for cooperating in the social cooperation version of the game must be discounted not only by the delay before the player's next turn, but also by the probability that the other player will reciprocate.

People's estimation of the probability of other people's future cooperation might be expected to be lower than their estimation of the probability of their own future cooperation. For this reason, a player who cooperates with her own future self in the alone game (who consistently chooses the lower current-trial reward) may defect from the interests of her partner in the together game. This, in fact, is what we found.[3]

Four groups of subjects were tested in a standard "transfer" design. One group played the game alone for forty trials. Another group played the game together for forty trials. The third group played alone for twenty trials (first phase) and then together for twenty trials (second phase). The fourth group played together for twenty trials (first phase) and then alone for twenty trials (second phase). Figure 7.3a shows the results averaged over four-trial blocks. Subjects playing alone came to cooperate on about 60 percent of the trials, while subjects playing together cooperated on about 20 percent of the trials. When subjects were switched from playing alone to playing together, cooperation decreased. When subjects were switched from playing together to playing alone, cooperation increased.

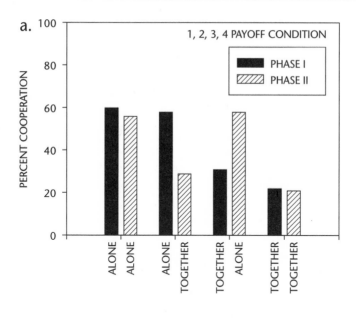

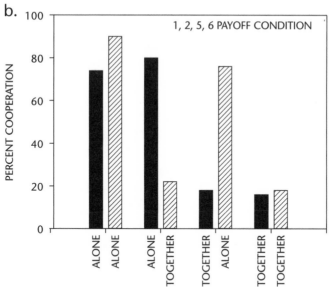

Figure 7.3. The results of Brown's first two experiments, subjects playing alone or together, with (a) small rewards in the upper boxes and (b) large rewards in the upper boxes.

Experience in the first phase with one condition seemed to have no effect on behavior in the second phase with the other condition.

With new subjects, Brown again performed the entire experiment as before, except that he increased the number of nickels in the two upper boxes (with the red doors) to 5 and 6 (rather than 3 and 4 as shown in Figure 7.2). This manipulation maintained the self-control (and prisoner's dilemma) contingencies but increased the larger delayed reward (the reward for cooperation). The reason for increasing the larger reward was to make sure that the alone condition presented a true conflict of motives rather than just a cognitive problem—a problem in practical arithmetic. If the alone condition were a true self-control problem, increasing the amount of the larger-later reward should increase self-control as it has done in many self-control experiments (Logue, 1988). If the alone condition were merely a problem in practical arithmetic, increasing the amount of the larger-later reward should have no effect. In a practical arithmetic problem, correct answers are not increased by increasing the amounts. (If Johnny goes to the store with $10 to buy groceries, just as many children will arrive at the right answer as if he goes to the store with $20.)

The results of Brown's second experiment, with the 5 and 6 nickels in the upper boxes, are shown in Figure 7.3b. Subjects in the alone condition cooperated on about 80 percent of the trials, rather than the 60 percent found with the smaller next-trial rewards—evidence that the alone condition does indeed test self-control.

What about the together condition? Increasing the amount of the next-trial rewards had no effect on the cooperation of subjects playing together; they still cooperated on about 20 percent of the trials. Recall that the benefit of cooperation in the together condition is realized only if the other player reciprocates. A crucial variable in the together game is a player's subjective estimation of the probability that if she cooperates, the *other* player will cooperate too. It is not surprising that increasing the amount of the next-trial reward (the reward to the *other* player) did not increase this subjective probability.[4]

In summary, the results of these experiments imply that a major variable distinguishing self-control from social cooperation is the probability of reciprocation of cooperation and defection. In self-control situations, where reciprocation is under the control of a single person, this probability may be high. Most people perceive a common interest between themselves today and themselves tomorrow. In prisoner's dilemma situations where the players have no common interest, this probability is inherently lower. An experiment by Forest Baker was designed to test the effects of reciprocation probability directly, and I will consider it shortly. First I need to describe (briefly) a third experiment by Jay Brown that further tested the analogy between self-control and social cooperation.

The key variable in this experiment was patterning of trials. Recall from Chapter 5 that patterning of trials (soft commitment) increased self-control of pigeons and humans under conditions of both simple and complex ambivalence. The effect of patterning is to broaden temporal scope—to cause decisions to be based on more abstract rather than more specific contingencies. If social cooperation is a consequence of correspondingly abstract choices, then patterning should increase social cooperation. In this third experiment with the game board, four new groups of subjects all played the game together at all times. The game board illustrated in Figure 7.2 was used except that, as in Brown's second experiment, there were 5 and 6 nickels rather than 3 and 4 nickels in the left and right upper boxes.

Instead of alone versus together, the conditions of the game were patterned versus unpatterned trials. The *unpatterned* trials condition was the same as the together condition of Brown's second experiment. In the *patterned* trials condition, both subjects playing together made four decisions at once. They indicated on a piece of paper out of the other subject's view whether, on each of the next four trials, they would choose the left box or the right box. Then the four trials were played out one by one. The player might have a red or green key on any of the four trials, but her choice on each trial was predetermined before the four-trial sequence began. The experimental design was again the standard transfer design with one group playing forty patterned trials, one group playing 40 unpatterned trials, and the other two groups switched in the middle. The results are shown in Figure 7.4.

Although the increase in cooperation due to patterning was not nearly as strong as that due to playing alone, patterning did significantly increase cooperative behavior as it increased self-control in prior experiments (note that when play was changed from one choice at a time to four choices at a time cooperation increased, and vice versa). This is more evidence that self-control and social cooperation are corresponding processes.[5]

The object of the experiment by Forest Baker, to be discussed next, was to directly test the theory that the crucial variable differentiating self-control from social cooperation is the probability of reciprocation. According

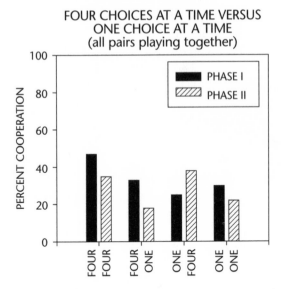

Figure 7.4. The results of Brown's third experiment (average of last four of twenty trials), subjects playing together, large rewards in the upper boxes, with patterned choices (four at a time) versus unpatterned choices (one at a time).

to the theory, subjects playing alone in Brown's experiments cooperated more than subjects playing together because the alone player's estimation of the probability that if she cooperated on this trial *she herself* would cooperate on subsequent trials was higher than the together player's estimation that if she cooperated on this trial *her partner* would cooperate on subsequent trials.

In Baker's experiment, probability of reciprocation was explicitly varied. The game was played together—not on a game board with another subject, but on a computer screen with the computer taking the place of the other subject. On the screen was a diagram with four boxes like the game board of Figure 7.2 but without keys and doors and with 5 and 6 nickels depicted in the upper boxes (as in Brown's second and third experiments). A bar on the screen grew in size in proportion to the money earned. As in the alone condition of Brown's second experiment, subjects chose between the left box with 1 or 5 nickels and the right box with 2 or 6 nickels. Whether they could choose between the upper two boxes (5 versus 6 nickels) or the lower two boxes (1 versus 2 nickels) depended on the computer. Between the subject's choices the computer would decide to highlight either the two upper boxes or the two lower boxes. The subject could choose only between the highlighted boxes. The subject's decision determined the computer's decision with a probability p. This probability, the probability of reciprocation by the computer, was the crucial experimental variable. Figure 7.5 illustrates the contingencies.

On the screen, in addition to the four boxes and the bar indicating winnings, were two spinners with white and black sectors. The proportion of the left spinner that was white was equal to p and the proportion of the right spinner that was white was equal to $(1 - p)$. That is, the right spinner was the inverse of the left. On a given trial, if the subject chose the left box with the lower number of nickels (if the subject cooperated), the left spinner was spun. If the spinner stopped with the white sector under the arrow, the upper boxes were highlighted on the next trial (that is, the computer cooperated); if it stopped with the black sector under the arrow, the lower boxes were highlighted on the next trial (that is, the computer defected). On the other hand, if the subject chose the right box with the higher number of nickels (if the subject defected), the right spinner was spun. Again, if the spinner landed on white, the upper boxes were highlighted on the next

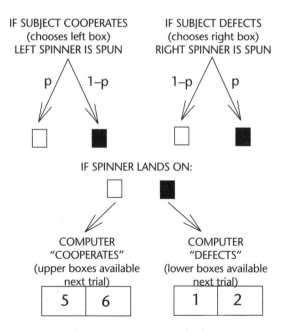

Figure 7.5. The contingencies in Baker's experiment.

trial (the computer cooperated), while if the spinner landed on black, the lower boxes were highlighted on the next trial (the computer defected).

The probability p was the probability of reciprocation. If the subject cooperated, the computer would cooperate with a probability equal to p and defect with a probability equal to $(1-p)$; if the subjected defected, the computer defected with a probability equal to p and cooperated with a probability equal to $(1 - p)$. Thus, the probability of reciprocation, implicit in Brown's experiments, was explicit and signaled by a discriminative stimulus in Baker's experiment.

There were five groups of subjects, each with a given probability of reciprocation: $p = 1, .75, .50, .25, 0$. With $p = 1$, the computer was playing tit for tat. If the subject cooperated on a given trial, the computer would surely cooperate; if the subject defected, the computer would surely defect. The $p = 1$ condition was equivalent to the alone condition in Brown's experiments; subjects would maximize earnings by always cooperating. With $p = .50$, the computer essentially flipped a coin to decide whether to cooperate or defect. Subjects would maximize earnings by always defecting (choosing the higher current-trial number of nickels), since cooperation with a computer would earn them nothing—not even gratitude. With $p = 0$, the computer cooperated only if the subject defected. That is, the computer was playing tat for tit. The subject should surely defect in this case since defection would both maximize reward on the current trial *and* get the computer to cooperate, thus maximizing reward on the next trial as well.[6]

Figure 7.6 shows Baker's results. The average degree of cooperation of each group at the end of one hundred trials was strongly affected by the probability of reciprocation.[7] This probability, explicitly varied in Baker's experiment, must have implicitly varied in Brown's experiments and been largely instrumental in determining the difference between the alone and together conditions.[8] Even though the actual reciprocation probabilities for the alone subjects in Brown's experiments equaled 1, lack of a clear discriminative stimulus and the complexity of the key and door contingencies may have reduced the subjective reciprocation probability for these subjects below 1.

What counts for cooperation is not the absolute probability of future cooperation or even the subject's subjective estimation of that probability. It is the nature of the prisoner's dilemma that it pays to defect regardless of the *absolute* probability that others will cooperate (or, in self-control situa-

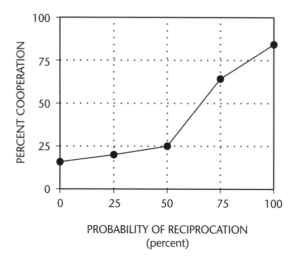

Figure 7.6. The results of Forest Baker's experiment (the average of the last fifteen of one hundred trials).

tions, the absolute probability of an individual's cooperating with his or her own future interests). The above experiments show that what counts is the *relative,* or *conditional,* probability, the probability of reciprocation over a series of opportunities to cooperate. The important question is not, Will others cooperate (or will I cooperate) in the future? but *If I cooperate now,* will others cooperate (or will I cooperate) in the future?

When self-control breaks down, as in cases of addiction, the probability of reciprocation plummets. The alcoholic who has quit a thousand times must also have started up again (defected) at least 999 times. For an alcoholic there may be no reason to cooperate today with the person who the alcoholic himself will be tomorrow. The probability that *that* future person, that incarnation of today's decisionmaker, will reciprocate today's drink refusal may well be low. It is not possible to change that probability at a single moment any more than it is possible, in Aristotle's analogy, for a single retreating soldier to turn and stop an enemy advance.

It is specific acts that have to be performed. Thus the establishment of self-control, as well as social cooperation, where none was before, requires a sort of faith. This faith is embodied in an act of imagination—acting as if something were true that is not in fact true—acting as if the probability of reciprocation is high when it has been low in the past.[9] Enough such acts will create the very thing imagined. For they are part of a still wider pattern of behavior, the pattern we refer to when we talk about the concept of "self." I turn now to the question, Why would a person ever perform an act of self-control or social cooperation when the probability of reciprocation is low?

Self and Self-Control

Reciprocation probability is crucial in differentiating between self-control and social cooperation, but it is not the only determinant of cooperative behavior. What about cases where the reciprocation probability is apparently zero, yet people still cooperate with each other? In other words, what about altruism in social situations? The social cooperation game of Figure 7.1 was played only once. It did not matter what other subjects chose, defection always paid more than cooperation. There was no chance for reciprocation, yet half of the people in the audience usually said they would cooperate if the situation were real. Those who defected seemed to profit.

What keeps us from defecting in similar situations in life? The usual answer is, altruism (see the appendix to this chapter). In the analogy between social cooperation and self-control, altruism corresponds to internal willpower, and it was argued as early as Chapter 1 that internal willpower is a concept that itself needs explanation. The same is true of altruism. *Why* are we ever altruistic? To approach this question, let us return to the analogy between self-control and social cooperation, this time from the perspective of complex ambivalence as exemplified by the multiperson prisoner's dilemma that introduced this chapter.[10]

The analogy between self-control and social cooperation has been pointed out by moral philosophers at least since Plato.[11] The fundamental issue addressed by ancient Greek philosophy was the relation between particular objects and abstract entities: abstract ideals for Plato; abstract categories for Aristotle (Rachlin, 1994).

The problem of self-control in the case of complex ambivalence, as defined in Chapter 3, is a conflict between particular acts such as eating a caloric dessert, taking an alcoholic drink, or getting high on drugs, and abstract patterns of acts strung out in time such as living a healthy life, functioning in a family, or getting along with friends. Recall the formal definition of complex ambivalence: If two alternative activities are available, a relatively brief activity lasting *t* units of time and a longer activity lasting T units of time, where $T = nt$ and n is a positive number greater than one, complex ambivalence depends on two conditions:

1. The whole longer activity is preferred to n repetitions of the brief activity.
2. The brief activity is preferred to the any t-length fraction of the longer activity.

A corresponding problem arises in everyday situations requiring social co-operation (ranging from littering to international arms control). Conflicts often exist between acts benefitting an individual (or a relatively small group) and acts benefitting a (larger) group. The social cooperation problem may be formalized in the same way as the self-control problem: two alternative activities are available; one maximally benefits an individual person, I; the other maximally benefits the group, $G = nI$. The classic case of such a conflict is "the tragedy of the commons" (Hardin, 1968), where overgrazing or overfishing depletes stock and harms the group of farmers or fishers as a whole (and all individuals in the long run) but, regardless of the level of stock at the moment, maximizes benefits for the individual. A New Bedford fisherman might well say, "However good or bad the fishing is, it is better to fish than not to fish." Still, if fishing is always chosen over not fishing, the fishing *will* eventually be bad for everyone.

Despite the closeness of the analogy between self-control and social co-operation, it is far from obvious that choice of more abstract alternatives in self-control situations (where delays are long) will correlate with or generalize to choice of more abstract alternatives in social choice situations (where probability of reciprocation is low). Social cooperation demands a more complex perception of individual self-interest than does self-control. In social cooperation situations, the benefits (to the individual) of cooperating are often very highly abstract (having a better self-image, an easy conscience, a sense of moral rightness) to the point of complete insubstantiality (going to heaven) (Caporael et al., 1989). The discrimination of such benefits from their lack is what we mean when we say that a person has a wide concept of *self*.

THE CONCEPT OF THE SELF.   A person's *self* is a functional interaction between behavior and environment. The reflection (or feedback) of behavior by the environment has been called reafferent stimulation (Held and Hein, 1958). Perhaps its most primitive form is reflection in an ordinary mirror. We move and our reflection moves correspondingly. It was thought for a while that the ability of certain organisms spontaneously to recognize themselves in a mirror's reflection would be a decisive test of their ability to conceive of themselves (Gallup, 1982).[12] But a self must be something more than simple reflection of movements in an ordinary mirror. To function in the development of a self, feedback must not only reflect behavior, it must reflect behavior in a meaningful way, positively or negatively. Reinforcement is just another name for positive reafferent stimulation; the value of the feedback is higher than the value of the behavior itself. (The bread is worth more to you than what you pay for it, otherwise you wouldn't buy it.) Punishment is merely another name for negative reafferent stimulation; the value of the feedback is lower than the value of the behavior itself.

All objects in the environment, including other organisms or other people, may serve as functional (positively or negatively valued) mirrors of our behavior. We step on the tines of the rake and the handle snaps back and hits us on the head—a distorted reflection of our own behavior; we say "Good morning" and our environment (in the form of a person we meet on the street) reflects back "Good morning." More significantly, we have too much to drink at a party and our spouse provides immediate feedback—reflecting our unpleasant behavior in unpleasant words (to be backed up later by the unpleasant sensations of a hangover). It is as if the world were a funhouse with distorting mirrors moving this way and that, and our conception of ourselves depends on steering our way through William James's "booming buzzing confusion" reflected back upon us. For a teleological behaviorist our selves are nothing but abstractions (reflected by the environment) of our own present and past behavior; our self-concepts are perceptions (discriminations) of those abstract reflections.[13]

This view of the self is a drastic departure from tradition (at least since Saint. Augustine). Traditionally, self-perception was conceived as a wholly internal process; better self understanding was supposed to come through better introspection. From the viewpoint of teleological behaviorism, however, the hermit who retires from the world in order to understand himself better is actually abandoning the set of mirrors—human society—from which he could best gain self-understanding. When we focus on inner dialogue, on inner pictures, we necessarily ignore our closest friends, our most intimate relations, the ones who see us and interact with us every day—mirrors where our selves are precisely and truly reflected.

SELF-CONTROL AS AN ABSTRACTION OF ENVIRONMENTAL FEEDBACK. The reafferent stimulation provided by our environments reflects both our immediate behavior and our behavior in the long run. Such stimulation, like a symphony or an opera or a novel, can be perceived on many levels. You might listen to a symphony for an individual melody or read a novel for an exciting turn of plot. On a wider level, you might listen for the structure of a movement or read for the plot of a chapter. On a still wider level, you might listen for the structure of the symphony itself or read for the structure of the novel itself—or, going still further, for the place of this piece in the work of the composer or author, and the work of the composer or author in the history of symphonies or novels. Similarly, you might perceive yourself reflected narrowly in the emotions of an evening or widely in the pattern of stimulation extending over a day, a month, a year, a lifetime, or beyond a lifetime.

Biological evolution has arranged matters so that for most species, most of the time, and for humans some of the time, behavior adaptive for the moment is also adaptive beyond the moment. The squirrel saves nuts not because its self-concept extends beyond the autumn and into the winter but rather because it wakes up one morning and suddenly finds burying nuts to be valuable in itself. The temporal breadth of a nonhuman animal's interest can, most of the time, remain narrow while Mother Nature takes care of the long view. A squirrel does not have and does not need a broad concept of self.

In human life, however, a conflict frequently arises between the long run and the short run. An alcoholic may strongly prefer having a scotch to having a soft drink, but also prefer strict sobriety to alcoholism. The preferred long-term pattern (strict sobriety) is inconsistent with the preferred short-term act (having a scotch). It is only when such inconsistencies arise that conformity to the preferred long-term pattern is labeled self-control. If such inconsistencies rarely or never arose (as in the life of the squirrel), there would be no need for self-control, hence no need for a self-concept extending beyond the moment.

DEGREES OF SELF AND SELF-CONCEPT.   It would be more correct to say that our human self-concept (deriving from the necessity for self-control in our environment) may be narrower or wider and that the squirrel actually has a self-concept, a narrow one, sufficient to its needs. Even a hungry rat rewarded by food for pressing a lever is to an extent controlling itself. The pattern of pressing the lever and eating takes longer (necessarily) than the act of pressing the lever alone. Pressing the lever, considered alone, is dispreferred to just sniffing in the corner of the cage; hence pressing the lever for food to be delivered within a fraction of a second is an instance of self-control and an instance of self-conception (albeit, a narrow one) by the rat. Correspondingly, even a slug has a self-concept—on a microscopic level. At the other extreme, strict sobriety may be narrow relative to still more valuable and wider patterns (social drinking, presumably).

Not that a person's self is equally wide in all areas. You could, over the same period, be an alcoholic, a nonsmoker, and a moderate gambler, taking risks sometimes, avoiding them at other times. Our selves are multidimensional but their essence is always behavioral patterning—behavior over time. Behavioral patterning in the context of local "temptations" (local preferences inconsistent with the pattern) is not just a reflection or a sign of self-control. It *is* self-control. A person cannot be an alcoholic inside his body and a teetotaler outside, nor the reverse. People *are* (abstractly and in the long run) what they *do.* (The qualifier "in the long run" distinguishes between the alcoholic and the social drinker who are both at the moment having a scotch.)

It is sometimes supposed that in a perfect world there would be no conflict between immediate desires and long-term values. The image of a natural human being living a natural life has this sort of framework—a place where our immediate desires are in harmony with our long-term best interests. But as Plato pointed out (*Philebos,* 21c), life in such a world would be the life of a slug. In such a world we would have no need of a wide self and we would therefore not have one. A person's self is not a mental appendix or mental decoration but a functional aspect of human life. Willpower, the ability to behave right now in conformance with a valuable long-term pattern of behavior—to turn down the scotch despite its immediate value, to choose sobriety over alcoholism—arises not from any introspection on our part, not from *insight,* but rather from what might better be called *outsight,* from our ability to abstract, from the booming buzzing confusion of the environment, reflections of our own behavior over long stretches of time.

SELF-CONTROL AND SOCIAL CONTROL.   It is customary to distinguish self-interested behavior, consistent with the goals of an individual, from altruistic behavior, consistent with the goals of someone else. Where these interests are in harmony (as in normal economic interchange), apparent altruism is normally explained in terms of self-interest. It is not considered altruistic to pay the grocer if he gives you something you want in return. But behavior where nothing is apparently received in return (such as volunteering at a hospital, anonymously donating to charity, rushing into a burning building to save a child) is considered altruistic because presumably no personal benefit accrues, no benefit to the *self*, but only social benefit, is involved. The personal satisfaction that we may derive from such acts is considered to be dependent not on fundamental self-interest but on socially imposed conscience (or superego), or an innate altruistic motive built into us and by its very nature distinct from our selfish motives (see appendix).

The first section of this chapter showed how social cooperation rests on self-control. This section goes on to argue that a higher level of social cooperation—altruistic behavior—also rests on self-control and thereby serves a crucial function for *individuals*. Consider the following informal demonstration that the functional self may extend beyond the limits of a person's skin. We asked one hundred Stony Brook undergraduates each to answer one of four questions below (25 subjects answered each question):

1. Which would you choose? (circle A or B)
   A. $100 for yourself
   B. $300 shared among yourself and the 5 people (friends or family) to whom you feel closest ($50 to each).
2. Which would you choose? (circle A or B)
   A. $100 for yourself
   B. $300 shared among yourself and 5 randomly selected students in this class ($50 to each).
3. Which would you choose? (circle A or B)
   A. $100 for yourself
   B. $300 shared among yourself and 5 randomly selected members of the Stony Brook community ($50 to each).
4. Which would you choose? (circle A or B)
   A. $100 for yourself
   B. $300 shared among yourself and 5 people randomly selected people from across the United States ($50 to each).

The results were what you would expect. Question 1 was answered "unselfishly" (B circled) by 20 of the 25 subjects, while all of the others were answered "selfishly" (A circled) by at least 23 of the 25 subjects.

It seems that people's concepts of their selves may include other people with whom they function together. Of course there is much more genetic overlap among families (question 1) than with classmates or schoolmates (question 2 or 3) or fellow citizens (question 4), but the same results ("unselfish" responses) apply when question 1 is rephrased to exclude blood relatives and include only the subject's closest friends or spouse.

The clearest connection here is a functional one. Imagine that the subject belongs to a basketball team needing equipment. Obviously $300 would buy more equipment than $100. The functional unit in this case is the team, not the individual. Recall the game used to introduce my lectures, discussed at the beginning of this chapter. Suppose I had said to the audience that all of the money earned was to be pooled and used for a common purpose, say to build more comfortable seats in the lecture hall. Then there would be no reason for anyone to choose X, a selection that would just reduce the value of the pool. The same applies to families and close friends. Although individuals are units of *choice*, groups of individuals may be units of reinforcement or punishment. Coaches of teams are always trying to get individual players to play as a unit—to make choices as individuals for the benefit of the group.

Failures to cooperate are common in real-life prisoner's dilemmas. The New Bedford fishermen mentioned previously each profited maximally by buying and sending out as many boats as possible, but ultimately, when all the fishermen began to do this, the common resource (the available fish) became depleted and the group as a whole suffered (the industry was devastated). The fishermen did have a common interest (in restraining their fishing), yet that interest was not obvious to them (the few surviving fishermen still deny it). It is thus of crucial social importance to understand how social situations may be manipulated to cause people to perceive an interest in common with others.

On a larger scale, the prisoner's dilemma is a warning not to rely wholly on pure competition to advance the common good. Although in most cases Adam Smith's "invisible hand" keeps overall good in line with individual benefit, sometimes (as in the case of the New Bedford fishermen), the invisible hand carries a sword. The interests of an individual, or a smaller group, generally operate in a much narrower time frame than the interests of a larger group. The interests of a corporation or firm are generally wider than those of individual administrators, who may only remain in their jobs for a limited time.

As the differential in group size expands, these interests may begin to conflict. Recall the illustration in Chapter 6 of the benefits of paying attention to sunk costs (the conflict between the comptroller and the president of a firm over whether to open a Fifth Avenue store). Decisions on hiring, promotion, maintenance, investment—almost all difficult business decisions—involve outcomes that arrive at different times. An effective administrator tries to discount future benefits realistically, but we have seen that long-term benefits are often difficult to quantify (and are no less real for that).

Altruism Reconsidered

We have seen that patterning increases self-control. We have seen Brown's third experiment that patterning increases social cooperation. Why should this be? In the terms of this chapter, why should temporal patterning of choices (a seemingly irrelevant process) expand the boundaries of the self? Figure 7.7 illustrates the analogy between self-control on the temporal dimension and social cooperation on the spatial dimension.

In Figure 7.7 a single person at successive moments in time, ranging from past to future, is compared to a person in a group of other people. Clearly, these conceptual individuals (person P at $t_{-n} \ldots , t_{-3}, t_{-2}, t_{-1}, t_0, t_1, t_2, t_3 \ldots t_n$) have a common interest; they all inhabit the same skin. Good habits benefit P over a sum of times (that is what we mean by good habits) even though they may impose a sacrifice at t_0 (now). Bad habits do the reverse. Individual development consists of a better and better perception of what might be called mutual self-interest (the interest of P at *all* times) while retaining an interest (nowadays considered "healthy") in our immediate self (the interest of P at t_0). As Ainslie (1992) has pointed out, these narrow versus long-term interests must often face the same (prisoner's) dilemma as the individual does versus society. Compressing the primrose path of Chapters 3 and 5 into a single day, consider P at t_0 (now) and P at t_1 (tomorrow morning). Let us again suppose that P is an alcoholic and arbitrarily assign points to events in his life as follows (this time with negative points indicating negative states):

Drinking while not having a hangover, 3 points.
Not drinking while not having a hangover, 0 points.
Drinking while having a hangover, −7 points.
Not drinking while having a hangover, −10 points.

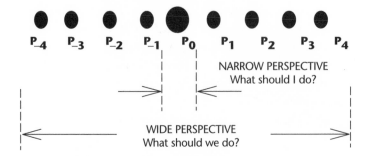

DIMENSION OF SOCIAL SPACE: SOCIAL DILEMMA

DIMENSION OF TIME: SELF-CONTROL

Figure 7.7. The analogy between the self-control dilemma (conflict between narrow and wide temporal perspectives) and the social cooperation dilemma (conflict between narrow and wide social-space perspectives).

Hangover or no hangover, the alcoholic is momentarily better off drinking than not drinking (with "hangover" standing for all the many deleterious effects of drinking). If he has no hangover, he can enjoy himself, put some pleasure in his life (going from 0 to 3 points). If he has a hangover, he can ameliorate its pain (going from −10 to −7 points). In either case he will be better off *now* if he drinks *now.*

His body is playing tit for tat with him, however. If he drinks now he will have a hangover tomorrow. Thus if he keeps drinking he will be in a continuous hangover state and lose 7 points every day whereas if he never drinks he will remain even every day (and, in the real world, be fit to pursue other pleasures). Just as the primary object of the prisoner's dilemma player (in Brown's or Baker's experiments) should have been to get her opponent to cooperate, the primary object of the alcoholic should be to avoid hangovers. Because the alcoholic's body is essentially playing tit for tat with him, if he chooses to defect (to have a drink now), his choices tomorrow will be just as if a prisoner's dilemma opponent had defected in return. If he chooses to cooperate (remain sober), his choices tomorrow will be just as if an opponent had cooperated in return. When we take these sorts of self-control situations into the laboratory, we find that the same patterning procedures (grouping trials together) that engender cooperation in the social prisoner's dilemma task engender cooperation in the individual game.

People like Trollope's Sir Felix, with extremely narrow self-conceptions, frequently make choices consistent with the interests of their narrow selves and in conflict with their wider selves. They are generally impulsive rather than self-controlled. All of us are successfully tempted at times by narrow interests; now, at the present moment (at t_0), we fail to cooperate with our past and future selves (t_{-n} to t_n). Just as the Stony Brook students who answered the questionnaire could not conceive of common interests with other Stony Brook students, so people with narrow self-concepts (all of us at times) do not perceive the common interests of our present selves with our selves of last year and next year.

As the previous section showed, the rewards of *social* cooperation are both delayed and probabilistic. Where rewards to an *individual* are delayed or probabilistic, patterning of trials serves to forcibly broaden self-perception. A person forced to make four decisions at a time cannot make one decision at a time. A drinker or a dieter who decides in advance on a monthlong pattern of drinking or eating is by definition better able to control himself than one who decides anew about each drink or each meal. The person who decides in advance is essentially making a group decision (P from t_{-n} to t_n) rather than an individual decision (P at t_0). Similarly, the person who develops effective social habits benefits from those habits.

On an individual level, people who commit themselves to a sanitarium (where eating or drinking will be rigidly controlled) are attempting to break a pattern of repeated defection in their normal environment by choosing in advance a weekly or monthly (self-cooperative) pattern. They expect that once they have begun to cooperate they will keep on cooperating outside the institution. On a social level, such commitment processes are not generally available. It is not feasible, for instance, to move to an authoritarian society (like Singapore) where social cooperation is rigidly enforced, as a sort of sanitarium, and then back to a permissive society (like ours).[14] The best alternative is consistently to cooperate within the permissive society. As I have argued above, this alternative is not just best for society but also best for the individual, for purely selfish reasons—*provided* we perceive our selfish selves broadly rather than narrowly in time.

Decision theorists find it a puzzle why people habitually leave tips at restaurants where they will never eat again (say on a highway). Leaving a tip at such a restaurant is obviously irrational when doing so is considered as an individual, isolated act. In fact, leaving a tip even at a restaurant where you *do* intend to eat again is irrational from the point of view of your self considered wholly at the present moment. By not leaving a tip, you benefit now; it is only that *other* person, the one who will inhabit your body at a later time, who may suffer.

Richard Price's 1992 book *Clockers* vividly illustrates the devastating effects of a ghetto environment where short-term social interactions dominate long-term ones. There, powerful short-term rewards (drugs, money, daily survival) overwhelm vague and abstract long-term rewards (health, family, friends). Consequently, everyone's self-concept is narrow in time, controlled by the clock rather than by the calendar.

Leaving tips is a pattern that (usually) serves us well in our society, a pattern that aids individual self-control. It may seem as though there is no connection between the benefit our tip confers on the next person who wanders into the restaurant where we will never return and the benefit conferred on us by the previous person's tip. But there *is* a connection—in the pattern we maintain in our behavior. It would be bad for us *personally, selfishly,* if we decided individually each time we went into a restaurant whether or not we should leave a tip. Decisions on a case-by-case basis are exactly the sort of (pseudorational) behavior (the lawyer's prisoner's dilemma advice) that would get us defecting all of the time.

It is not possible to tease apart the individual and social benefits of such acts. Most altruistic acts are, like tipping, personally profitable a lot of the time. Giving to charity is often observed and frequently rewarded by society. The relation between generosity and its rewards, however, is vague and indistinct. Generosity for most of us (like sobriety for the alcoholic) is not profitable and would not be chosen considering only its case-by-case (narrow) reinforcement. Consequently the way for most of us to profit from generosity (and the way for an alcoholic to profit from sobriety) is to pattern our behavior abstractly—to choose to be a generous (or a sober) person.

It is in aid of making such choices that narrative—biographical and autobiographical—derives its function (Bruner, 1997). The internal *mechanism* by which a personal narrative may gain control of a person's behavior is a subject for neuroscience. Here we are concerned with the *function*, the purpose of that mechanism in human life. Saying "I am a generous (or a sober) person" provides a discriminative stimulus that functions to group generous (or sober) behavior into positively (if vaguely and indistinctly) reinforced patterns—to classify behavior into acts consistent with one's self—acts reinforced in the long run and as a group.

In order to pattern our behavior in this way (and reap the consequent rewards), we must forgo making decisions on a case-by-case basis. Once we do that, there will come times in choosing between selfishness and generosity when we will be generous even when generosity is explicitly unreinforced or even punished. In other words, we will behave altruistically. Such altruism is not only compatible with a wider selfishness, it is a *necessary component* of a wider selfishness.

In an environment (like at least some of ours) where tit-for-tat behavior (do unto others as they do unto you) is more or less the norm, altruistic acts are clearly selfish. Those of us who live in such environments can come to perceive the social good as our good in the same way as we can come to perceive our long-range good as our immediate good—by developing good habits. But good habits require a certain kind of faith in the future. If you were born yesterday and were going to die tomorrow (a situation approached by some of the characters in *Clockers*), there would be no advantage in behaving well—such behavior would have no function. Still, our larger society demands a wider self. The mother who, without thinking twice, runs into the burning building to save someone else's child is behaving altruistically but she is also behaving selfishly. *By* her behavior she has teased out of her booming, buzzing environment an abstract reflection of herself.

Appendix: Group Selection

The material in this chapter is analogous to the arguments of some evolutionary biologists for group selection. Recently, Sober and Wilson (1998) presented a compelling case for group selection of altruism. A highly simplified version of their argument runs as follows. Consider a population of organisms divided into several relatively isolated groups (tribes, for example). Within each tribe are some altruists and some selfish individuals ("egoists") interacting with each other repeatedly in multiperson games similar to prisoner's dilemma—such as the one with which I introduce my lectures, except that instead of monetary reward the players receive more or less fitness (ability to reproduce). In these games the altruists tend to cooperate while the egoists tend to defect. Within each group (as in prisoner's dilemma) altruists always lose out to egoists. However, those groups originally containing many altruists grow much faster than those originally containing many egoists—because cooperation benefits the group more than defection does.

Consider the case of teams, such as basketball teams, playing in a league. It is commonly accepted that, all else being equal, teams with individual players who play unselfishly will beat teams with individual players who play selfishly; however, within each team, the most selfish players will score the most points. Imagine now, instead of scoring points and winning or losing games, the teams competed for reproductive fitness. Then teams with a predominance of unselfish players would rapidly grow in numbers, while those with a predominance of selfish players would grow slowly or (in competition for scarce resources) shrink—the group effect. Although, within each team, selfish players would still increase faster than unselfish ones (the individual effect), this growth could well be overwhelmed by the group effect.

As time goes on, the *absolute* number of unselfish individuals (altruists) could increase faster across the whole population than the *absolute* number of egoists, even though within each group the *relative* number of altruists decreases. If the groups remained rigidly divided, eventually—because the relative number of altruists is always decreasing within each group—the absolute number would begin to decrease as well. However, if before this point is reached, the groups mixed with each other and then re-formed, the process would begin all over again and altruists might maintain or increase their gains.

Again, this is a highly simplified version of the argument. The essential point is that while individual altruists may always be at a disadvantage relative to egoists, groups of altruists may be at an advantage relative to groups of egoists.

The reader may recognize the analogy of the above argument to the central argument of the chapters of this book on complex ambivalence; instead of individual organisms versus groups of organisms, we have individual acts versus patterns of acts; instead of survival of the fittest, we have choice of the most valuable. My view in this book is that an altruistic behavioral pattern may be more valuable than repeated selfish acts even though individual altruistic acts are always less valuable than individual selfish acts.[15] Thus, altruism may evolve within the lifetime of the individual just as it may evolve across generations of individuals. Although the mechanisms of selection and variation may differ strongly between biology and psychology, the evolutionary process requires not a particular mechanism, but merely the principles of selection and variation themselves (Staddon, 1993, pp. 56–62).

Nothing in the present book argues against group selection. Organisms may be born with greater or lesser biological tendencies to be altruistic. But it does not follow from group selection that altruistic behavior is incompatible with a larger individual selfishness. Sober and Wilson consider only two forms of human selfishness: that selfishness which desires maximization of consumer goods and that which desires "internal, psychological benefits" (p. 2). They do not consider individual selfishness in the long run and in the abstract. They say that "evolutionary biologists often work from the outside in" (p. 193) but do not consider the possibility of psychology's also working from the outside in. They leapfrog over the behavioral contingencies that cause behavioral change (contingencies analogous to the group selection processes they have just developed) and proceed directly to "delve below the level of behavior" (p. 194) to an internal cognitive mechanism hypothesized to mediate between the biological selective process and altruistic behavior.

Their cognitive psychology may well be correct but it is not evident to this reader how (or even whether), according to their psychology, altruism may emerge from selfishness over an organism's lifetime. If the implication is that we are born with fixed proportions of selfish and altruistic motives and that experience cannot teach us to alter those proportions, then their theory is not as optimistic as Sober and Wilson seem to think; it will not be of much use to those of us trying, despite our weaknesses, to live a better life.

Notes

Introduction

1. The poem is Whitman's "When I Heard the Learn'd Astonomer":

> When I heard the learn'd astronomer,
> When the proofs, the figures, were ranged in
>   columns before me,
> When I was shown the charts and diagrams,
>   to add, divide, and measure them,
> When I heard the astronomer when he lectured
>   to much applause in the lecture-room,
> How soon unaccountable I became tired and sick,
> Till rising and gliding out I wander'd off by myself,
> In the mystical moist night air, and
>   from time to time
> Looked up in perfect silence at the stars

2. I do not imply here that squirrels are less susceptible to bad habits than humans are—quite the reverse. But in natural environments (those in which their species evolved) temptations to bad habits are less likely to arise than in artificial environments such as the psychology laboratory.

1. Habit and Willpower

1. Even more important for self-control, as later chapters will show, are the social support and the temporal patterning in people's lives (sabbaths, holidays, daily rituals) that religions provide.

2. Most contemporary philosophers are strongly antibehavioral. They regard behaviorism as at best narrow and at worst immoral. Recently, however, behaviorism, very much like the teleological behaviorism espoused here, has been revived within philosophy (see Stout, 1996).

3. At least, this is what should be happening in a mature cognitive science. But cognitive theory today is highly fractionated. Every domain and subdomain has its own theory (it sometimes seems that each theorist has his or her own theory) independent of or even incompatible with all the others. Perhaps this is all to the good. As cognitive theory evolves, useful theories will emerge and useless ones fall away.

4. Although behaviorists tend to agree that these are the two main determinants of behavior, they disagree on what to call them. The names chosen here are as noncommittal and general as the author can make them.

2. Simple Ambivalence

1. A motive is in this sense like a probability. The probability of an event, such as that of a particular coin coming up heads, can never be totally known. As more and more events of the same kind (coin flips) accumulate, the relative frequency of a given outcome (heads divided by flips), approaches a given value. The coin is either "fair" (if relative frequency approaches 0.5)or "biased"(if it approaches another fraction). But there is always an above-zero possibility, however minute, that the fraction observed in the past will be contradicted by a preponderance of future events. (A coin that seemed biased may, as flips accumulate, seem fair and vice versa.) The same is true of motives. And just as the ultimate indeterminacy of probabilities does not prohibit a quantitative science of physics based on probabilities of events, it does not prohibit a quantitative (and behavioral) science of psychology.

2. The procedures and results illustrated are amalgams of studies reported by Ainslie (1974), Fantino (1966), Green et al. (1981), Rachlin and Green (1972), and others. In these studies pigeons at first sample both alternatives. Eventually preferences emerge, as indicated in the text. For convenience of representation, the buttons are arranged vertically in Figure 2.4 rather than horizontally as they were in the test chambers used in the studies. Unless otherwise indicated, the pigeons were tested in twenty to forty trials daily for two to ten weeks at each condition.

3. It does not do this because it fails to discriminate between 10 and 14 seconds. A pigeon would choose a food delivery delayed by 10 seconds over an equal amount of food delayed by 14 seconds on nearly 100 percent of its choice opportunities, showing sensitivity to the time difference between the rewards.

4. They would eventually cross, however, if delay ($t_B - t_A$) were indefinitely increased.

5. Other amounts and several longer delays were also utilized in this experiment. Only the $1,000 amount was tested with all three groups. Further, there was some evidence that the longer hypothetical delays were beyond the children's

time horizons. (The sixth graders were indifferent among delays of 5, 10, and 25 years.) Older adults, who might well have died before collecting, severely discounted money at the longer delays.

6. These are the nominal rewards. The actual rewards are also (perhaps largely) social. The child would like the experimenter to return (a smaller-sooner reward), but the experimenter implies that her approval (a larger-later reward) depends on how long the child waits.

7. Waiting time is also sensitive to a host of other variables, such as the experimenter's instructions and whether the smaller reward is exposed or hidden. I will discuss these stimulus variables in Chapter 6.

8. I assume here that all else is equal. But of course waiting for the bus is a function of many other variables such as baby-sitters at home, susceptibility to cold, and experience with the bus system. Moreover, a sensible person would have previously established a working rule such as: Wait no more than 10 minutes, then hail a cab (see Chapter 6).

9. Of course, this is a gross oversimplification. Subsequent chapters will refer to more complex evolutionary mechanisms. The point here is just that increasing a reward's delay tends to decrease the probability of its receipt and that this tendency is stronger in primitive than in civilized societies.

10. The procedure of Figure 2.8 and the results described correspond to those of an experiment by Ainslie (1974).

11. If b were rewritten as c/k and $k \to 0$, the form of Equation 2.3 would become exponential. However, as noted, empirical discount functions are rarely exponential in form.

3. Complex Ambivalence

1. I presented the principles of this chapter and of the rest of the book in condensed form in an article (Rachlin, 1995) printed with commentary by psychologists and philosophers, plus my response to the commentary.

2. I have chosen the symphony example because of the relatively fixed temporal character of music. The assumptions in the text reflect my own preferences, perhaps not those of the reader. Of course there are times when a coherent excerpt, a movement, might be preferred to a whole symphony, an act to a whole play, a chapter to a novel, and so forth. But it would seem to be rare for a fixed three-minute or 3-page excerpt of a work, ending anywhere, to be preferred to the whole work or a coherent section of it. A person may well prefer to read an entire novel or nonfiction book, say, to a three-page short story or article. But he or she may also prefer reading the short story or article to reading the first three pages (not a whole chapter) of the book.

3. Enjoyment and recognition are not the same thing, however. Enjoyment does

not depend strictly on recognition. You may readily recognize a song when its beginning or end or middle is lopped off, but you are unlikely to enjoy it.

4. When we come to discuss Figure 3.8, and in subsequent chapters, the primrose path will be made continuous so that instead of outcome values after various *numbers* of choices to drink, the path will represent outcome values at various *rates* of consumption of the addictive substance.

5. For an extended discussion of the relation of melioration to maximization see Rachlin and Laibson (1997).

6. The concept of reinforcement and punishment used throughout this book rests on Premack's (1965) theory. Reinforcement and punishment are defined in terms of relative positions of activities on a value scale. Reinforcement is the contingency of a higher-valued activity on a lower one; punishment is the (forced) contingency of a lower-valued activity on a higher one. Value is in turn determined by choice experiments in which both reinforcer and reinforced (punisher and punished) activities are alternatives. Premack's wholly behavioral theory is the most internally consistent, noncircular, and empirically supported of all reinforcement theories. It has been extended by the matching law (Herrnstein, 1997) and economic demand theory (Rachlin et al., 1976), but its basic assumptions and predictive power remain intact.

7. They need not be straight either. Melioration depends on relative rather than absolute values, so the same behavior is predicted through a range of topological distortions of the parallelogram ABCD. The straightness of the lines is nevertheless a simplification. Herrnstein and Prelec describe several cases of curved underlying functions. For example, moderate levels of drinking may increase rather than decrease both future value of drinking and future value of not drinking. Perhaps moderate drinking is beneficial for health. This effect would make lines AD and BC of Figure 3.8 rise for a short distance in the region of point A and then fall. Line AC representing average value would rise and fall as well. I shall discuss this case further in Chapter 5.

4. The Lonely Addict

1. Chapter 4 expands on and restates the material of Chapter 3 in economic terms. It is written in a somewhat more technical style than previous chapters and contains material from two recent articles by the author (Rachlin, 1997a, forthcoming).

2. Some of this difference may be due not to tolerance for the drug, but to tolerance for its harmful side effects. Still, tolerance of aversive side effects cannot counteract tolerance for the addictive substance itself.

3. Even addictive activities involve skill acquisition at low levels. Many addictions are "acquired tastes." The first cigarette burns your throat, the first beer tastes

bitter. The solid line of Figure 4.1a should have been drawn with a slight downward dip at the leftmost edge. The intent of the figure, however, is not to accurately reflect variations in any particular set of addictions but to show dominant or overall trends.

4. This is a simplification. Rarely is overall utility simply the average of a series of local utilities. As the previous chapter indicates (see Figure 3.4), the organization or pattern of local utilities contributes to the value of overall utility. (The whole may be greater than the sum of its parts, as the gestalt psychologists said.) In these more complex cases overall utility may rise to a maximum and fall, even as local utilities monotonically decrease. The point of the present chapter is that even where overall utilities are merely the average of local utilities, a conflict may develop between maximization of local and overall utilities. When overall utilities are greater than the average of local utilities, the conflict is exacerbated.

5. Although in some it may well not be condemned. In Richard Price's fictional ghetto neighborhood in *Clockers,* addiction and dope dealing are the norm. American middle-class values are portrayed as rare and indeed maladaptive in that environment.

6. Steven Hursh and his colleagues have developed precise methods to compare the elasticity of demand for different drugs and for the same drug under different biological and treatment conditions. These methods provide a way to evaluate both treatments and public policies aimed at reducing demand for (hence consumption of) drugs. See Hursh and Winger (1995) for a review of these studies.

7. The sensitivity is not necessarily the same in both directions. Price decreases have been found to have a stronger effect on consumption of cigarettes than price increases. A reason for this ratchet effect will be discussed later.

8. Cocaine treatment programs that have both increased the cost of drugs and provided alternative activities have produced much higher levels of abstinence than have other treatments of cocaine dependence (Higgins et al., 1995; Silverman et al., 1996).

5. Soft Commitment

1. A similar experiment was done by Eisenberger et al. (1989) with rats as subjects. The rats normally preferred a small reward that required an easy response (pressing on a light lever) to a large reward that required a difficult response (pressing on a heavy lever). Yet when the rats had to run back and forth in a runway a number of times prior to pressing the lever, the preferences reversed.

2. Although the pattern of responding generated by fixed-interval schedules ulti-

mately (after many months of daily testing and many thousands of exposures) becomes rigid, it is initially (after two or three weeks of daily exposures), as in this experiment, much more varied than is the fixed-ratio pattern.

3. The concept of economic complementarity of a commodity consumed at one time with another commodity consumed at another time has been labeled "adjacent complementarity" by Becker (1996). Although in the pigeon example the two time periods are indeed adjacent (SS or LL, immediately following the 31 pecks), there is no inherent requirement that they be so. In fact, the central principle of this book—that of self-control by construction of patterns arching over time—depends on economic complementarity of temporally nonadjacent components.

4. That is, I am making the simplifying assumptions inherent in the concept of melioration. Instead of the continuous discounting implied by exponential or hyperbolic discount functions, I am assuming the existence of a window (of a fixed time period, a fixed number of trials or the duration of a given stimulus) within which utility is evenly distributed and outside of which utility is completely discounted.

5. Figure 5.3 will complicate this situation somewhat, but still leave it far from real life. The reader should remember, though, that any science is a simplification of real life. For example, the fact that a physicist cannot predict the exact path of a leaf as it falls from a tree does not make physics any less useful.

6. The fact that in Figures 5.2 and 5.3 utility is always positive does not mean that addiction is not harmful. The util scales in the figures are interval scales (like Centigrade and Fahrenheit temperature scales) where the zero point is arbitrary. Perhaps a more realistic picture of the harmfulness of addictive activities would put the zero point of utility at or just below point A. Then high rates of consumption of X would be associated with negative utility.

7. This game is a within-subject version of a between-subjects prisoner's dilemma. I will examine the between-subjects version and its relation to self-control in Chapter 7.

8. The conception of freedom as potential behavioral variability differs from Skinner's (1971) conception of freedom as positive as opposed to negative reinforcement.

9. This technique resembles diets that work by restricting foods eaten to a given class—steak, grapefruit, cabbage soup, it does not seem to matter. Reduction of diet variability eventually becomes aversive, and eating is reduced. The difference is that the present technique imposes a temporal pattern (a weekly total) on the variability reduction.

10. Although in Figures 5.2 and 5.3 it is possible to go below 3 utils (to zero) in local utility, even a single Y-choice raises *average* utility—just as at the other extreme in Figure 5.2 a single X-choice lowers average utility.

11. As Ainslie (1992) points out, this is not always the case. A teleological analysis needs to look at patterns of behavior in the context of still larger patterns. Considered in their context, impulsive behaviors may sometimes be reinforced by events other than the addictive activity itself. An alcoholic may, by getting drunk, avoid or reduce the severity of punishment for behavior normally considered to be antisocial—aggression or spousal abuse as examples. For some binge drinkers, drinking may be only a discriminative stimulus for aggressive or abusive behavior—a stimulus in the presence of which aggressive or abusive behavior has been reinforced or at least has gone unpunished.

6. Rules and Probability

1. In a still wider extension, an animal's history of reinforcement may be conceived as extending to its evolutionary history. Although this book occasionally discusses evolutionary processes, it concentrates on behavioral change within an organism's lifetime.

2. The cognitive psychologist takes exactly the opposite view, maintaining that both first and second subjects are using the rule to solve the problem—the second subject, directly; the first, through construction from experience. Of course, both points of view are valid. Which you take will depend on whether your conceptions of learning and knowledge refer primarily to events within the organism (as do those of the cognitive psychologist) or whether those conceptions refer primarily to the interaction over time between the organism as a whole and its environment (as do those of the teleological behaviorist).

3. Still, we have seen that in much simpler tasks (such as fixed-ratio schedules of reinforcement) pigeons do treat response sequences as units. The crucial difficulty for pigeons is not in organizing responses into units but in treating those units as coherent discriminative stimuli.

4. Actually there were many more categories, but any single pigeon saw only four. We will follow along with these four categories as an example.

5. As Plato declared, and as other philosophers have since emphasized, abstract entities are no less real than specific ones; they are in fact *more* real because they last longer and maintain their properties even though their particulars may change (as a melody remains the same in different keys).

6. Nevertheless, as indicated in previous chapters, patterning can get out of hand and become obsessive. It can become a "revolt against indulgence." That is, simple patterning is a kind of impulsiveness with respect to complex patterning.

7. If the child knew when the experimenter would return, expected waiting time would of course decrease as time went by without her return. But the child has no idea of when the experimenter will return. The only hint he has is how long

he has already waited. The longer he has waited, the longer he can expect to wait, and the less probable it becomes that the experimenter will come back at all (she could have forgotten about him). Therefore, the longer he waits, the more the large reward is discounted, and the more likely he will be to ring the bell for the small reward.

8. This reasoning explains why longer waiting in the delay of gratification experiment is correlated with positive evaluations by teachers and parents, with intelligence, with higher SAT scores many years later, and with a host of other variables.

9. Unfortunately, it is not possible to reward or punish our own behavior. You can pat yourself on the back when you have done a good job, and that may serve as an effective signal that the job has been done. But unless there is also some *extrinsic* reward (as social acceptance or improved health was for our dieters), behavior will not change. Self-reward is like an intrapersonal Ponzi scheme, or like taking money from one pocket and putting it into another. It just does not work.

10. For cognitive psychologists, prior experience lays down an internal representation of itself in a person's neurocognitive system. The discriminative stimulus then activates that representation. The behaviorist does not deny the existence of internal mechanisms but does challenge the conception of those mechanisms as internal representations. For a behaviorist, prior experience comes into focus in temporally extended behavior of the whole person, rather than inside the person's head.

11. It has been argued that delay discounting is fundamental and that all apparent probability discounting is really delay discounting (Rachlin et al., 1986), and it has been argued that probability discounting is fundamental and that all apparent delay discounting is really probability discounting (Mischel and Grusec, 1967; Rotter, 1954). The debate has not been settled and may never be settled. It may not be meaningful. Henceforth I shall adopt whichever view applies best to the problem at hand.

12. Instead of adding a common delay between the first and second stages as in the delay commitment procedure, I have here multiplied by a common probability. Multiplying by a probability is equivalent to adding odds against. Although multiplication by common probabilities does not necessarily correspond to common additions of odds against, Equation 6.3 (with the amounts and probabilities used) predicts the preference reversal that we found.

13. Assuming that $k = 1$ in Mazur's discount equation (Equation 2.2), and assuming that the number of losses in a substring equals its delay, the discounted values reading left to right are

$$+1, 0, -.33, -.67, -.67, +1, +1, +1, -.33, +1.$$

The sum of these numbers is $+3$, which would be the subjective value of the whole string.

14. State-run lotteries are even worse than casinos. The bets are low, the wins are high, and the vast majority of lottery bettors never win—the substring is infinite in length. A more fundamental attraction of lotteries is that people consistently overvalue gambles with very small probabilities of winning. All nonzero probabilities below about one in ten thousand are subjectively "rounded up" to that number (Rachlin, Siegel, and Cross, 1994). A million-dollar lottery ticket with true one-in-a-million odds would be worth just $1. But the same ticket, rounded up to one-in-ten-thousand odds, would be *subjectively* worth $100. That is why reducing the odds of winning a lottery (already well below one in ten thousand) has no effect on the number of tickets sold, whereas increasing the amount of the prize proportionally increases the number of tickets sold (Lyons and Ghezzi, 1995).

7. Self-Control and Social Cooperation

1. I thank Gerry Mackie for bringing this theory to my attention.

2. In the standard prisoner's dilemma, however, pairs of players usually choose simultaneously on each trial (Rapoport and Chammah, 1965) whereas in this study the choices were made sequentially. In the standard repeated prisoner's dilemma game, each player must choose on each trial not knowing what the other player chose on that trial. With the standard procedure, as with the procedure used here, regardless of the other player's choice, defecting maximizes reward on the current trial, and consistent cooperation maximizes reward in the long run.

3. Performance in these sorts of experiments is strongly affected by the degree to which subjects are allowed to communicate with each other outside of their actual play (Caporael et al., 1989). Such communication was not allowed during the experiment. Of course, it is possible that earlier subjects spoke about the experiment to later ones. One can only hope that whatever extra-experimental communication took place was randomized across conditions. It is a problem associated with human subject experimentation in general.

4. "Subjective probability" is not meant to imply an internal state but rather the effective degree of probabilistic discounting—akin to Kahneman and Tversky's (1979) decision weight.

5. The results of a similar group of experiments that used playing cards rather than a game board (Silverstein et al., 1998) were replicated by the experiments described here.

6. In Baker's experiment the probability of reciprocation at which it makes no difference whether the subject cooperates or defects may be calculated as follows: $5p + 1(1 - p) = 2p + 6(1 - p)$. The solution is $p = .63$. Reward in Baker's experiment would therefore have been maximized if subjects with $p = 1.0$ and .75 had cooperated on all trials and subjects with $p = .50, .25,$ and 0.0

had defected on all trials. Subjects approached but did not reach maximization. Some evidence exists that in similar situations, after many trials, subjects will come to maximize (Goodie, 1997).

7. In further experiments Baker's subjects played the game without being able to see the spinners; in other experiments, also without spinners, Baker's subjects were under the impression that they were playing against another subject rather than a computer; in still other experiments, the probability of reciprocation was sharply increased or decreased for each subject halfway through the experiment (as in Brown's experimental design). These manipulations tended to slightly flatten the slope of the function of Figure 7.6, but the effect of reciprocation probability on cooperation remained very strong.

8. There is an enormous literature on the prisoner's dilemma game. Axelrod (1997, p. xi) calls it "the *E. coli* of the social sciences." Many of the studies within mathematics and economics are theoretical and concern the logic of the game and methods of developing effective strategies in its variants. Some studies have pitted one strategy against another in computer simulations. In these simulations, tit-for-tat has proven highly effective even against much more sophisticated strategies (Axelrod, 1980). Probably the greatest number of applications of game theory have been in the area of evolutionary biology (see the appendix to Chapter 7).

Within psychology, a series of illuminating experiments on reciprocity, pitting individuals against fixed strategies, has been performed by Komorita, Parks, and their colleagues (see Komorita and Parks, 1994, for a review). The object of the studies was to develop methods to encourage cooperation rather than to explore the correspondence between cooperation and self-control, but the results are entirely consistent with this correspondence. For example Komorita, Hilty, and Parks (1991) varied delay of reciprocity and found that immediate reciprocity engendered more cooperation than delayed reciprocity. This is exactly what would be expected if delay, so important in self-control, were an underlying discounting variable in social situations as well. Komorita, Parks, and Hulbert (1992) varied the proportion of (simulated) group members in a many-person game who used a "reciprocal strategy" (tit for tat). Increasing the proportion of members of an *N*-person group playing tit for tat is similar to increasing probability of cooperation in a two-person game (as Baker did) in the sense that both manipulations increase subjects' control over their opponents' behavior and hence over their own future alternatives. The effect of this manipulation was the same in both cases—an increase in cooperation by the subject.

9. The term *imagination* need not mean a picture in the head. Here it refers to action in the absence of a discriminative stimulus as if that stimulus were present. For the teleological behaviorist, a person successfully imagining a lion in

the room would run screaming from the room rather than dreamily reflecting on its mane and its tail. (The latter person is imagining a picture of a lion rather than an actual lion.) Imagination is *acting*, not dreaming; vividness of imagination is not vividness of interior image but of overt behavior. A vivid imagination is not just an aid or tool in acting on the stage. Rather, for a teleological behaviorist, acting *is* imagining (Rachlin, 1994).

10. Here again is the crucial difference between teleological behaviorism on the one hand and cognitive or physiological psychology on the other. When faced with behavior for which there is no apparent immediate external cause (such as altruism) the cognitive or physiological psychologist tends to assume that the cause of the behavior lies inside the organism—somewhere else in space. The teleological behaviorist resists this move, called by Stout (1996) the Internal Shift. Instead, the teleological behaviorist assumes that the cause of the behavior lies not somewhere else in space but somewhere else in time—in the organism's temporally extended environment.

11. Ainslie (1992), Platt (1973), Schelling (1971), and many others have also stressed this correspondence. And, as illustrated by the Trollope quote, it has been pointed out in literature.

12. Although only humans and certain species of monkeys seem to recognize themselves spontaneously, even pigeons may be trained to do it (Epstein, Lanza, and Skinner, 1981).

13. The difference between "self" and "self-concept" is a difference between behaving in a complex pattern and discriminating between that pattern and others. It corresponds to Aristotle's distinction between thought and perception. A thought, for Aristotle, is a complex behavioral pattern involving perception, imagination, and motivation. The behavior of which perception is composed is much simpler. All it needs is consistent categorization—like pressing button A or button B. Of course, when the perception is of one's own behavioral patterns, the more complex patterns need to precede the simpler perception. Still, you may perceive patterns in another person's behavior before exhibiting them in your own. You may perceive patterns in another person's behavior before *perceiving* them in your own—even though you are exhibiting them. See Rachlin (1994, 1997b) for a further discussion.

14. It is far from clear, moreover, that such shuttling would work. The stimuli of the Singapore environment may well gain control of social cooperation, while those of the United States continue to signal rewards for defection. Nor is it a good idea simply to move to Singapore. The rigid aversive contingencies there bring everyone's immediate interests (in avoiding punishment) forcibly into line with the group's interest, thereby making human life like the life of a squirrel—or an ant, or a slug.

15. In this book, "altruism" is a tendency to behave altruistically in particular in-

stances but consistently with selfishness in the long run. Group selection also defines altruism in terms of an extension of selfishness—a selfishness of the group (vis-à-vis other groups) over social space. If altruism were defined so as to eliminate any selfish motive, however broadly conceived, then this book would deny the existence of altruism. But so would group selection.

References

Aczl, J. 1948. On mean values. *Bulletin of the American Mathematical Society, 54,* 392–400.

Ainslie, G. 1974. Impulse control in pigeons. *Journal of The Experimental Analysis of Behavior, 21,* 485–489.

———1992. *Picoeconomics: The strategic interaction of successive motivational states within the person.* New York: Cambridge University Press.

Ainslie, G., and R. Herrnstein. 1981. Preference reversal and delayed reinforcement. *Animal Learning And Behavior, 9,* 476–482.

Ainsworth, M. D. S., and J. Bowlby. 1991. An ethological approach to personality development. *American Psychologist, 46,* 333–341.

Allais, M. 1953. Le comportement de l'homme rationnel devant le risque: Critique des postulats et axiomes de l'école americaine. *Econometrica, 21,* 503–546.

Axelrod, R. 1997. *The complexity of cooperation: Agent based models of competition and collaboration.* Princeton, N.J.: Princeton University Press.

Axelrod, R. 1980. Effective choice in the prisoner's dilemma. *Journal of Conflict Resolution, 24,* 3–25.

Balsam, P. 1988. Selection, representation, and equivalence of controlling stimuli. In R. C. Atkinson, R. J. Herrnstein, G. Lindsay, and R. D. Luce, eds., *Stevens' Handbook of Experimental Psychology.* Vol. 2; *Learning and Cognition.* 2nd ed., pp. 112–165. New York: Wiley.

Baum, W. M. 1974. On two types of deviation from the matching law: Bias and undermatching. *Journal of the Experimental Analysis of Behavior, 22,* 231–242.

———1994. *Understanding behaviorism.* New York: Harper Collins.

Baum, W. M., and H. Rachlin. 1969. Choice as time allocation. *Journal of the Experimental Analysis of Behavior, 12,* 861–874.

Becker, G. S. 1976. *The economic approach to human behavior.* Chicago: University of Chicago Press.

————1996. *Accounting for tastes.* Cambridge, Mass: Harvard University Press.

Becker, G. S., and K. M. Murphy. 1990. A theory of rational addiction. *Journal of Political Economy, 96,* 675–700.

Brazelton, T. B., B. Koslowski, and M. Main. 1974. The origins of reciprocity: The early mother-infant interaction. In M. Lewis and L. Rosenblum, eds., *The effect of the infant on its caregiver.* New York: Wiley, pp. 49–76.

Brown, J., and H. Rachlin. 1999. Self-control and social cooperation. *Behavioral Processes, 47,* 65–72.

Brownell, K. D., G. A. Marlatt, E. Lichtenstein, and G. T. Wilson. 1986. Understanding and preventing relapse. *American Psychologist, 41,* 765–782.

Bruner, J. 1997. A narrative model of self-construction. In J. G. Snodgrass and R. L. Thompson, eds., *The self across psychology: Self-recognition, self awareness, and the self concept,* Annals of the New York Academy of Sciences, vol. 818, pp. 145–162.

Calvino, I. 1988. *Six memos for the next millennium.* Cambridge, Mass.: Harvard University Press.

Caporael, L. R., R. M. Dawes, J. M. Orbel, and A. J. C. van de Kragt. 1989. Selfishness examined: Cooperation in the absence of egoistic incentives. *Behavioral and Brain Sciences, 12,* 683–739.

Castro, L., and H. Rachlin. 1980. Self-reward, self-monitoring, and self-punishment as feedback in weight control. *Behavior Therapy, 11,* 38–48.

Catania, A. C., B. A. Matthews, and E. Shimhoff. 1982. Instructed versus shaped human verbal behavior. *Journal of the Experimental Analysis of Behavior, 38,* 233–248.

Cerutti, D., and A. C. Catania. 1997. Pigeon's preference for free choice: Number of keys versus key area. *Journal of the Experimental Analysis of Behavior, 68,* 349–356.

Chung, S. H., and R. J. Herrnstein. 1967. Choice and delay of reinforcement. *Journal of the Experimental Analysis of Behavior, 10,* 67–74.

Davison, G. C., and J. Neale. 1994. *Abnormal psychology,* 6th ed. New York: Wiley.

DeGrandpre, R. J., and W. K. Bickel. 1996. Drug dependence as consumer demand. In L. Green and J. H. Kagel, eds., *Advances in behavioral economics.* Vol. 3; *Substance use and abuse,* pp. 1–36. Norwood, N.J.: Ablex Publishing Co.

de Villiers, P. A. 1977. Choice in concurrent schedules and a quantitative formulation of the law of effect. In W. K. Honig and J. E. R. Staddon, eds., *Handbook of operant behavior,* pp. 233–287. Englewood Cliffs, N.J.: Prentice-Hall.

Eisenberger, R., F. Weier, F. A. Masterson, and L. Y. Theis. 1989. Fixed ratio schedules increase generalized self-control: Preference for large rewards despite high effort or punishment. *Journal of Experimental Psychology: Animal Behavior Processes, 15,* 383–392.

Epstein, R., R. F. Lanza, and B. F. Skinner. 1981. "Self-awareness" in the pigeon. *Science, 212,* 695–696.

Fantino, E. 1966. Immediate reward followed by extinction versus later reward without extinction. *Psychonomic Science, 6*, 233–234.

———1998. Behavioral analysis and decision making. *Journal of the Experimental Analysis of Behavior, 69*, 355–364.

Fisher, E. B., Jr. 1996. A behavioral-economic perspective on the influence of social support on cigarette smoking. In L. Green and J. H. Kagel, eds., *Advances in behavioral economics*. Vol. 3; *Substance use and abuse*, pp. 207–236. Norwood, N.J.: Ablex Publishing Co.

Gallup, C. G., Jr. 1982. Self-awareness and the emergence of mind in primates. *American Journal of Primatology, 2*, 237–248.

Goodie, A. S. 1997. Base rate neglect under direct experience. *Dissertation Abstracts International.*

Green, L., E. B. Fisher, S. Perlow, and L. Sherman, 1981. Preference reversal and self-control: Choice as a function of reward amount and delay. *Behavior Analysis Letters, 1*, 43–51.

Green, L., A. F. Fry, and J. Myerson. 1994. Discounting of delayed rewards: A life span comparison. *Psychological Science, 5*, 33–36.

Green, L., and J. H. Kagel. 1996. *Advances in behavioral economics*. Vol. 3; *Substance use and abuse.* Norwood, N.J.: Ablex Publishing Co.

Green, L., and H. Rachlin. 1991. Economic substitutability of electrical brain stimulation, food and water. *Journal of the Experimental Analysis of Behavior, 55*, 133–144.

———1996. Commitment using punishment. *Journal of The Experimental Analysis of Behavior, 65*, 593–601.

Hackenberg, T. D., and S. A. M. Axtel. 1993. Humans' choices in situations of time-based diminishing returns. *Journal of the Experimental Analysis of Behavior, 59*, 445–470.

Hardin, G. 1968. The tragedy of the commons. *Science, 162*, 1243–1248.

Hayes, S. C., A. J. Brownstein, J. R. Haar, and D. E. Greenway. 1986. Instructions, multiple schedules, and extinction: Distinguishing rule-governed from schedule-induced behavior. *Journal of the Experimental Analysis of Behavior, 46*, 137–148.

Held, R., and A. V. Hein. 1958. Adaptation of disarranged hand-eye coordination contingent upon re-afferent stimulation. *Perceptual and Motor Skills, 8*, 87–90.

Herrnstein, R. J. 1961. Relative and absolute strength of response as a function of frequency of reinforcement. *Journal of the Experimental Analysis of Behavior, 4*, 267–272.

———1997. H. Rachlin and D. Laibson, eds., *The matching law: Papers in psychology and economics.* Cambridge, Mass: Harvard University Press.

———1991. Experiments on stable suboptimality in individual behavior. *American Economic Review, 81*, 360–364.

Herrnstein, R. J., G. F. Loewenstein, D. Prelec, and W. Vaughan, Jr. 1993. Utility maximization and melioration: Internalities in individual choice. *Journal of Behavioral Decision Making, 6,* 149–185.

Herrnstein, R. J., and D. Prelec. 1992. A theory of addiction. In G. Loewenstein and J. Elster, eds., *Choice over time,* pp. 331–360. New York: Russell Sage Foundation.

Herrnstein, R. J., D. Prelec, and W. Vaughan, Jr. 1986. An intra-personal prisoners' dilemma. Paper presented at the ninth symposium on Quantitative Analysis of Behavior: Behavioral Economics, at Harvard University.

Herrnstein, R. J., and W. Vaughan, Jr. 1980. Melioration and behavioral allocation. In J. E. R. Staddon, ed., *Limits to action: The allocation of individual behavior,* pp. 143–176. New York: Academic Press.

Heyman, G. M. 1996a. Resolving the contradictions of addiction. *Behavioral and Brain Sciences, 19,* 561–610.

————1996b. Elasticity of demand for alcohol in humans and rats. In L. Green and J. H. Kagel, eds., *Advances in behavioral economics.* Vol. 3; *Substance use and abuse,* pp. 107–132. Norwood, N.J.: Ablex Publishing Co.

Heyman, G. M. and L. Tanz. 1995. How to teach a pigeon to maximize overall reinforcement rate. *Journal of the Experimental Analysis of Behavior, 64,* 277–298.

Higgins, S. T., A. J. Budney, W. K. Bickel, G. J. Badger, F. E. Foerg, and D. Ogden. 1995. Outpatient behavioral treatment for cocaine dependence: One-year outcome. *Experimental and Clinical Psychopharmacology, 3,* 358–363.

Hineline, P. N. 1977. Negative reinforcement and avoidance. In W. K. Honig and J. E. R. Staddon, eds., *Handbook of operant behavior,* pp. 364–414. Englewood Cliffs, N.J.: Prentice-Hall.

Hursh, S. R. 1978. The economics of daily consumption controlling food- and water-reinforced responding. *Journal of the Experimental Analysis of Behavior, 29,* 475–491.

Hursh, S. R., and G. Winger. 1995. Normalized demand for drugs and other reinforcers. *Journal of the Experimental Analysis of Behavior, 64,* 373–384.

James, W. 1890/1981. *The principles of psychology.* Cambridge, Mass.: Harvard University Press.

Kahn, L. M., and J. K. Murnigham. 1993. Conjecture, uncertainty, and cooperation in prisoner's dilemma games: Some experimental evidence. *Journal of Economic Behavior and Organization, 22,* 91–117.

Kahneman, D., and A. Tversky. 1979. Prospect theory: An analysis of decisions under risk. *Econometrica, 47,* 263–291.

Kirby, K. N., and R. J. Herrnstein. 1995. Preference reversals due to myopic discounting of delayed reward. *Psychological Science, 6,* 83–89.

Komorita, S. S., J. R. Hilty, and C. D. Parks. 1991. Reciprocity and cooperation in social dilemmas. *Journal of Conflict Resolution, 35,* 494–518.

Komorita, S. S., and C. D. Parks. 1994. *Social dilemmas*. Dubuque, Iowa: Brown & Benchmark.

Komorita, S. S., C. D. Parks, and L. G. Hulbert. 1992. Reciprocity and the induction of cooperation in social dilemmas. *Journal of Personality and Social Psychology, 62,* 607–617.

Kudadjie-Gyamfi, E. 1998. Patterns of behavior: Self-control choices among risky alternatives. Ph.D. dissertation, State University of New York at Stony Brook.

Kudadjie-Gyamfi, E., and H. Rachlin. 1996. Temporal patterning in choice among delayed outcomes. *Organizational Behavior and Human Decision Processes, 65,* 61–67.

Loewenstein, G., and D. Prelec. 1992. Anomalies in intertemporal choice: Evidence and interpretation. In G. Loewenstein and D. Prelec, eds., *Choice over time,* pp. 119–146. New York: Russell Sage Foundation.

Logue, A. W. 1988. Research on self-control: An integrating framework. *Behavioral and Brain Sciences, 11,* 665–679.

Lyons, C. A., and P. M. Ghezzi. 1995. Wagering on a large scale: Relationships between ticket sales and game manipulation in two state lotteries. *Journal of Applied Behavioral Analysis, 28,* 127–137.

Mahoney, M. J. 1974. Self-reward and self-monitoring techniques for weight control. *Behavior Therapy, 5,* 48–57.

Marlatt, G. A., and J. R. Gordon. 1980. Determinants of relapse: Implications for the maintenance of behavior change. In P. O. Davidson and S. M. Davidson, eds., *Behavioral medicine: Changing health lifestyles,* pp. 410–452. New York: Brunner/Mazel.

Mazur, J. E. 1987. An adjusting procedure for studying delayed reinforcement. In M. L. Commons, J. E. Mazur, J. A. Nevin, and H. Rachlin, eds., *Quantitative analyses of behavior.* Vol. 5; *The effects of delay and of intervening events on reinforcement value,* pp. 55–73. Mahwah, N.J.: Erlbaum.

McMorrow, M. J., and R. M. Foxx. 1983. Nicotine's role in smoking: An analysis of nicotine regulation. *Psychological Bulletin, 93,* 302–327.

Millar, A., and D. J. Navarick. 1984. Self control and choice in humans: Effects of video game playing as a positive reinforcer. *Learning and Motivation, 15,* 203–218.

Miller, W. R., J. M. Brown, T. L. Simpson, N. S. Handmaker, T. H. Bien, L. F. Luckie, H. A. Montgomery, R. K. Hester, and J. S. Tonigan. 1995. What works? A methodological analysis of the alcohol treatment outcome literature. In R. K. Hester and W. R. Miller, eds., *Handbook of alcoholism treatment approaches.* 2nd ed. Boston: Allyn & Bacon.

Mischel, W., and J. Grusec. 1967. Waiting for rewards and punishments: Effects of time and probability on choice. *Journal of Personality and Social Psychology, 5,* 24–31.

Mischel, W., Y. Shoda, and M. Rodriguez. 1989. Delay of gratification in children. *Science, 244,* 933–938.

Navarick, D. J., and E. Fantino. 1976. Self control and general models of choice. *Journal of Experimental Psychology: Animal Behavior Processes, 2,* 75–87.

Nevin, J. A., and K. Liebold. 1966. *Psychonomic Science, 5,* 351–352.

Northcraft, G. B., and G. Wolf. 1984. Dollars, sense, and sunk costs. A life-cycle model of resource allocation decisions. *Academy of Management Review, 9,* 225–234.

Olton, D. S. 1979. Mazes, maps, and memory. *American Psychologist, 34,* 583–596.

Ostaszewski, P., L. Green, and J. Myerson. 1998. Effects of inflation on the subjective value of delayed and probabilistic rewards. *Psychonomic Bulletin and Review, 5,* 324–333.

Platt, J. 1973. Social traps. *American Psychologist, 28,* 641–651.

Premack, D. 1965. Reinforcement theory. In D. Levine, ed., *Nebraska symposium on motivation: 1965,* pp. 123–179. Lincoln: University of Nebraska Press.

Price, R. 1992. *Clockers.* Boston: Houghton Mifflin.

Rachlin, H. 1970. *Introduction to modern behaviorism.* San Francisco: W. H. Freeman.

———1978. A molar theory of reinforcement schedules. *Journal of the Experimental Analysis of Behavior, 30,* 345–360.

———1994. *Behavior and mind: The roots of modern psychology.* New York: Oxford University Press.

———1995. Self-control: Beyond commitment. *Behavioral and Brain Sciences, 18,* 109–159.

———1997a. Four teleological theories of addiction. *Psychonomic Bulletin and Review, 4,* 462–473.

———1997b. Self and self-control. In J. G. Snodgrass and R. L. Thompson, eds., *The self across psychology: Self-recognition, self-awareness, and the self concept.* Annals of the New York Academy of Sciences, vol. 818, pp. 85–98.

———Forthcoming. The lonely addict. In W. K. Bickel and R. E. Vuchinich, eds., *Reframing health change with behavioral economics.* Mahwah, N.J.: Erlbaum.

Rachlin, H., R. Battalio, J. Kagel, and L. Green. 1981. Maximization theory in behavioral psychology. *Behavioral and Brain Sciences, 4,* 371–417.

Rachlin, H., and B. Burkhard. 1978. The temporal triangle: Substitution in instrumental conditioning. *Psychological Review, 85,* 22–48.

Rachlin, H., A. Castrogiovanni, and D. Cross, 1987. Probability and delay in commitment. *Journal of The Experimental Analysis of Behavior, 48,* 347–353.

Rachlin, H., and L. Green, 1972. Commitment, choice and self-control. *Journal of the Experimental Analysis of Behavior, 17,* 15–22.

Rachlin, H., L. Green, J. H. Kagel, and R. C. Battalio. 1976. Economic demand theory and psychological studies of choice. In G. Bower, ed., *The psychology of learning and motivation.* Vol. 10. New York: Academic Press.

Rachlin, H., L. Green, and B. Tormey. 1988. Is there a decisive test between matching and maximizing? *Journal of the Experimental Analysis of Behavior, 50,* 113–123.

Rachlin, H., and D. Laibson, eds. 1997. *The matching law: Papers in psychology and economics.* Introduction to Part III, pp. 189–193. Cambridge, Mass.: Harvard University Press.

Rachlin, H., A. W. Logue, J. Gibbon, and M. Frankel. 1986. Cognition and behavior in studies of choice. *Psychological Review, 93,* 33–45.

Rachlin, H., E. Siegel, and D. Cross. 1994. Lotteries and the time horizon. *Psychological Science, 5,* 390–393.

Raineri, A., and H. Rachlin. 1993. The effect of temporal constraints on the value of money and other commodities. *Journal of Behavioral Decision Making, 6,* 77–94.

Rapoport, A., and A. M. Chammah. 1965. *Prisoner's dilemma.* Ann Arbor: University of Michigan Press.

Robins, L. N. 1974. The Vietnam drug user returns. Special Action Office Monograph: Series A, Number 2. Washington, D.C.: Government Printing Office.

Roske, I., I. Baeger, R. Frenzel, and P. Oehme. 1994. Does a relationship exist between the quality of stress and the motivation to ingest alcohol? *Alcohol, 11,* 113–124.

Rotter, J. B. 1954. *Social learning and clinical psychology.* Englewood Cliffs, N.J.: Prentice-Hall.

Schelling, T. 1971. The ecology of micromotives. *Public Interest, 25,* 61–98.

Schuster, C. R., K. Silverman, S. Harrell, R. Brooner, E. Cone, and K. Preston. 1995. ASP as a predictor of treatment outcome in a contingency management program for cocaine abusers. Poster presented at the annual meeting of the American College of Neuropsychopharmacology, San Juan, Puerto Rico.

Siegel, E., and H. Rachlin. 1996. Soft commitment: Self-control achieved by response persistence. *Journal of the Experimental Analysis of Behavior, 64,* 117–128.

Siegel, S. 1976. Morphine analgesic tolerance: Its situation specificity supports a Pavlovian conditioning model. *Science, 193,* 323–325.

————1988a. Pavlovian conditioning, drug tolerance and dependency and withdrawal and treatment issues. National Institute on Drug Abuse Research Monograph No. 84.

Siegel, S. 1988b. State dependent learning and morphine tolerance. *Behavioral Neuroscience, 102,* 228–232.

Silberberg, A., R. Bauman, and S. R. Hursh. 1993. Stock optimizing: Maximizing reinforcers per session on a variable-interval schedule. *Journal of the Experimental Analysis of Behavior, 59,* 389–400.

Silverman, K., S. T. Higgins, R. K. Brooner, I. D. Montoya, E. J. Cone, C. R. Schuster, and K. L. Preston. 1996. Sustained cocaine abstinence in methadone maintenance patients through voucher-based reinforcement therapy. *Archives of General Psychiatry, 53,* 409–415.

Silverstein, A., D. Cross, J. Brown, and H. Rachlin. 1998. Prior experience and patterning in a prisoner's dilemma game. *Journal of Behavioral Decision Making, 11,* 123–138.

Skinner, B. F. 1938. *The behavior of organisms: An experimental analysis.* New York: Appleton-Century-Crofts.

———1971. *Beyond freedom and dignity.* New York: Knopf.

Sober, E., and D. S. Wilson. 1998. *Unto others: The evolution and psychology of unselfish behavior.* Cambridge, Mass.: Harvard University Press.

Solnick, J. W., C. Kannenberg, D. A. Eckerman, and M. B. Waller. 1980. An experimental analysis of impulsivity and impulse control in humans. *Learning and Motivation, 1,* 61–77.

Solomon, R. L. 1980. The opponent-process theory of acquired motivation. *American Psychologist, 35,* 691–712.

Staddon, J. E. R. 1993. *Behaviorism: Mind, mechanism and society.* London: Duckworth.

Stevenson, M. K. 1986. A discounting model for decisions with delayed positive or negative outcomes. *Journal of Experimental Psychology: General, 115,* 131–154.

Stout, R. 1996. *Things that happen because they should.* Oxford: Oxford University Press.

Terrace, H. S. 1993. The phylogeny and ontogeny of serial memory: List learning by pigeons and monkeys. *Psychological Science, 4,* 162–169.

Trollope, A. 1875/1982. *The way we live now.* Oxford: Oxford University Press.

Tversky, A., and D. Kahneman. 1982. Evidential impact of base rates. In D. Kahneman, P. Slovic, and A. Tversky, eds., *Judgment under uncertainty: Heuristics and biases.* New York: Cambridge University Press.

U.S. Department of Health and Human Services. 1988. *The health consequences of smoking: Nicotine addiction. A report of the Surgeon General.* DHHS Publication No. 89–8411. Washington, D.C.: Government Printing Office.

Vuchinich, R. E., and J. Tucker. 1996a. The molar context of alcohol abuse. In L. Green and J. H. Kagel, eds., *Advances in behavioral economics.* Vol. 3; *Substance use and abuse,* pp. 133–162. Norwood, N.J.: Ablex Publishing Co.

———1996b. Alcohol relapse, life events, and behavioral theories of choice: A prospective analysis. *Experimental and Clinical Psychopharmacology, 4,* 19–28.

Wanchisen, B. A., T. A. Tatham, and P. N. Hineline. 1992. Human choice in "counterintuitive" situations: Fixed- versus progressive-ratio schedules. *Journal of the Experimental Analysis of Behavior, 58,* 67–86.

Wasserman, E. A., C. L. DeVolder, and D. J. Coppage. 1992. Nonsimilarity-based conceptualization in pigeons via secondary or mediated generalization. *Psychological Science, 3,* 374–379.

Wolffgramm, J. 1990. Free choice ethanol intake of laboratory rats under different social conditions. *Psychopharmacology, 101,* 233–239.

Wolffgramm, J., and A. Heyne. 1995. From controlled drug intake to loss of control: the irreversible development of drug addiction in the rat. *Behavioural Brain Research, 70,* 77–94.

Yamagishi, T., and K. Yamagishi. 1994. Trust and commitment in the United States and Japan. *Motivation and Emotion, 18,* 129–166.

Young, T. 1983. The demand for cigarettes: Alternative specifications of Fujii's model. *Applied Economics, 15,* 203–211.

Index